CHRONIC YOUTH

NYU SERIES IN SOCIAL AND CULTURAL ANALYSIS

General Editor: Andrew Ross

Nice Work If You Can Get It: Life and Labor in Precarious Times
Andrew Ross

City Folk: English Country Dance and the Politics of the Folk in Modern America
Daniel J. Walkowitz

Toilet: Public Restrooms and the Politics of Sharing
Edited by Harvey Molotch and Laura Norén

Unhitched: Love, Marriage, and Family Values from West Hollywood to Western China
Judith Stacey

The Sun Never Sets: South Asian Migrants in an Age of U.S. Power
Edited by Vivek Bald, Miabi Chatterji, Sujani Reddy, and Manu Vimalassery

Chronic Youth: Disability, Sexuality, and U.S. Media Cultures of Rehabilitation
Julie Passanante Elman

Chronic Youth

Disability, Sexuality, and U.S. Media Cultures of Rehabilitation

Julie Passanante Elman

NEW YORK UNIVERSITY PRESS
New York and London

NEW YORK UNIVERSITY PRESS
New York and London
www.nyupress.org

References to Internet websites (URLs) were accurate at the time of writing.
Neither the author nor New York University Press is responsible for URLs that
may have expired or changed since the manuscript was prepared.

LIBRARY OF CONGRESS CATALOGING-IN-PUBLICATION DATA
Elman, Julie Passanante.
Chronic youth : disability, sexuality, and U.S. media cultures of rehabilitation / Julie
Passanante Elman.
pages cm. — (NYU series in social and cultural analysis)
Includes bibliographical references and index.
ISBN 978-1-4798-4142-4 (hardback) — ISBN 978-1-4798-1822-8 (pb)
1. Teenagers—United States. 2. Problem youth—United States. 3. Youth—United States—
Conduct of life. I. Title.
HQ796.E553 2014
305.2350973—dc23
2014017279

New York University Press books are printed on acid-free paper,
and their binding materials are chosen for strength and durability.
We strive to use environmentally responsible suppliers and materials
to the greatest extent possible in publishing our books.

Manufactured in the United States of America

10 9 8 7 6 5 4 3 2 1

Also available as an ebook

For Dave, the magic that holds the sky up from the ground.

CONTENTS

ACKNOWLEDGMENTS

The journey to this book has been a long and labyrinthine one: a life in four cities at four different institutions on two continents, a few very stressful years on the academic job market, and new additions to our family. My journey began as a graduate student in American studies at George Washington University, an intellectual community in the truest sense: a vibrant place where faculty and students work with integrity and generosity to enrich one another's lives and scholarly pursuits. The department provided me with instruction, travel grants, funding, and a dissertation completion fellowship. Thanks to Katie Brian, Chad Heap, Dave Kieran, Jeremy Hill, Cameron Logan, Jim Miller, and especially to mababy Ramzi Fawaz, one of the most amazing colleagues I've ever known. I also thank the GWU faculty/graduate student disability studies reading group and my dissertation committee, Kip Kosek, Todd Ramlow, Gayle Wald, and Abby Wilkerson, for their trenchant questions. Melani McAlister's unflagging support and rigorous feedback made my work better, and I treasure her friendship, sense of humor, and yoga allegories. Robert McRuer is one of the smartest and most generous human beings I've ever encountered; his unwavering faith in me bolstered me in many moments of self-doubt. The spirit of this community remains with me and sustains me.

My time in the Department of Social and Cultural Analysis (SCA) at New York University reshaped the contours of my work. My colleagues' deep commitment to political activism and social justice enriched this manuscript. There I had the privilege of developing the university's first-ever undergraduate disability studies course, and I thank my many wonderful students for their insight and energy. I am grateful for the conversations, feedback, professional mentoring, and especially the moral support I received as I worked on this book while balancing the intense labor of job applications. Andrew Ross prodded me when I needed prodding, and I am thrilled to release this book as part of the Social and Cultural Analysis series. My faculty writing group, Toral Gajarawala, Maggie Gray, Krishnendu Ray, and Thuy Linh Tu, as well as Lisa Duggan, Lezlie Frye, Gayatri Gopinath, Jennifer Morgan, Crystal Parikh, Josie Saldaña, Rayna Rapp, and Nikhil Pal Singh, offered invaluable feedback as I revised. I learned much about institution building and collegiality from Faye Ginsburg in our work on the NYU Council for the Study of Disability. I especially thank Crystal Parikh for her laughter and friendship; Anne

Rademacher for her consoling cooking; Thuy Linh Tu for her incomparable sense of humor and compassion; and Nikhil Singh, who took me under his wing as mentor and friend during some of my toughest moments. When I felt mired or afraid, you all reminded me, often over a nice glass of scotch, that my work was valuable and necessary. Finally, I treasure Emily Martin, not only for enhancing my work but also for continually showing me what type of scholar and person I'd like to be. I hope each of you sees your contributions in the pages that follow, because you've changed my work for the better.

I am very grateful to New York University Press, especially Eric Zinner and Alicia Nadkarni, for their commitment to publishing disability studies work and for the energy and creativity they brought to this project. I am indebted to the two anonymous New York University Press reviewers for their intellectual rigor and generosity. Portions of this book appeared previously in *Television and New Media* and the *Journal of Literary and Cultural Disability Studies*, and I thank them for their permission to reprint this material as well as their anonymous journal reviewers, whose feedback enriched my revisions. Thanks to Michael Crawford for the permission to reprint his cartoon and to Riva Lehrer for allowing her incredible artwork to appear on the cover. I am grateful to the archivists at the Paley Center for New Media and also to Martin Tahse for taking the time for two interviews about the *After School Specials*. Allison Perlman and Elana Levine also read an early version of the second chapter and were valuable interlocutors. Other colleagues and friends enriched my thinking, including Cynthia Barounis, Michael Bérubé, Eli Clare, Petra Kuppers, David Mitchell, Alondra Nelson, and Sharon Snyder. I had many opportunities to work through the concepts in this book at conferences and invited lectures, and I thank the audiences, respondents, and fellow panelists for their productive questions and critiques.

Prior to joining the University of Missouri, I spent a brief time at University College Dublin in the Republic of Ireland, and I benefitted much from conversations with my colleagues and students. I am honored to be part of Mizzou's Women's and Gender Studies Department, a dazzling community of supportive and passionate women scholars. Teaching relief in my first year as well as generous research and travel support were vital to the completion of this book. My colleagues here in Missouri have enriched my work and my life. I am thankful to Shelda Eggers, Elisa Glick, Joan Hermsen, Mary Jo Neitz, Srirupa Prasad, Enid Schatz, and especially my intrepid faculty mentors and friends, Rebecca Dingo and Linda Reeder, who have offered me solid advice, feedback, intellectual comradeship, and delectable food! I look forward to my future in this community as it continues to flourish.

My wonderful George Washington University writing group has provided round-the-clock intellectual and emotional support over the years. Kyle Riismandel helped make the book's historical arguments more sophisticated and staved off despair with his unrivaled hilarity. Laurel Clark Shire always saw the big picture of my work and soothed me with her insight and baking prowess. There are few readers with Laura Cook Kenna's attention to detail, and I thank her for always reminding me that "it doesn't need to be redeemed; it just needs to be revised." Finally, I thank Stephanie Ricker Schulte, a rare and brilliant treasure, for her diligence in pruning my ten-line sentences (though a few may remain, not for lack of trying), for always telling me the truth, for dancing with me on the peaks, and for easing the pain of the valleys. I am ever brimming with awe and gratitude for all of you, my chosen family. Long live The Trust.

This book would not have been possible without the support of my loved ones in Washington, DC, New York, and Missouri. Thanks especially to my friends Javier Cortes, Jeremy Hill, Nancy Goldman, Nate Goldman, Gary Husslein, Judy Husslein, Mary Stilwell, and Glenn Rice. For hours of song-filled decompression, I thank my many beloved musician friends, Shannon Canfield, Tracy Greever-Rice, Erica and Jamie Kroll, and finally, Kevin Strait and David Goldman, the big brothers I always wished for and now have. Thank you to my fantastic extended family, especially Michael J. G. Cain, Jim Cain, Tom and Joan Cain, Missy Doebley, Elizabeth Elman, Larry and Cheryl Elman, RoRo and Rick Johannson, Jonathan Laurans, Chris and Doug Shaffer, and Carrie Manzo, who always asked when "that friggedy book" would be done. My late grandparents, Joseph and Ann Passanante and Frances Cain, showed me the value of hard work and family. None of this would have been possible without my parents, Kathleen and Dennis, who shower me with unconditional love, support, and enthusiasm, and my incredible sister, Amanda Passanante, my first and always best friend. Thank you to my baby boy, Everett, for filling my mornings with smiles and for napping well so I could finish this book. Being a Mama to you has already been an amazing journey. Finally, to Dave, my best friend and lover, I love you more than I could ever say for making me laugh like no other; for holding me in my darkest places; for moving around the world and back again chasing after my dreams; for being an incredible father to our boy; for building Fretboard Coffee with passion and integrity; and of course, for making music with me along the way. Getting to spend the past, present, and future with you and our son is the greatest gift I will ever receive.

Introduction

From Rebel to Patient

A dark-haired teenaged boy prepares to attend a Fourth of July beach party to celebrate the nation's bicentennial and to pursue the pretty girl next door. After packing the essentials, his sunglasses and shorts, he makes sure there is enough oxygen in his air tanks for the voyage. As the boy shields his eyes from the sun, his parents carefully navigate his plastic-enclosed stretcher's wheels through the deep sand and toward the other teenagers, who gleefully dance to rock music or dive for errant volleyballs. Later in the evening, as fireworks streak across the darkened sky, the girl of his dreams finally sits beside him. He had been attempting to avoid the merciless stares of the other partygoers all evening, but now, through his clear plastic window onto the world, he awkwardly avoids her eyes for an entirely different reason. Shyly, he slips his fingers into a thick black plastic glove to take her hand. The sparks quickly fizzle, however, when he discovers that she has only flirted with him to win a bet with another boy. Watching helplessly as she scampers away to join a group of chuckling boys, he angrily beats the clear walls of his antiseptic bubble in betrayal. He demands that his parents return him to his hospital room, the only place this disabled teenager, born without a functional immune system, might be safe from germs if not from a broken heart.

The boy was the teen heartthrob John Travolta. He was playing the fictional character Tod Lubitch in *The Boy in the Plastic Bubble* (1976), a made-for-TV romantic drama that was loosely based on the highly publicized lives of two young children without functioning immune systems, David Vetter III and Ted DeVita, "bubble boys" who lived and died in isolation from the germ-filled outside world. ABC's bubble-boy-meets-girl-next-door teen romance may seem a bit bizarre at first—just a peculiar bit of 1970s ephemera. However, rather than interpreting *The Boy in the Plastic Bubble* as a medical drama or an otherworldly story about a rare disability, critics at the time uniformly recognized it as a classic adolescent coming-of-age narrative. In the words of Tom Shales, a TV critic for the *Washington Post*, "Any teenager who feels isolated, picked on, or odd should be able to identify with

Travolta" and his immunocompromised character, Tod.[1] Transforming the medicalized human interest story of the bubble boy into a teenaged love story, the movie juxtaposes a U.S. Independence Day celebration with the humiliation of Tod's failed romantic encounter to accentuate his emasculating dependence. This pairing not only links his disability to a failed (or queer) masculinity and heterosexuality, but also configures his broader failure to achieve autonomy as an issue that is entwined with national belonging, or citizenship. Within the story's logic, Tod, queered by his inability to touch others (most tragically the girl he loves), must overcome his disability not just to become heterosexual but also to become an adult and a citizen. Television critics unanimously interpreted Tod's isolating disability as a metaphor for adolescent identity crisis and resolution—not because this pairing is at all essential, but because the articulation of adolescence with disability and queerness was becoming such a pervasive representational convention across so many different U.S. cultural realms by the 1970s.

Spotlighting the figure of the developing teenager as a site of pop cultural, medical, and governmental intervention, *Chronic Youth* argues that teen identity crises help to link the destinies of youth to the national future and that cultural understandings of youth as a "disabling condition" have been central to this project. But how did this rendering of "normal" adolescence as a disability to be overcome become the stuff of common sense? And more broadly, how has this articulation served as a way to "police the crisis" not only of adolescence but also of the normative social order?[2]

The teenager has appeared in history and culture as an anxious figure, the repository for American dreams and worst nightmares, national and individual success and the imminent danger of failure. As culture, policy, and medicine work to address the paradigmatic teen identity crisis (or, the teen *as* crisis), these spheres also acknowledge the possibility and peril of a future citizen who may yet be anything. This is a proto-citizen who may not turn out straight or gender-normative, may not be white, may not be nondisabled, may not be a productive worker who adheres to the economic and cultural values of U.S. capitalism. Teenagers are potentially normative and potently pathological, unfinished projects whose indeterminacy provokes the anxiety inherent in this chrono-social category of adolescence. Charles Acland argues that common cultural concerns over "youth in crisis" are always less about real teenagers or their real problems and more about "an anxiety concerning the reproduction of social order."[3] In this framework, youth is understood as having "no fundamental essence *except* as a problem, as a crisis of value, of economics, or of resources."[4] Conceptualizing teenagers as a crisis of value has been a lucrative strategy for a variety of industries and institutions, including pop cultural, governmental, medical, pharmaceutical, and juridical ones. But the story of how the rebel became the patient is much more than a story of simple market demand.[5]

In part, this idea of "teens as/in crisis" derives from essentializing theories of the biological or psychological nature of adolescence. To be a teenager is to be besieged by raging hormones while at the mercy of an incomplete brain. Such figurations of the teenager offer up adolescent bodies as perennially volatile and unstable or as problems to be managed. In spite of a variety of cultural studies of the social construction of identity, such essentialist figurations of adolescence also conjure a body that is remarkably impermeable to historical change or cultural difference. Depictions of adolescence as a universal psychological or bodily stage of temporary crisis evacuate the history of youth as an identity category akin to (and indeed, affected by) race, class, gender, sexuality, or dis/ability, whose cultural and political meaning continues to change radically over time. While the biological and hormonal process that sociologists, psychologists, and physicians have named "adolescence" certainly exists, this book imagines "teen" as a shifting cultural figure that serves as a paradigmatic crisis to be overcome in order to achieve the role of adult citizen, a rational and stable subject position that is established in contrast to the unstable and irrational teen. Although ideas about teen emotional volatility, rebelliousness, generational conflict, or sexual waywardness often circulate in U.S. culture as timeless facets of teens' "true" physiological nature, this commonsense perception of teen nature actually comprises many sedimentary layers of culture and history from the turn of the twentieth century to the present.

Whether in psychologists' offices, in classrooms, or on television screens, approaches to representing or managing individual identity crises always collide with and construct broader cultural crises over national and economic health, development, and futurity. Cultural theorists of youth, including Stuart Hall and Dick Hebdige, first analyzed youth through the lens of subculture to examine how young people, as a subordinated group, have challenged the hegemonic norms of a dominant (adult) culture, often through their consumption patterns.[6] Building on this work, *Chronic Youth* analyzes the teenager as a cultural figure through which broad threats to the normative order—racial, gendered, disabled, or sexual—have been negotiated and contained. This book details how the teenager has transitioned from rebel to patient in order to show how this teen transformation has participated in an ongoing normalization of a culture of rehabilitation, or the idea that endless self-surveillance and enhancement are not only innately healthy but also central to good citizenship.

After World War II, a U.S. economic boom revealed that teens could be a lucrative market segment. Then post-1968 youth movements demonstrated that teenagers could be powerful and political if their potency was properly channeled. By the early 1970s, popular media and literary producers quickly responded to this call by creating new pedagogical modes of storytelling for teen audiences that openly addressed a variety of "real" teen problems, like parental alcoholism, sex, sexually transmitted diseases, and teen pregnancy. This new, problem-driven, teen-specific entertainment emerged within and across multiple mediums through established media industries and formed a new genre of teen popular culture that I call "rehabilitative edutainment." Cultural industries, as well as policy makers and parents, imagined rehabilitative edutainment to be a realistic, socially relevant, and entertaining variety of popular culture that would be healthy and informative for impressionable teen consumers. They also depicted youth crises and offered a "serious" address of teen proto-citizens as an opportunity to sell products that appear to be directed at a formerly neglected segment of the consumer market. This commercial vision found political traction in a country that had been shaken by national scandals like Watergate and Vietnam (both of which have been characterized as the nation's "loss of innocence") as well as by post-1968 social movements that exposed the many exclusions of the white middle-class suburban bliss of Cold War American dreams.

Chronic Youth focuses on how these rehabilitative cultural narratives exerted power on everyday lives, shaping norms of embodiment, knowledge about youth, sexuality, and disability, and policies for regulating teen behaviors through medicine *and* media. Often state- or community-endorsed, this problem-driven formula's ubiquity both revealed and incorporated cultural perceptions about popular media's powerful effects on developing citizenry.[7] Rather than perpetuate Cold War fears about mass media's potential to incite juvenile delinquency, a new coalition in the 1970s and after, including parents, policy makers, regulatory institutions, and media producers, attempted to wield that influence to create socially responsible media designed to develop productive and empathetic teen citizens. By addressing its teen characters and viewers in a tone that was more diagnostic or preventative than punitive, rehabilitative edutainment asserted a therapeutic function for popular culture and, along with that, a sense of its legitimate contribution to rather than corruption of society's youth. This problem-driven formula soon prevailed as the dominant mode of address for teen audiences, and in turn, it rehabilitated the image of formerly denigrated media forms, like television or paperback novels, as productive rather than damaging to youth citizenship development.

From the immunocompromised Tod Lubitch, to the stuttering ice-skating boys of ABC's *After School Specials* (1972–1994), to the love-struck girls with cancer of Lurlene McDaniel's *Six Months to Live* (1989), rehabilitative edutainment also prominently featured narratives of disability. Ableist representations of disability as tragic or inspirational had long been a staple of American cultural representation for audiences of all ages without a corresponding cultural awareness about the damaging nature of disability stereotypes or a realization of the ubiquity of disability images. In addition to critiquing ableist or stereotypical representations of disability, disability studies scholars have shown how popular media rarely portrays the fullness or political realities of disabled lives and instead uses disability as corporeal otherness that signifies otherwise intangible character traits.[8] Amputated limbs continue to connote villainy, while fatness implies wealth or greed, and a critique of this representational taxonomy of disability often still "falls on deaf ears."[9] In other words, disability pervades representation not on its own terms, but rather, in the words of David T. Mitchell and Sharon L. Snyder, as "the materiality of metaphor."[10] Rehabilitative edutainment for teenagers certainly falls within this broader representational history of ableist representations of disability as tragic, undesirable, or inspirational. However, *Chronic Youth* offers a provocative new analysis of how American cultural producers, policy makers, and medical professionals have mobilized discourses of disability to cast adolescence as a treatable "condition" rather than a willful (or potentially criminal) waywardness. Rather than a physical condition solely rooted in the body, disability is, in Rosemarie Garland-Thomson's words, a historically shifting "attribution of corporeal deviance" that is "not so much a property of bodies as a product of cultural rules about what bodies should be or do."[11] Discourses of disability enflesh sets of cultural rules that regulate all bodies, whether disabled or not. Thus rehabilitative edutainment's narratives feature stutters, mobility impairments, and chronic illnesses as undesirable embodiments and obstacles to development in order to signify the otherwise intangible instability of "normal" adolescence and provide strategies for its containment.

Chief among these narratives has been the inspirational story of "overcoming" disability to "achieve" able-bodiedness. Overcoming narratives reinforce the superiority and desirability of the able body in contrast to the disabled body by rendering disability an undesirable obstacle to be overcome or otherwise eliminated. Thus, in the words of Eli Clare, such narratives rest on the ableist idea that "disability and achievement contradict each other and that any disabled person who overcomes this contradiction is heroic."[12] Nevertheless, overcoming narratives have been popular and enduring in the

United States because they reinforce the ideals of American liberalism: productivity, freedom, and self-reliance as central to good citizenship. Rehabilitative edutainment uses disability, as the materiality of metaphor, to establish and teach cultural rules about what teen proto-citizens should be *becoming*. Overcoming disability corporealizes the abstract metamorphosis that is teen coming of age, constructing it as a process of overcoming limitations or obstacles (often, their very bodies) to achieve coherent and stable (read: able-bodied and heterosexual) adulthood. In this sense, a recurrent cultural narrative about teenagers' overcoming their disabling adolescence has also provided a collective story of citizenship that binds rehabilitating/maturing teenagers inextricably to ideas about national belonging and health.

Rehabilitative edutainment's ableist narratives of overcoming disability also provided a crucial strategy for regulating teen sexuality. Amid a U.S. cultural rejection of the sexual repression that allegedly characterized the Cold War, the development of sexuality was increasingly attached not only to ideals of democratic freedom ("liberation") but also to healthy citizenship for all people, whether young or old. Thus, by the 1970s, neglecting entirely issues of sexuality in teen popular culture was no longer a viable option. On the screen and across their pages, striving for able-bodiedness became linked to achieving heterosexuality in plotlines within which teen protagonists reached adulthood when they demonstrated that they had not only achieved able-bodiedness but also formed a "healthy" heterosexual romantic relationship with an able-bodied partner.

Queer scholars such as Lauren Berlant and Lee Edelman have shown that "the Child" has often functioned as an affective rallying point for seemingly apolitical investments in a "better future," but such investments are always political, as they further entrench heteronormativity (and, disability studies scholars would add, able-bodiedness) as a shared ideal of citizenship.[13] However, when they maintain a polar opposition between adults and children, queer theories of childhood largely neglect the particular histories, cultures, and symbolic value of adolescence. The instability of adolescence, as in-between-ness, crisis, and becoming, became useful to the affective and political arrangement of post–sexual liberation citizenship as it coalesced around heterosexuality and able-bodiedness. While there are certainly many continuities between children and teenagers, in terms of their political-affective cultural value and the tactics used to police their sexualities, the *inevitably* sexual teenager, at risk of having an unwanted pregnancy, a sexual identity crisis, or a sexually transmitted disease, has not always functioned in popular culture or public policy as a figure of sexual innocence like the Child, especially when the teenager in question is nonwhite, disabled, queer, or poor.[14]

This book builds on valuable queer scholarship of citizenship, affect, and childhood to consider how teens have been imagined and addressed as developing proto-citizens—something more than "infantile citizens" or "queer children"—whose proper acquisition of self-discipline and "healthy" sexual development was imagined as particularly crucial to the nation's future.[15] Often in opposition to vulnerable and sexually innocent children in need of protection, teens had emerged, by the 1970s, as sexual proto-citizens in need of citizenship training to proactively navigate a new culture of sexual openness and gender trouble in the wake of sexual liberation and second-wave feminism. However, as teenagers' maturation into "normal" heterosexuality or traditional gender roles was far from assured in advance, it had to be carefully managed through healthy rehabilitative edutainment, lest the increasing sexual explicitness of a post-1970s popular culture that was "wallowing in sex" be cast as a corrosive or dangerous influence on youth development.[16]

Yet, as *Chronic Youth* will show, this new form of citizenship affected a broader swath of the population than teenagers alone. Rehabilitative citizenship took root as citizenship became imagined as a cultural or emotional attachment rather than a form of national political belonging. By the 1980s, this transition in the character of citizenship became articulated increasingly through a privatized (or what Berlant refers to as an "intimate") political discourse that spotlighted personal morality and the family. The body of the teenager and its management through self-discipline provided nothing less than a template for naturalizing cultural citizenship *as* governmentality, as a never-ending and participatory process of emotional and physical self-regulation, in relation to the "intimate public sphere" of the United States.[17]

Chronic Youth is thus also part of a growing body of scholarship that theorizes the relationship among heteronormativity, able-bodiedness, and citizenship—and conversely, the configuration of queerness and disability as sites of "deviant" sexuality that lie outside acceptable citizenship.[18] When overcoming disability stands in metaphorically for "coming of age," rehabilitative narratives equate a partnership of able-bodiedness and heterosexuality with healthy, mature adulthood. This linkage of heterosexuality and able-bodiedness as the "healthy" or natural outcome of development participates in a broader cultural process that Robert McRuer has named "compulsory able-bodiedness," or the set of diverse cultural rules that continually establish able-bodiedness as pre-discursively natural in contrast to disability, which appears as an undesirable aberration.[19] Paradoxically, even as rehabilitative edutainment offered a new challenge to paternalism by addressing teenagers proactively rather than protectively, its rehabilitative logic relied on and perpetuated an ongoing infantilization of disabled and queer bodies. Within the entwined systems of compulsory able-bodiedness and heterosexuality, adolescence, queerness, and disability have been positioned as interrelated sites (or passing "stages") of abnormality that require development, intervention, and normalization until and unless they are overcome. This book builds on generative theoretical work on compulsory heterosexuality and able-bodiedness by providing a historical account of the mediated, gendered, and age-related processes through which adolescence, able-bodiedness, and heterosexuality operated to form the very regulatory norms that govern what counts as good media or productive citizenship. Just as the "impaired teenager" has changed over time, so have the varied expressions of compulsory able-bodiedness and heterosexuality.

The common thread uniting the two dominant images of teen life traced in *Chronic Youth*, those of the rebel and the patient, is a fundamental understanding of the teenager as a problem to be managed and solved. Both on- and off-screen, teenagers, while still threatening to social norms *and* threatened by a variety of bad influences, were recast from post–World War II rebels in need of punishment to patients in need of a treatment regimen. They became development opportunities, ripe for sexual, emotional, and bodily instruction and compassionate intervention. Highlighting the figure of the developing teenager as s/he appeared in popular culture, government policy, and medical discourse, *Chronic Youth* traces how adolescence became "cripped"—namely, how disability became an enforced category for youth, whose marginal citizen-position and problematic sexuality became marked by their imaginary and requisite disabling.[20] In representing adolescence as a disability, popular representations advocated the decriminalization of adolescence while simultaneously pathologizing the space of maturation that exists between childhood and adulthood.

Of course, the association of adolescence with disability also had diverse cultural effects that varied drastically in relation to race, class, gender, and sexuality. As the final chapter shows, the medicalization of white middle-class teenagers from the 1970s onward also coincided with (and, in many ways, facilitated) the ongoing criminalization and incarceration of nonwhite youth.[21] Thus, while the discourse about teen bodies that this book historicizes produces *all* teen bodies that do not conform as always-already deviant, pathologized, subjected, and cripped, it spotlights some teens—such as school shooters or "superpredators"—as figures of excess that bear an unequal brunt of that cripping. Coming of age became recast as a gradual process of rehabilitation, one that proactively involved teenagers in their own decision making and self-fashioning through the work of pedagogical popular culture and, with increasing frequency by the twentieth century's close, medical and pharmaceutical intervention for some, criminalization for others, and surveillance for all. On the broadest scale, *Chronic Youth* uncovers how representations of adolescence, sexuality, and disability, as sites of development, management, and investment, helped to naturalize a culture of rehabilitation as coterminous with good citizenship not just for those deemed disabled—but for all of us.

Cripping Adolescence

By analyzing a variety of cultural materials, *Chronic Youth* innovatively shows how disability became attached to *other* forms of embodied experience that have been deemed undesirable, such as adolescence, queerness, or immaturity, while able-bodiedness became synonymous with "healthy" attributes like maturity, productivity, or heteronormativity. However, disability has been discursively (and often implicitly) attached to adolescence at various points in U.S. history and in diverse cultural locations that precede post-1968 rehabilitative edutainment. In many ways, disability, as a "metaphoric abstraction" for adolescence, became such a compelling and pervasive representational taxonomy and ideology by the 1970s because disability and adolescence had been intimately entangled disciplinary sites from the turn of the twentieth century onward.[22] Governmental institutions, from local to national, from juridical to educational, and later, social scientific and psychological disciplines expressed fears over the management of adolescence and used historically shifting terminologies like "savagery," "feeblemindedness," "juvenile delinquency," "deviance," and later, "neurological (under)development." Policing the sexuality, emotional expressiveness, embodiment, and behavior of teenagers—whether through specters of the savage, the rebel, or the patient—has been central to enforcing the normative social order and its ideal of democratic citizenship.

A new Romantic ideal of childhood as a stage of sexual innocence and play (as opposed to labor) took root in the Victorian era in stark contrast to what G. Stanley Hall first described, in 1904, as the "storm and stress" of adolescence. Yet storm and stress at the turn of the twentieth century, as countless scholars of youth history have shown, encompassed much more than volatile adolescent bodies. Hall's codification of adolescence, for instance, manifested cultural anxieties about white middle-class men's loss of strength and vigor due to the "overcivilizing" impulses of American modernity—an overcivilization to which a "savage" adolescence served as a crucial antidote.[23] Likewise, "generational conflict," often perceived to be transhistorically characteristic of adolescent psychology, first emerged to name an anxiety about the Americanization of immigrants and the perceived distance and loss of cultural traditions between young second-generation immigrants and their parents.[24] Thus, cultural anxieties about the rapid pace of modernity—industrialization, urbanization, and the racial and ethnic diversification of the national body through immigration and the Great Migration—triangulated within anxieties about adolescent behavior.

However, fears over the "proper development" of individuals, economies, and even nations were not only articulated through ideas about a body's generation or age but also through measurements of its capacity. Two emergent and co-constitutive Progressive-era ideologies of development and productivity, eugenics and Taylorist scientific management, relied on cultural narratives and understandings of Darwinian theories of evolutionary development. Both systems inexorably shaped cultural constructions of adolescence, race, and dis/ability. Amid the rise of industrial capitalism, "scientific management" of the workplace demanded ever more rigorous standardization and efficiency of workers. Meanwhile, using overlapping rhetorics of race, disability, and age, eugenic thinkers established Western culture as the pinnacle of development, capacity, and efficiency in opposition to other non-Western cultures, which were deemed less developed, more "infantile" or "primitive" by comparison. Eugenics formed what Snyder and Mitchell call a "diagnostic regime," comprising diverse and interwoven branches of scientific inquiry, including psychology, sexology, and anthropology; forms of reproductive control; and educational technologies, such as classrooms and IQ tests.[25] In this context, disabled people were increasingly remanded to custodial institutions (especially during their childbearing years) as eugenics defined them as a "subnormal" population whose bodies were deemed inferior and "unfit" for the new demands of modern labor as it standardized workers' bodies and systematized their function.

Through Progressive-era mechanisms that were deeply infused with eugenic philosophies and modern techniques of disciplining the body, cultural ideas about disability and its management linked directly to concerns over the sexuality of adolescent bodies. While rebellion among adolescent boys might ensure future generations of virile, white American male entrepreneurs, female "delinquency" usually corresponded to allegations of promiscuity and allied with the eugenic designation "feebleminded," a capacious term that operated to police gender, sexuality, class, and race within this new social order. As Michael Rembis shows, late nineteenth-century medical doctors, psychologists, educators, and reformers undertook a systemic program to diagnose and treat rebellious behavior associated with young urban women, a project that led to the establishment of juvenile courts and sex-specific institutions designed to punish, segregate, and cure adolescent girls who were labeled deviant, defective, or delinquent.[26] Within a eugenic diagnostic regime, regardless of whether or not young women were "truly" disabled or simply poor, sexually active, or nonwhite, disability was used as a common "justification for inequality," transforming deviant traits or behavior into undesirable embodiment.[27] Disabled persons—institutionalized, abused, or neglected—were joined by sexually "mismanaged" teen bodies that were also policed and segregated using designations of disability. Through overlapping and mutually reinforcing discourses of racial, sexual, and disabled "deviance," reproductive controls based on eugenic notions of the heredity of deviant behavior played out in the sexual containment and policing of adolescent bodies to ensure and protect future "fit" generations.[28] Thus, the eugenic management of the future, the quest to ensure the continuance of a white, middle-class, able-bodied, heterosexual ideal by regulating "undesirable" sexuality, formed one of the earliest cultural convergences of disability, sexuality, race, and adolescence.

However, the conventional origin story for the teenager—as not only a body undergoing the biological changes of adolescence but also a particularly unruly social creature—does not typically include Progressive-era overlaps between disabled and adolescent bodies as, in Acland's words, "crises of value or resources."[29] Rather, the black leather–coated postwar rebel remains one of the most enduring images of American adolescence. When high school became compulsory by the 1940s, teenagers emerged as a distinct social group, while adolescence (at least for members of the white middle and elite classes) increasingly became defined as a period of suspended maturation devoted to schooling prior to employment and adult responsibility. Teenagers also became a lucrative market segment for a variety of films, television shows, rock-and-roll music, and clothing. *Rebel without a Cause* (1955), alongside other midcentury images of juvenile delinquency such as *The Wild One* (1953), *Blackboard Jungle* (1955), and *Teen-Age Crime Wave* (1955), emerged and entrenched a variety of cultural understandings of the "nature" of adolescence—namely, that teen rebellion was natural but also dangerously pathological, without obvious cause yet somehow essential to American coming of age.

The mystifying rebel personified a growing cultural panic about juvenile delinquency and a more generalized anxiety about the power of mass media. Toward the end of World War II, social scientists, the Children's Bureau, the Federal Bureau of Investigation, and journalists argued that juvenile delinquency was on the rise, in spite of the lack of evidence of an increased crime rate among young people.[30] Apart from the visual and narrative danger rebel movies presented to impressionable youth, even the rock-and-roll soundtrack to *Blackboard Jungle* was considered a bad influence. One year prior to the film's release, Frederic Wertham, a neurologist and psychiatrist, penned his infamous *Seduction of the Innocent* (1954), which warned that mass media, especially comic books, contributed to an increase in juvenile delinquency and homosexuality. In what became popularly known as the "comic book hearings," Wertham appeared as an expert witness before the Senate Subcommittee on Juvenile Delinquency, led by U.S. Representative Estes Kefauver, to discuss the causal relationship between "dangerous media" and "bad teenagers."

Although cultural fears about adolescent rebellion led to the censure of an array of teen media and music, Leerom Medovoi persuasively argues that the figure of the rebel, epitomized by the adolescent "bad boy," was crucial to maintaining Cold War American conformity rather than antithetical to it because the dissident rebel preserved America's image as a democratic space of self-expression and self-fashioning.[31] At the same time, Medovoi argues, these narratives performed rebellion's containment by disciplining and reabsorbing bad boys (and girls) into the safe conventions of suburban life, heteronormativity, and traditional gender roles. As a figure of dissent and nonconformity, the rebel was essential to notions of American participatory democracy and to the correlation of democracy with Americanness itself. Yet the rebel also figured prominently in representations that characterized all post–World War II teenagers as perennially angst-ridden potential criminals, who were dually threatening to society and threatened by a variety of external forces. Rather than simply relying on parents to discipline teens, the government, through the Judiciary Committee, intervened to police teenagers as potential criminals. The government also offered a new cultural understanding of media, when it argued that the regulation of media was crucial to the regulation of youth and, more generally, to the preservation of a healthy nation during Cold War anticommunist struggles. Along with a variety of other "external forces," like unstable families (especially those with overbearing mothers or absent fathers) or delinquent friends, dangerous media might adversely impact adolescent development and lead to national decline.

While the image of the delinquent teenager dominated the Cold War cultural imagination and media landscape, by the mid- to late 1960s, cultural understandings of adolescence began undergoing a radical shift, largely due to the concurrent politicization and psychologization of "identity." Medovoi argues that the concept of identity figured heavily in the "ideological terrain" of the Cold War, with "adolescence playing the pivotal role."[32] The first use of the term "identity" in relation to youth development occurred in Erik H.

Erikson's *Childhood and Society* (1950), which, by 1963, had become required reading for university courses in sociology, psychology, and social work. However, it was Erikson's subsequent study, *Identity: Youth and Crisis* (1968), that fully elaborated his famous concept of "identity crisis," a period of "role confusion" usually occurring in adolescence, when a person feels conflicting internal and external pressures as s/he searches for a clearer sense of self and the role s/he will play in society. Although Erikson believed that identity crises could happen at any stage of the life cycle, identity crisis quickly became commonsense vernacular used to characterize adolescence. Crucially, Erikson's new formulation shifted the predominantly externalizing sociological vocabulary used to describe 1950s teenagers (rebels without cause who were besieged by bad external influences like unstable families, violent media, or delinquent friends) to internalizing medical diagnoses, a shift that validated teen angst as deriving from a very real mind-body process that was simultaneously normal and pathological. Problem-driven narratives in rehabilitative edutainment would capitalize on this vocabulary by the 1970s, gaining popularity and legitimacy as "realistic" portrayals of teen identity crisis and assisting audiences in imagining the developmental space between childhood and adulthood as legitimately fraught with real difficulty rather than willful or nonsensical resistance against adults.

By the late 1960s, from Vietnam War draft resistance, to the Chicago riots following the 1968 assassination of Martin Luther King Jr., to the birth of the disability activists' independent living movement at UC-Berkeley, "youth" had also become a politically charged identity rather than solely a developmental category. Far from rebellion "without a cause," 1960s youth countercultural movements represented a politically engaged rebellion of a new kind. "Don't trust anyone over thirty," the mantra of the free speech movement, emblazoned buttons and formed a rallying cry in speeches and manifestos that politicized generational conflict as a rejection of conventional social mores and political ideals. Identity and crisis became a way of fomenting and negotiating identity-based political movements, such as those for civil rights, gay and lesbian liberation, women's liberation, disability rights, and black nationalism. At the same time, critics of the counterculture mobilized the same rhetoric of identity crisis in order to dismiss youth protest as immaturity—a passing stage of youthful craziness that threatened to fragment the cohesive identity of the nation—rather than legitimate it as political consciousness.

This brief overview suggests that a crip history of teens as crisis-ridden subjects matters not just for youth studies but also for the broader fields of U.S. media, cultural, and political history, because discourses of adolescence have been crucial in rendering heteronormativity, able-bodiedness, and emotional management synonymous with maturity and, ultimately, with productive citizenship. Although "teen" and "disability" may at first seem like unrelated categories, both have been understood as abnormal (and undesirable) bodily states and as problematic sexual sites in different but intimately related ways. As such, both have called forth forms of discipline that combine bodily, psychological, and cultural forms of rehabilitation. Within and around these bodies, rehabilitation coalesced into a culture.

Rehabilitative Citizenship

To "rehabilitate" means "to restore" "to a former capacity," "to a former state (as of efficiency, good management, or solvency)," or "to . . . bring to a condition of health or useful and constructive activity."[33] These definitions reflect the complex discursive locations of rehabilitation, a dynamic interplay among bodies, capacities, medical knowledge, social services, personal growth, and norms of productive labor that are at once economic and cultural. Most often, rehabilitation, as a medical and cultural language, invokes ideas about disability and able-bodiedness, where disability appears as undesirable "loss" and able-bodiedness as coveted "wholeness"—a past wholeness, marred by disability, and the future wholeness promised by successful and ongoing commitment to rehabilitation. Yoking capitalist values ("efficiency," "good management," and "solvency") to individual health, rehabilitation describes a set of relationships that are simultaneously cultural, bodily, and economic: an entanglement of healthy bodies and healthy economies, once threatened and then restored. Pivoting from queer theories of temporality, I suggest that rehabilitation is only partly a "straight" linear developmental narrative of "overcoming" disability or "growing up."[34] Rather, it also requires a sort of polytemporal desire. It involves longing nostalgically for the past, figured as a lost previous state of imagined wholeness or integrity, but one that is recoverable (in the ever-receding future) through disciplined individual effort and collective desire in the present. Rehabilitation, at its core, is a self-making project involving perpetual self-discipline and self-surveillance. It has become attached to the notions of liberal individualism and good citizenship that scaffold our commonsense ideas about democracy and citizenship.

However, rehabilitation, as a practice or set of beliefs, did not always exist. In contrast to earlier models of disability as a pathology to be cured or eliminated, rehabilitation marked the appearance of something new as it emerged around World War I. Although the pathologization, segregation, and institutionalization of the disabled had (and have) not completely disappeared, by the second half of the twentieth century, argues the historian Henri Jacques Stiker, rehabilitation "ended up dominating the idea of cure."[35] In addition to the rise of prosthetics for wounded soldiers, rehabilitation encompassed other physical, mental, and social therapies meant to facilitate disabled people's "reintegration" into society.[36] As rehabilitation "moved out in front of the hospital," treatment regimens for disability and disease relocated to the social and cultural realm rather than remaining exclusive to the medical sphere.[37]

To illustrate this cultural shift, one particular story of rehabilitation's emergence is especially illuminating. During World War II, a psychoanalyst in the Mt. Zion Veterans' Rehabilitation Clinic observed veterans who "had neither been 'shellshocked' nor become malingerers, but had through the exigencies of war lost a sense of personal sameness and historical continuity."[38] The war had shattered the veterans' senses of self into "bodily, sexual, social, occupational fragments, each having to overcome again the danger of . . . its evil prototype[s]."[39] The psychoanalyst's list of "evil prototypes" included "the crying baby, the bleeding female, the submissive nigger, the sexual sissy, the economic sucker, the mental moron—all prototypes the mere allusion to which could bring [the veterans] close to homicidal or suicidal rage followed by varying degrees of irritability or apathy."[40] This elaborate assemblage of "evil prototypes" that threatened a soldier's war-traumatized body and mind featured a variety of sexual, racial, and bodily categories—femininity ("bleeding female"), blackness ("submissive nigger"), homosexuality (figured as effeminacy in the "sexual sissy"), and disability ("mental moron"), among others—as terrifying obstacles to development and coherence. In the case of the shattered soldier, these prototypes were also specters of *former* developmental obstacles that he must now confront *again* in order to resynthesize the fragments into a coherent identity. At the same time, the word "prototype" suggests a powerful ambivalence. The quest for a coherent identity might be a perpetually unfinished project (and perhaps especially for the variety of categorically deviant bodies the psychoanalyst lists!) because such undesirable, fragmented, and "evil" figures might *always* be part of us. Perhaps these prototypes are not only potential nightmare "futures" resulting from poor development, but also ongoing "presents," originating conceptual bedrocks around which all selves form. This particular account of veterans in a World War II rehabilitation clinic takes a rather surprising turn, however, when the psychoanalyst explains straightforwardly that "the same central disturbance" he observed in war-wounded soldiers appeared "in severely conflicted young people whose sense of confusion is due, rather, to a war within themselves, and in confused rebels and destructive delinquents who war on their society."[41] Of course, the psychoanalyst-storyteller was none other than the preeminent developmental psychologist Erik H. Erikson. The "central disturbance" Erikson discovered in wounded war veterans was "identity crisis."

Arguably one of the most dominant and lasting conceptual frameworks for adolescence, the concept of identity crisis was born out of the rehabilitative convergence of disability and sexuality.[42] By observing (and depathologizing) veterans who had been previously diagnosed as mentally ill, Erikson had invented a new diagnostic term for "normal" people who were undergoing difficulties. As identity crisis moved "out of the hospital" to become firmly affixed to commonsense understandings of the chrono-social category of adolescence as a universally experienced stage, the necessity of rehabilitation began extending to *all* bodies, regardless of disability status or age.

Thus within and alongside the story of the teen's transition from rebel to patient is not only the story of how cure gave way to rehabilitation but also how rehabilitation became attached to citizenship. I use the term "rehabilitative citizenship" to describe how rehabilitation has become attached to what it means to be a good citizen, often through seemingly apolitical discourses of "health" or "growth." I argue that its ascendance marks a broader cultural, economic, and historical shift toward governmentality from 1970s-era post-Fordism to neoliberalism and globalization of the 1990s and beyond. Governmentality, a term coined by Michel Foucault, describes the process by which power in advanced liberal democracies, which was formerly centralized in the nation-state (or in institutions such as the hospital, to invoke the rehabilitation model), morphs into the diffuse biopolitical power of individual self-surveillance. While "cure" implies an end to the management of a body, rehabilitation produces the body as forever incomplete—a ripe market for commodities and site for governmentality, both of which promote endless enhancement, flexibility, and self-regulation as voluntary, desirable, and liberating. Rehabilitative citizenship reframed individual citizenship, not as guaranteed in advance by the nation-state but rather as an endless "contractual" negotiation that is contingent on perpetual self-surveillance and healthy (read: normative) behavior.[43] *Chronic Youth* shows how rehabilitative citizenship emerged in overlapping cultural locations of adolescence, sexuality, and disability, including medical knowledge and authority, cultural representation, strategies of emotional management, and governmental policy.

However, beginning to unpack the history and culture of rehabilitative citizenship requires first contextualizing its emergence within a 1970s economic and cultural turn toward "self-help" and its eventual alignment with two intertwined core values of neoliberalism: "privatization" and "personal responsibility." Rehabilitation subjected everyone—not just the previously pathologized bodies of the disabled—to a process of self-management that was configured as essential to maintaining healthy, productive citizenship. Historians and sociologists have characterized self-help culture's meteoric rise in the 1970s and 1980s as part of a broad cultural "turn inward" or a "triumph of the therapeutic."[44] The self-help industry's diverse and lucrative offerings included "pop" psychological and self-improvement literature, television shows, radio programs, and seminars, as well as personal coaching.[45] With the establishment of a "twelve step culture" and the media popularity of the self-help guru John Bradshaw in the early 1970s, the phrase "inner child," a personification of trauma that impeded proper development into adulthood, came into circulation alongside "codependency" as two prevailing terms of an emergent self-help movement. Mobilizing rhetorics of adolescence and disability, the self-help movement emphasized personal "growth" or "overcoming" obstacles to "achieve your full potential." The self-help industry capitalized on strategies of individual empowerment that had been pioneered by liberal progressive "depathologizing" movements such as feminist "consciousness raising" or the countercultural slogan "power to the people." However, while those in social movements fought for equality, social recognition, and the downward redistribution of power and wealth, the self-help industry converted their dissident rhetoric into a profitable industry, offering consumer-driven "cultural citizenship" that promoted "resistance through consumption" and identity-based market segmentation as an alternative (and hollow homage) to participation in social movements.[46] By the 1990s, Erikson's "evil prototypes" had become lucrative niche markets.[47]

Self-help culture, as well as the rehabilitative ethos that formed its infrastructure, was a tactic of governmentality that positioned perpetual work on the self as essential to achieving maturity, health, capacity, and good citizenship. Rehabilitation rests on ableist notions of embodiment involving the language and activity of "return"—a return to a state of able-bodied normalcy or stability—through "personal effort." Historically, this form of self-regulating rehabilitative citizenship became equated with healthiness just as post-Fordist economic deregulation—or the idea that markets are *also* healthiest when self-regulating—ascended as a hybrid economic-cultural philosophy that claimed to promote economic "recovery." From the 1970s onward, images of rehabilitation became inextricable from endless calls for personal responsibility to promote national health, a type of self-rehabilitation that formed the cultural underpinnings of U.S. neoliberalism.

As rehabilitation became normalized as a youthful rite of passage by the twentieth century's close, "disability" likewise no longer always signified pathology or even difference. In a post–Americans with Disabilities Act (ADA) United States, disabled people, through strategies of "reasonable accommodation" and "universal design" as well as through cultural representation, were integrated as productive fellow citizens who formed part of the U.S. multicultural tapestry. Yet although the ADA formed part of a shift in cultural attitudes about disability and provided the framework for legal redress against disability prejudice in the workplace in 1990, an ADA Restoration Act was necessary eighteen years later, because those claiming discrimination by invoking it lost their cases more than 80 percent of the time.

Although rehabilitation operates through discourses of inclusion, disability is rendered an undesirable and transitory obstacle to be surpassed through individual *will*, or in neoliberalism-speak, through "personal responsibility" and "hard work." Rehabilitation's integrative ideal also requires a damaging pattern of cultural erasure as a prerequisite for granting social inclusion— a pattern also at work in liberal multiculturalist movements of the 1990s. Namely, rehabilitation chooses and spotlights the disabled, proclaiming a desire for their inclusion, but paradoxically only so that they are "made to disappear."[48] In Stiker's tragically prescient words, rehabilitation emblematizes "[s]ociety's wish . . . to make identical *without making equal . . .* to efface [disabled people's] difference but not establish them on the same level economically and socially."[49] Neoliberalism's philosophy of personal responsibility acts as an important counterpart to rehabilitation. As complementary systems, they elide how ongoing structural inequalities, based on race, class, gender, sexuality, or dis/ability, continue to affect education, employment, health care, and access to citizenship and instead prioritize the individual will to overcome adversity as the key determinant of success.

One can see this rehabilitative logic at work in various arenas. As many queer studies scholars have shown, gay men and lesbians have been tacitly included in mainstream society and culture, provided that they assimilate to the norms of a new "homonormativity." Homonormativity is characterized by "a politics that does not contest dominant heteronormative assumptions and institutions" such as marriage, domesticity, or consumption, but rather "upholds and sustains them" while bolstering broader neoliberal tactics of economic privatization.[50] Contemporaneously, prevailing "color-blind" racist practices of "postracial" America maintain that any acknowledgment of ongoing racism is itself racist in a culture that celebrates achievement regardless of race, color, gender, or sexual orientation despite tacitly perpetuating ongoing structures of inequality. Any attempt to remedy historically produced inequality becomes recast not as legitimate redress but as an "entitlement" of "special interest" groups amid an ongoing neoliberal privatization of government-administered social safety nets. Agile rehabilitative logics offer inclusion in exchange for assimilation to dominant cultural norms and individual overcoming.

Likewise, by the end of the twentieth century, a more general rehabilitative language of effacement began to circulate in relation to disability—one that did not characterize disability as a "difference" but rather as a more general "obstacle" or struggle. Banal statements such as "Aren't we *all* disabled in some way?" epitomized this shift. Well-intentioned phrases like this invite empathy by emphasizing a shared experience of hardship. They are integrative at heart. They imply that disabled people are "just like (the presumed nondisabled) *us*." This will to integrate formed rehabilitative edutainment's core ethos.

However, this philosophy also suggests that minor inconveniences experienced by the nondisabled are somehow the same as those experienced by disabled people as they navigate inaccessible environments, employment, and social stigma on a daily basis. This rehabilitative logic dangerously erases an ongoing history of disabled exclusion, abuse, institutionalization, and neglect by negating the specificity of disabled experience. Perhaps most dangerously, it reifies compulsory able-bodiedness as the normative ideal through a seemingly benevolent sleight of hand: it invites disabled people to aspire to and achieve integration by negating or overcoming their disabilities (rather than, say, confronting and critiquing structural barriers or prejudices) and bestows the privileges of citizenship (in contractual exchange for lifelong overcoming). In other words, cultural outsiders—disabled, nonwhite, or queer—are integrated *conditionally* into society only if they assimilate perfectly to the dominant norms of that society, which remain unmarked and largely unchanged. Moreover, though integration remains conditional, dominant social norms appear more inclusive and are often celebrated as progressive.

By the time of global neoliberalism's arrival, rehabilitation had come to encompass so much more than notions of capacity and dis/ability. Rehabilitation is predicated on the belief "that if you devote sufficient resources, it is possible to reduce the distance and bring each person, however great the burden she carries, to reoccupy a normal place in the group of the able (the normal)."[51] A rehabilitative contractual exchange has become normalized as the very condition of citizenship and social recognition for everyone, in varying degrees. This results in the discursive mobility and even celebration of formerly pathological identities, like homosexuality or disability, especially in the marketplace. The next four chapters evidence this depathologizing shift by showing the broad proliferation of stories about disability, adolescence, and sexuality across a variety of cultural media platforms from the 1970s to the present. However, this kind of integration comes at a high cost: no matter how great the burden we carry, we must always adapt to existing social structures rather than radically dismantle, disrupt, or resist them. The idea that "everyone is disabled in some way" and can overcome obstacles with sufficient pluck ensures that inequitable structures—those that continue to privilege dominant identities, such as white, male, able-bodied, heterosexual, or affluent—remain unchallenged. Rehabilitation, unlike cure, is an endless project of self-surveillance; of flexibility to circumstances that shift under your wheels, feet, or crutches; and of endless adaptation to increasingly hidden forms of structural inequality in an age of inclusion.

Rehabilitative citizenship, formed at the intersection of rehabilitation and identity crisis, has become a central treatment regimen for managing, through discourses of health and personal responsibility, the shifting demands of post-Fordism, an era defined by unrelenting crisis that is at once social, global, and economic.[52] As a conceptual framework, rehabilitative citizenship combines ways of thinking theoretically, historically, and culturally. In terms of history, it articulates the body and its regulation to broader histories of sexual liberation, disability rights, and other post-1968 social movements; to the rise of popular psychology and self-help culture; and finally, to the economy and culture of neoliberalism. Rehabilitative citizenship is also a way of thinking theoretically and culturally about how two familiar narratives of development, "coming of age" and "overcoming disability," became intertwined in "healthy" popular media for teenagers and emerged as a new strategy of neoliberal governmentality. Cripping adolescence reveals a culture of rehabilitation that has become so naturalized that, by the end of the twentieth century, it no longer requires disability to further its reach. If we all have disabilities to overcome, as a culture of rehabilitation insists, then we have nothing to change but ourselves. We can all accept personal responsibility for our circumstances rather than selfishly complain about ongoing structural inequality—or in other words, we can all just "grow up."

Medicinal Media

Although teen coming of age has often appeared as a universal stage of development, this growth process required intense cultural work. Rehabilitative citizenship has figured around three key areas of intervention. First, it conjures sedimented histories of disability and adolescence by casting adolescence as a disability and "coming of age" as a process of "overcoming" disabling adolescence that is simultaneously normal and pathological. Second, as an outgrowth of sexual liberation politics and history, rehabilitative citizenship operates through adolescence as a form of sexual containment that fosters "healthy" (hetero)sexual development for teenagers as equivalent with stable (or "capable") adulthood. In so doing, it reifies mutually reinforcing systems of compulsory able-bodiedness and compulsory heterosexuality. Finally, as rehabilitation is transmitted through "socially responsible" popular culture, it constructs perpetual self-surveillance as essential to good citizenship as well as individual and collective health.

Proponents of rehabilitative edutainment often suggested that it was a necessary alternative to the disingenuous, puritanical, or intolerant images of adolescent life that had been offered up by their post–World War II predecessors. Young adult authors and television producers as well as parents and parenting experts who were fascinated with new sciences of the teen brain certainly all intended—in different ways and in different cultural moments—to connect proactively with teenagers through an honest effort to devise more progressive and nonjudgmental ways of dealing with difficult coming-of-age issues. They often claimed that their approach might yield "more authentic" representations of adolescence or disability than previous offerings. However, in this book, I do not endeavor to establish, through interviews or audience research, a representative sample of what "real" teenagers "really" thought about rehabilitative edutainment texts as they consumed them, although this might be an interesting line of inquiry. Cultural representations of teenagers usually correspond very little to the lived realities of actual teenagers, just as popular representations of disability, in which disability functions as metaphor, rarely encapsulate the full diversity of disabled people's real, lived experiences. No matter how earnest their intentions, cultural producers' claims for rehabilitative edutainment's authenticity functioned as legitimating cultural capital, not just for this new pedagogical popular media but also for emergent neoliberal capitalist values that the genre enshrined as essential to healthy youth development: structural injustices recast as individual pathologies to be overcome and the portrayal of compulsory able-bodiedness, gender normativity, and heterosexuality as equivalent with maturity. From this vantage, it matters less whether cultural representations of teenagers correspond closely to the lived realities of actual teenagers than how those representations function culturally to promote particular values, affects, or politics. *Chronic Youth* examines what was thinkable about adolescence and dis/ability in particular moments to establish how commonsense ideas about their nature participated in cultural debates about national affiliation, emotional maturity, cultural citizenship, normative embodiment, medical power, and media and their regulation.

The following four chapters map the historical and cultural operations of rehabilitative citizenship by tracing figurations of adolescence and disability as they emerged in 1970s educational entertainment for "normal" teenagers.[53] Arranged chronologically, the individual chapters emphasize how specific texts each formed part of a broader, neoliberal rehabilitation project addressed to the teen. However, these individual texts also functioned in concert as a new popular media genre and tactic of governmentality as they drew from a burgeoning self-help culture. Rehabilitative edutainment was one venue in which people with diseases and disabilities became culturally visible in entirely new ways amid the uneven processes of American deinstitutionalization, the Vietnam War, and post-1968 depathologizing movements, albeit in narratives that reinforced compulsory able-bodiedness as a normative citizenship ideal.[54]

Engaging in textual and discursive analysis, the book situates close readings of popular narratives spotlighting disability and adolescence—made-for-TV movies, television series, best-selling and serialized young adult novels, and parenting books—alongside and within larger cultural debates about medical knowledge and technology; media regulatory discourses; post-1968 social movements; and theories of youth development, as they were established and analyzed in contemporaneous news media and government policy. This integrative methodology attends to specific experiences, texts, and mediums as well as to their participation in broader discourses and allows readers to glimpse the multiple and uneven processes that constitute a U.S. cultural history of disability, adolescence, sexuality, and neoliberalism. While my study includes close readings of texts to elucidate their complex narrative operations, my broader analysis shows how pop cultural representations of disability and teens—representations with broad audiences and significant cultural capital—played a significant role in making profits for media and medical industries by recasting their offerings as essential rather than damaging for developing citizens and by presenting rehabilitation as coterminous with citizenship. Many of the cultural texts analyzed in *Chronic Youth* are likely familiar to readers. They all were (and, in many cases, continue to be) extremely popular. Yet none of the texts featured in the book's chapters has ever been analyzed in current scholarship. In many ways, these texts are not exceptional. They do not constitute the core of a national culture (if there really is such a thing), but they have helped naturalize a culture of rehabilitation, offered up as a normal and compulsory "rite of passage" into adulthood.[55] This culture continues to shape the ways we imagine and enact privatization—of politics and citizenship—in the intimate public sphere of the nation.

In chapter 1, I analyze the cultural importance of the disabled 1970s cultural icon, "the bubble boy," by surveying representations of "real" bubble boys, David Vetter III and Ted DeVita, alongside the made-for-television movie *The Boy in the Plastic Bubble* (1976), which was an early example of "disease-of-the-week" television programming, a core form of rehabilitative edutainment. News stories and movies about the bubble boy linked sexual exploration with space exploration and manly self-sacrifice with self-making, and the boy became a figure through which Americans negotiated ambivalence about technology, masculinity, and sexuality in a new sexually liberated world. Specifically, I analyze how "disabled martyrdom" ensured American narratives of technological progress and masculine, heterosexual coming of age as they were presented in news media accounts of the bubble boys and in the fictional dramatization of their lives. This chapter shows how two conjoined rehabilitative narratives, "overcoming sexual repression" and "overcoming disability," became co-constitutive expectations of teen coming of age, such that adulthood was represented as the achievement of heterosexuality and able-bodied masculinity.

In chapter 2, I turn to another set of made-for-television movies that became a cultural institution: ABC's famous *After School Specials*. Despite their widespread popularity, the *Specials* have often been ridiculed for their overt didacticism and hokey "problem novel" storylines. I make these episodes, however, into objects of serious scholarly inquiry, contextualizing the *Specials* within the history of television regulation, educational broadcasting, and concerns about teens' relationship to a new, post–sexual revolution sexual culture of the 1970s. I argue that the series presented a disciplined vision of sexual liberation for teen viewers, combining (sex) educational value with sexual titillation. By linking heteronormativity and ability, the *Specials* presented coming-of-age lessons through stories of the healthy overcoming of disability, and the series linked that overcoming to proper heterosexual development. This chapter argues that the series ushered in a new openness about teen sexuality even as it reconsolidated heterosexist and ableist norms. The *Specials* also engaged in another cultural project of rehabilitation: an effort to transform the popular image of television itself by countering older fears about TV's deleterious effects on youth with a new form of entertaining *and* socially responsible programming.

By considering age, affect, and disability in relation to television history, these chapters extend recent comparative media studies scholarship that emphasizes how the cultural work of reality television facilitated a new form of self-surveilling viewership as central to "good citizenship."[56] *Chronic Youth* emphasizes how television interacted with other mediums and how increasing popular transmission of medical knowledge and a new visibility of disability produced new modes of storytelling. In so doing, it makes clear that a culture of perpetual reinvention not only significantly predates reality television (showing up, instead, in the 1970s) but has also relied particularly upon the teen viewer as an object of regulation around which to reframe ideas about what counts as responsible and engaged viewership and citizenship.

Problem-driven popular culture for teenagers increasingly sought to manipulate affects, such as fear and sadness, to create teachable moments for impressionable citizens. By the 1970s, this strategy also permeated a new young adult (YA) literature market, the subject of this book's third chapter, which spotlights another key moment in the genealogy of rehabilitative citizenship: the neoliberal transition to affective labor and its role in the development of the intimate public sphere. This chapter traces the emergence and proliferation of a subgenre of the YA problem novel that I call "teen sick-lit." Published largely in the 1980s as part of a long history of sentimental literature about illness for women, these books were aimed at teen girl readers and featured love stories about teen girls and boys with life-threatening illnesses. Surveying the work of the best-selling YA authors Lurlene McDaniel and Jean Ferris, this chapter analyzes the affective labor of sadness as a crucial growth-inducing emotion that tragic disability narratives were best suited to convey.[57] The books issued emotional challenges to teen readers through yet more representations of teens as patients, physically imperiled subjects who needed to overcome and rehabilitate. Just as ABC's *After School Specials* rehabilitated television, teen sick-lit countered critiques of YA novels as vapid (in comparison to classical literature) and, instead, cast themselves as a rehabilitative influence on both teenagers and the culture of teen reading understood as incapacitated by the televisual and digital age. Bridging new scholarship about affect, representation, and citizenship with insights from disability studies, this book considers how "the depressed teen" became not only a developmental imperative but also a profitable market for popular culture (and later for pharmaceuticals).

While the presumed audience for *After School Specials*, disease-of-the-week movies, and teen sick-lit traditionally has been white, male, heterosexual, middle-class, and able-bodied, the works examined here ironically demonstrate the degree to which young women have been crucial participants. Although youth subculture studies have focused mainly on boys, *Chronic*

Youth examines how young women's roles in rehabilitative edutainment were central to its cultural work, although female characters often appeared in representations as less active and outward-directed than their stereotypical male counterparts, disabled or otherwise. Along with other rehabilitative edutainment offerings for teens, teen sick-lit functioned as a popular and pedagogical form of emotional self-management that addressed teen girls directly and reinforced neoliberal discourses of personal responsibility and flexibility.

Although the commonsense alignment of disability and adolescence may have begun as a storytelling convention, disability had become much more than a metaphor by the end of the twentieth century, as it animated criminal, neurological, and pharmaceutical debates about teen depression and violence. Specifically, this book's final chapter focuses on the rise of "neuroparenting," my term for a new model of parenting teenagers that incorporates new neuroscientific discoveries to explain how "typical teen" attributes like impulsiveness or emotional explosiveness are neurologically rooted rather than culturally constructed. Broader discourses of genetics and neuroscience in the 1990s "Decade of the Brain" attempted to prove that other valences of identity, such as race, class, gender, and sexuality, as well as violent behavior, were neurologically and/or genetically rooted rather than socially constructed. Meanwhile, the "teen mind" was reengineered into the "teen brain." This chapter traces how news media and parenting books used the language of disability to translate neuroscientific studies of the adolescent brain into proof that teens were "brain damaged," "disabled," or always-already mentally ill rather than just willfully misbehaving. By articulating the history of media representation with that of medical technology, this chapter builds on scholarship in technological history, disability studies, and feminist science studies to critique the ways medical knowledge and rehabilitative edutainment have participated in constructing, visualizing, and medicalizing adolescence.[58]

As this chapter demonstrates, medicalization and rehabilitation had intensified and expanded into a range of other cultural locations by the twentieth century's close. These sites ranged from parenting advice literature about managing your teen's "disabled" and incomplete brain, to American school shooting and teen "superpredator" epidemics, and even to federally endorsed counterterrorist surveillance technologies used to scan and detect teens "at risk" for depression or violent behavior. By analyzing cultural depictions of white school shooters alongside those of black and Latino "superpredators," we see that the post-1970s rehabilitation of white middle-class suburban teens both required and facilitated the increasing criminalization, institutionalization, and incarceration of "unrehabilitatable" Others (i.e., nonwhite, queer, or disabled teenagers) by the 1990s.

Chronic Youth tracks power and resistance within and through cultural production. Scholarship in youth subculture studies has posed important challenges to essentializing understandings of adolescence. However, analyses of youth culture have often proceeded from a generational conflict narrative of teen consumer resistance that is determined in advance: either teens consume cultural products selling a kind of prefabricated signal of rebellion, or cultural analysts, from a variety of academic disciplines, read teen consumer choices as always-already resisting a normative (adult) cultural order.[59] This narrative evacuates the historical and cultural specificity of youth dissidence; moreover, when teen "resistance" becomes little more than a transhistorical effect of the market or the prediscursive nature of adolescence, a particular vision of able-bodied middle-class white male adolescence problematically stands in as universal.

That said, to argue, as *Chronic Youth* does, that cultural conceptions of adolescence have been overdetermined by rebellion or that rebellion has been commodified is certainly not to suggest that resistance is nonexistent. A primary strain of disability activism and scholarship has been its critique of ableism in popular media; although disabled youth often have been left out of youth subculture studies, many young disabled people were galvanized into activists by contesting stereotypical televisual and literary images of disability. In each cultural moment, teenagers surely read and viewed against-the-grain in ways that did not contribute by default to the legitimacy of rehabilitative edutainment or to the broader neoliberal paradigms of which it is part. The first chapter demonstrates how made-for-TV movies about disability and disease embraced a certain politics of sexual liberation to offer resistive ethical critiques of the inhumanity of medical technology and the "disabling" effects of youth sexual repression. The second and third chapters excavate how television and popular literature for teenagers opened up discussions about teen sexuality and gender nonconformity that were not simply protective or paternalistic foreclosures but also proactive opportunities to resist cultural anxieties about youth sexuality. Amazon customer reviews of all-too-saccharine YA literature posted by teen readers, as well as the eventual emergence of parodies of ABC's *After School Specials*, offer cultural traces of teen resistance to the narrative logic of rehabilitative edutainment.[60] This book's final chapter excavates how anti-prison activist-scholars as well as youth activists in psychiatric survivor, anti-psychiatry, and MadPride movements have contested an ongoing rehabilitative cultural drift toward pathologizing discourses of "faulty brain wiring" and pharmaceutical treatments, which has had drastically different ramifications for disabled and queer youth and youth of color. However pervasive the disciplines of rehabilitative citizenship became (or continue to become), cultural texts remain polysemic. By tracing the tactics of discipline employed by rehabilitative edutainment, I do not mean to suggest that they ever operated seamlessly or without resistance. Narratives are never wholly repressive or resistive, and teen audiences of their cultural moment did not simply imbibe their ideologies uncritically. As it turns out, rebels and patients are not always so easily or discretely separated.

A sweeping cultural redefinition of adolescence as a pathological but treatable "condition" has powerfully shaped our contemporary understandings of youth. However, this book's conclusion argues that cripping adolescence in cultural production has had its greatest cultural impact not simply on how Americans think of youth but how they have grown to accept the logic of rehabilitative citizenship as normal. Post-1970s youth culture naturalized endless self-management and transformation by mapping it onto "normal" teen bodies that everybody regards as already changing. This cultural transition away from post–World War II externalizing sociologies of juvenile delinquency and toward post-1968 internalizing psychological understandings of teen angst—namely, away from the rebel and toward the patient—was neither accidental nor ahistorically essential. In fact, it took root within a broader cultural turn away from collective bargaining and toward a neoliberal model of personal responsibility. In this sense, teens, as crisis-ridden, cripped subjects, became convenient figures for (mis)managing the perpetual crisis that is neoliberal capitalism. *Chronic Youth* traces a genealogy of adolescence and disability to begin to map and historicize the chronic state of neoliberal crisis—because the post-1968 teenager, we will see in retrospect, was a crucial canary in the coalmine in the development of a rehabilitation culture that encourages us all to imagine ourselves as perpetually unfinished projects.

1

Medicine Is Magical and Magical Is Art

Liberation and Overcoming in The Boy in the Plastic Bubble

[Y]ou'd see that I'm not a cripple. And that there's nothing wrong
with me except that I can't get out of here until they tell me it's
okay. . . . I'm so sick of it. I'm so sick of feeling like a hospital case.
Like some weirdo kid who can't even breathe normal air because
he might get sick and die. I just wanna be like a man. Someone that
you could care about, and not feel sorry for.
—Tod Lubitch in *The Boy in the Plastic Bubble* (1976)

Medicine is magical, and magical is art.
The boy in the bubble and the baby with the baboon heart.
And I believe these are the days of . . . lasers in the jungle somewhere
Staccato signals of constant information
A loose affiliation of millionaires and billionaires and baby,
These are the days of miracle and wonder. This is the long distance call.
The way the camera follows us in slo-mo. The way we look to us all.
The way we look to a distant constellation that's dying in a corner of the sky.
These are the days of miracle and wonder. And don't cry, baby. Don't cry.
—Paul Simon, "The Boy in the Bubble," *Graceland* (1986)

In 1986, Paul Simon released his Grammy Award–winning *Graceland*, an
album that blended American rock and roll with the unique vocal and rhyth-
mic stylings of the South African musical group Ladysmith Black Mam-
bazo in the era of apartheid. An international success, the album's first track
sardonically declared medicine "magical" and the cultural moment of its
release, "the days of miracle and wonder."[1] In this song, Simon gave voice to
countercultural anxieties about rapid technological change in an era characterized by the death of American manufacturing and the unflagging upward
redistribution of wealth and power into the hands of "a loose affiliation of
millionaires and billionaires." The song was called "The Boy in the Bubble,"
a title that invoked the cultural memory of David Vetter III, a "bubble boy"

who was born without an immune system, lived his entire life in a plastic enclosure, and died two years prior to *Graceland*'s release.

In its outward look from the bubble, the song chronicled the screaming pace of technological change across multiple fields in the 1980s by emphasizing vertigo-inducing shifts of time, distance, scale, and space. A series of colliding images form its breathless lyrics: increasing militarization ("[t]hese are the days of lasers in the jungle, lasers in the jungle somewhere"); the incessant drone of globalizing communications technologies ("staccato signals of constant information"); and finally, the ethically ambiguous legacies of death-defying medical experiments ("the boy in the bubble and the baby with the baboon heart"). "The Boy in the Bubble" was a frenzied sketch of the globalizing media-saturated world of post-Fordism as well as the increasing emotional and physical distance wrought by new technologies. The song encapsulated this convergence in one thrumming phrase about constant surveillance: "the way the camera follows us in slow-mo." Through the cultural figure of the bubble boy, who lived in isolation from human touch, "The Boy in the Bubble" described a world never more "in touch" with its farthest reaches, through cables, telescopes, and cameras, but never more "out of touch" with humanity. Its haunting refrain, "This is the long distance call," reminds listeners that its critique was perhaps already too late.

As this song suggests, the cultural memory of the boy in the bubble persisted long after David Vetter III's death in 1984. The bubble boy has appeared as the swindled *Trivial Pursuit* player Donald Sanger (Jon Hayman) of *Seinfeld* (1992) or the sexually repressed Jimmy Livingston (Jake Gyllenhaal) of Disney's romantic comedy *Bubble Boy* (2001).[2] Most recently, he has even become the namesake of the Spanish indie-electronica band, Niño Burbuja (Bubble Boy). However, perhaps the most familiar incarnation of this story was the ABC made-for-TV movie *The Boy in the Plastic Bubble* (1976), about an immunocompromised teenaged boy in love with the girl next door. All of these pop cultural narratives were based on the lives of David Vetter III and the lesser-known Ted DeVita, two boys with immune disorders, who lived in plastic enclosures for a significant portion of their lives. David Vetter's short life was highly mediated. Newspapers and news magazines covered his story with fervor, weaving a triumphal tale of technological innovation and medical mavericks in the era of space exploration. ABC, CBS, and NBC ran nearly thirty reports on Vetter until his untimely death, and for years thereafter, television news and newspapers commemorated the anniversaries of David's birth and death by recounting his story alongside an update on the status of medical research on immune deficiencies. Years after his death, his story has often been framed as a cautionary tale about unchecked medical power—a tale elaborated by medical historians, bioethicists, and documentary film-makers.[3] Countless doctors argued that insights gleaned from David's and Ted's confinement and treatment contributed to advancements in clinical immunology and gene therapy that resulted in better treatment options for immune disorders writ large and did so before HIV/AIDS became a highly publicized epidemic.

Cultural figures like the bubble boy unite cultural images of "the cripple" and "the queer," which are always "[i]nvested with meanings that far out-strip their biological bases," as they are made to function as "taxonomical" figures against which normal bodies are sorted.[4] Thus, in fictional and non-fictional representations alike, the bubble boy always exceeded David's and Ted's actual bodies. As the bubble boy appeared in songs, films, television shows, and made-for-TV movies, he pervaded American culture less as a real disabled person with human needs, desires, and emotions and more as an abstracted cultural figure through which Americans negotiated unrelent-ing technological progress, burgeoning sexual liberation, and their ethical consequences for humankind.

In journalists' and doctors' accounts of heroic medicine, David and Ted were extremely valuable as what I call "disabled martyrs" who shored up discourses of national and technological progress in the post–World War II era—an era that, as this chapter will show, was characterized by new assessment mechanisms for and ambivalence about technology's increas-ing encroachment on American life. Journalists and scientific authorities cast this technological progress narrative as a coming-of-age narrative in which vulnerable boys became self-sacrificial men, a narrative of disabled martyrdom that reconsolidated a national pride assured by technologi-cal progress—often by eliding or ignoring the ways the boys themselves resisted the medical management of their bodies. Journalists and doctors recast David and Ted as self-possessed, manly explorers who "chose" their own fates rather than passive test subjects. Alongside the ongoing blood-shed of the Vietnam War and highly visible young veterans returning to American shores with various physical and psychological disabilities, this spotlighting of disabled boys' coming of age also served as a displacement of wartime violence and American imperialism in favor of heroic medi-cine's saving vulnerable children, highlighting the actual inextricability of Simon's twin technologies: the "boy in the bubble" and the "lasers in the jungle somewhere."

However, journalistic reportage was not the only medium through which people formed ideas about technology and science in relation to the bubble.

Produced by Aaron Spelling and directed by Randal Kleiser, *The Boy in the Plastic Bubble* first aired on ABC at 9 p.m. on November 12, 1976. The movie hybridized elements of David Vetter's and Ted DeVita's stories to form "Tod" Lubitch. It boasted a star-studded cast, including young John Travolta as well as Diana Hyland, a former star of the popular prime-time soap opera *Peyton Place* (1964–1969), and Robert Reed, the all-American dad of *The Brady Bunch* (1969–1974), as Tod's parents.[5] *The Boy in the Plastic Bubble* was part of a historically specific trajectory in television programming in the late 1960s and 1970s—the "made-for-TV" movie—that increasingly introduced sexually themed and "disease-of-the-week" programming and aimed for "realistic portrayals" of major news stories. However, while the news media narrated the story of a real-life bubble "boy" who could not be hugged or kissed by his mother, significantly *The Boy in the Plastic Bubble* opted against adherence to the media's dominant narrative. Instead, it drastically transformed the story from the tale of an untouchable child at the cutting edge of exciting medical research into a romantic coming-of-age story in which a teen boy leaves the bubble for love and sexual intimacy. This chapter analyzes the type of cultural work this narrative reimagining of coming of age undertook in its historical moment.

In particular, this chapter contends that the cultural figure of the bubble boy, as it was relocated into the fictional television coming-of-age tale of a "bubble man," forced questions of medical ethics *through* sexual politics in an era of rehabilitative citizenship. The movie rescripted the bubble boy's exit from the protective bubble not as a heroic self-sacrifice for the advancement of medical knowledge but as the natural pursuit of (hetero)sexual liberation and self-actualization, in an era in which sexuality and pleasure were becoming increasingly politicized in youth sexual liberation movements. By prioritizing sexual coming of age over medical cure, this fictional televisual rendering of teen romance in the bubble dramatized cultural contestations about the management of sexuality, masculinity, and disability in an era of rapid medical and technological innovation and shifting post–sexual revolution sexual culture.

Beyond the complex bioethical issues provoked by the bubble, cultural representations of the bubble boy raised important questions about the relationship between sexual liberation and disabled overcoming narratives. Queer scholars have argued that the sexual revolution, emblematized by the availability of birth control and abortion, was mainly a revolution in heterosexuality, as nonheterosexual sex and pleasure were marginalized from public discourse about sex and liberal feminism maintained "compulsory heterosexuality" as both liberatory and natural. The sexual revolution was also, in many respects, largely a revolution in adulthood and able-bodied-ness. Increased policing of the boundaries of childhood sexual innocence as well as the containment of teen sexuality within compulsory heterosexuality accompanied the politicization of sexual identity in the era of sexual libera-tion. These combined processes also worked to infantilize disabled adults as nonsexual and pathologize crip pleasures as deviant or queer.

However, this chapter argues that disabled overcoming became articu-lated to emergent understandings (and disciplinings) of "liberation" in the 1970s, while cultural notions of "liberation," in various forms, became increasingly essential to and formative of regimes of compulsory heterosex-uality and compulsory able-bodiedness. By narrating Vetter and DeVita as disabled martyrs for medical advancement *through* a coming-of-age frame-work, this chapter shows how the cultural figure of the bubble boy—forged at the intersection of science, science fiction, and heterosexual romance—made visible the cracks in the foundation of the liberationist ethos that has come to characterize post-1968 histories of sexuality. Namely, "overcoming repression" became enfleshed as overcoming disability. This discursive over-lap asserted the naturalness (and healthiness) of heterosexuality and simul-taneously destabilized it. Fictional and nonfictional accounts of the bubble boys imagined that by submitting to medical technology, boys could be brave disabled martyrs for national progress—a progress heavily invested in a philosophy of technology's triumph over the frailty of the body in the days of miracle and wonder. However, only by exiting the bubble and *choosing* normality over protection—even if it meant death—could bubble boys become men.

Technological Triumphalism, Nationalism, and the Bubble

In 1971, David Vetter III was born in Houston, Texas, with a rare genetic dis-order called Severe-Combined Immunodeficiency Syndrome (SCID). The disease generally affects male children and leaves them without any immu-nity to even the most basic infections. David arrived one year after his par-ents, David Joseph Vetter and Carol Ann Vetter, lost a son, David II, to the same disease. Doctors at the Baylor College of Medicine had warned the Vetters, who already had a daughter, that any of their sons would have a 50 percent chance of being born with SCID. However, they suggested that if the Vetters conceived another son who tested positive for SCID, they could facil-itate a completely sterile birth by placing the child in an isolator to protect him until they found a cure for SCID. Led to believe that a cure was immi-nent and eager to try for another baby, the Vetters trusted in the doctors' optimism and conceived David Vetter III eight weeks after the death of their previous son. Journalists covering David's story noted that the Vetters decided against an abortion once they learned the sex of their unborn son not only because they were Roman Catholic but also because they desperately wanted a boy.[6] Doctors delivered David by caesarean section and placed him in an "isolator," the "bubble" in which he would live out his next twelve years, four months, and seventeen days. The bubble was filled with sterilized toys, and a teacher educated David in the hospital throughout his time in the bubble. Over the course of his short life, he made a few highly publicized forays into the "outside world," traveling to his parents' home and the zoo using a child-sized spacesuit donated by the National Aeronautics and Space Administration (NASA).

During this era of medical experimentation with immune deficiency diseases, there was very little public discussion of the ethical issues posed by David's life in the bubble. Twelve years after David's initial confinement, a cure for SCID still eluded doctors, so David's doctors, Ralph Feigin and William Shearer, suggested performing a bone marrow transplant, using marrow donated by his sister, Katherine, in the hopes that it would jump-start his immune system. Although his initial responses to the transplant were positive, David fell ill for the first time in his life, experiencing diarrhea, fever, and severe vomiting a few months later. At this point, he left the bubble and ventured into the outside world unprotected for the first and last time on February 7, 1984. He died fifteen days later. Unbeknownst to the doctors, the bone marrow contained traces of a dormant strain of the Epstein-Barr virus, which facilitated the growth of Burkitt's lymphoma, a rare cancer that produced countless tumors throughout his body and caused his death.

While David became the most familiar "bubble boy," another boy in isolation from both germs and the public eye would provide additional inspiration for fictional representations of life in a germ-free bubble. Born in 1962—nearly ten years before David—Ted "Teddy" DeVita was diagnosed with aplastic anemia at the age of ten by his father, Dr. Vincent DeVita, a renowned oncologist at the National Institutes of Health (NIH). Upon his diagnosis, his family relocated Ted from his home to a place they all called "The Room," a completely sterile laminar airflow room in "13-East" in the NIH's Clinical Center in Washington, DC.[7] Ted's story entered the media only after an NIH medical board received an anonymous letter accusing Dr. Vincent DeVita of an "abuse of privilege." The source argued that Dr. DeVita had exploited his NIH position to ensure treatment for his son while denying equal treatment for another boy who ultimately died from the same disease.[8] The medical board found that Ted's treatment was justified because his care had been "a valuable if only partly successful experiment."[9] Although doctors expected Ted to enter remission or die within a few months of his sequestration in 1972, he lived in The Room until May 27, 1980, when he died at age seventeen of an iron overload from too many blood transfusions.

David and Ted were placed in sterile environments within a year of one another. However, unlike the Vetters, who generally cooperated with media outlets seeking to write about their son, the DeVita family and the NIH generally kept Ted and his treatment out of the press.[10] In her book about sibling loss, *The Empty Room: Surviving the Loss of a Brother or Sister at Any Age*, Elizabeth DeVita-Raeburn, Ted's younger sister, described the family's dismay over the uninvited media sensationalism that eventually surrounded Ted in "pre-AIDS days . . . before health and talk shows regularly trotted out people with rare medical afflictions."[11] She recalls being barraged by phone calls and lamented that the *National Enquirer* sent a photographer to Ted's funeral, in spite of the DeVitas' best efforts to retain their privacy. According to DeVita-Raeburn, this absence of "rare medical afflictions" in the news media made her brother's and David's stories "big news," which caused the boys to persist as "strange, abstract figures in American pop culture."[12]

Mysterious maladies may not have been popular talk show fare at the time of Ted's death, but the "poster child" was already a well-recognized image of disability through which technological innovation and medical miracles were entwined and publicized. David became more iconic than Ted DeVita not only because Ted's family suppressed his story, but also because David's childhood status meant that his image, more so than Ted's, suited the established representational conventions of the poster child. A twentieth-century outgrowth of the nineteenth-century freak show, the poster child hybridized the medical model of disability, the visual spectacle of the freak show, and the charity model of the late nineteenth and early twentieth centuries.[13] As various disability studies scholars have shown, a relationship of pity between the observer and the spectacularized body on display was not a component of the freak show, which emphasized the extraordinariness rather than the wretchedness of the displayed "freak." By contrast, the poster child's raison d'être was to evoke charitable pity from the nondisabled. Historically, poster children emerged before World War II in service of the March of Dimes fundraising campaign to cure polio, undertaken by the National Foundation for Infantile Paralysis. The first poster child was Donald Anderson, who came to the March of Dimes in the 1940s. In the aftermath of a serious outbreak of polio in Hickory, North Carolina, the foundation produced posters featuring child survivors of the epidemic. Print advertisements emphasized the combined heroism of innovative doctors and charitable donors, spotlighting the cure rather than the voices, perspectives, or desires of disabled people. The posters often featured a sad and disabled "before" image juxtaposed with a triumphant after image of the same child, smiling and walking proudly in living testament to the curative power of generous donations.

Another media text in the genealogy of the poster child, the telethon, had also become a television institution during David and Ted's isolation. The best-known telethon was the twenty-one-hour annual Labor Day Muscular Dystrophy Association (MDA) Telethon (1966–2012), hosted by Jerry Lewis. Featuring tragic and inspirational stories of disabled "victims" of muscular dystrophy, the show elicited donations by activating pity in viewers, a practice that angered disability rights activists, who annually protested the event until its cancellation in 2012. Displayed to invite pathos and charity from nondisabled "givers," the poster child of the telethon, according to the disability historian Paul Longmore, enables nondisabled contributors to engage in a transaction he calls "conspicuous contribution": through their donations to disabled "takers," donors prove that they are still members of "a moral community" in spite of their participation in a capitalist system defined by conspicuous consumption.[14] Two culturally dominant figurations of disability, the telethon and the poster child, overwhelmingly spotlighted disabled children rather than adults, and this elision has bolstered the ongoing infantilization and neglect of disabled adults. Such visual conventions denied disabled people's autonomy and individuality as well as produced a hierarchical viewing relationship between the presumed-superior nondisabled onlooker and the disabled body on display—a form of objectification that elided the poster child's subjectivity and instead spectacularized his medical diagnosis. These images celebrated cure rather than human diversity and represented disability as a personal misfortune to be overcome or mitigated through individual dispensations of charity rather than through broad cultural, political, or economic reform.

Characterized exclusively by the pathos of his isolation from the "normal" outside world, David Vetter, as portrayed by the media, conveniently fit the well-established representational trope of the poster child. Describing his environment as "womb-like," the press constructed David as an "infantile citizen," a docile citizen-subject who never resisted the medical management of his body, its representation by news media, or its mobilization in discourses of patriotism.[15] Journalists assiduously crafted an image of normality and contentment tinged with pathos in their portraits of life in the bubble. They described him as "like any normal, healthy, 3-year-old boy" in that he "jumps up and down, sometimes plays rough and giggles when he is tickled."[16] They also juxtaposed images of David's normal upbringing with an emphasis on the tragic nature of his predicament. In nearly every article written about him, reporters lamented that his mother had never kissed him.[17]

Meanwhile, testimonies from David's psychiatrists assured onlookers that he exhibited "no emotional problems." The inclusion of expert psychological opinions on David's mental state subtly expressed ambivalence about the bubble—namely, that it might ensure his physical safety at the expense of his emotional and psychological growth. In fact, one article suggested that David's radical normality might even compel psychologists to reconsider timeworn theories of childhood development because his isolation might be optimizing his development by "remov[ing] certain subtle impediments" to growth.[18] What doctors meant by "subtle impediments" remains unclear (interactions with peers? overprotective parents? skin-to-skin contact?), but nearly every story featured an expert opinion that reassured readers that David was psychologically normal in every respect.

David, depicted as an acquiescent child, stood in stark contrast to Ted DeVita and the fictional Tod Lubitch, recalcitrant teenagers who questioned and resisted medical authority, national belonging, and the costs of technological progress. Journalists described Ted DeVita as "a typical 17-year old youth" of above-average intelligence.[19] His room contained a stereo set, television, books, records, two Les Paul electric guitars, a telephone, a commode and shower, and even a small recording studio. While in The Room, Ted had school lessons and also undertook hobbies, including playing guitar, performing magic tricks, and operating a ham radio.[20] According to the press, just as David allegedly never resented his confinement, Ted "never thought of himself as a prisoner"; a friend quoted in an article written about him after his death said, "He controlled his environment. . . . He didn't want pity. I never heard him complain once."[21] Ted was older than David when he entered the bubble, and articles played up his rebellious teenaged identity, reporting that Ted "liked Shakespeare and 'Star Trek,' played electric guitar, grew a beard, drank too much champagne last New Year's Eve, and bickered with his kid sister." The same article emphasizes his commonality with his nondisabled friends, noting that "only one thing"—his disease and confinement—"separate[d] him from his peers." Rather than reflecting the mother-son pathos so characteristic of stories about David, journalists highlighted Ted's quasi-adulthood and his teenaged rebelliousness when they reported his drinking too much champagne and playing rock and roll. Instead of discussing his familial relationships, articles emphasized his friendships and autonomy, as a specially designed helmet enabled "the dark-haired teen-ager" to make trips into the outside world, most often rock concerts in the VIP box at the Capital Centre.

Optimistic post–World War II cultural perceptions of medicine and technology informed the decision to put David and Ted into isolation. According to the bioethicist Bruce Jennings, by the 1970s "medicine was on a roll."[22] Medical innovation had triumphed over numerous diseases, most notably polio, in the previous decades. The triumphant discovery of the iron lung and the Salk vaccine inexorably shaped American cultural perceptions of medical technology as a powerful force for the public good, especially when narrativized through the innocent poster child, saved by medical innovation and charitable donation. Post–World War II Americans witnessed the first successful open-heart surgery and the first kidney transplant, while medical achievements of the mid-1960s included the patenting of the first artificial heart; the development of the heart-lung machine; hundreds of heart transplants, with varying degrees of success; the widespread use of contraceptive pills; and the advent of the first commercially available, noninvasive fetal monitors, manufactured by Hewlett-Packard and aptly named "The Babysitters." Indeed, a *Life* magazine special issue cover in September 1962 trumpeted the arrival of "The Take-Over Generation," referring to multiple breakthroughs by "young men and women" in "government, science, space, business, education, religion and the arts."[23] The cover featured a photograph of a doctor peering into a microscope alongside a man observing a rocket. Finally, just as the development of new prosthetics had inexorably changed the post–World War II cultural landscape, the sophistication of battlefield medicine during the Vietnam War reduced war casualties and increased the number of young disabled veterans returning home. Amid all of these new forms of technological control over the body, the mid-1970s also witnessed a victory over immune-deficiency, embodied by an adorable baby boy in a bubble.

Celebratory representations of the real and fictional bubble boys actively blurred the rhetorical and visual boundaries between science and science fiction. Imbued with a visual rhetoric of liberation from the bubble, pervasive iconography of exploration—spacesuits and extraterrestrials—in stories of the bubble forged a linkage among masculinity, exploration, and technological triumphalism. NASA imagery, references to *Star Trek*, and actual astronauts make repeated appearances in narratives and images of David and Ted. For instance, reporters often referenced Ted's *Star Trek* fandom in pieces written about him. He once attended a *Star Trek* convention wearing his protective helmet—a trip outside that his sister recalled as "the only time Ted wasn't stared at."[24] Another teen boy who liked Ted's "costume" greeted him with the signature hand gesture of the *U.S.S. Enterprise*'s half-Vulcan First Officer Spock (Leonard Nimoy), and this anecdote, repeated in various stories of Ted's life, represented him as somehow extraterrestrial, or, in the words of his sister, as "a sci-fi kid come to life."[25] His sister also recalls when astronauts came to visit Ted during his stay at NIH, a visit that was also dramatized in *The Boy in the Plastic Bubble* through a brief guest appearance by Buzz Aldrin as Tod Lubitch's special visitor.

Likewise, David Vetter had a few highly publicized forays into the outside world, to the zoo and to his suburban home, using a $50,000 child-sized spacesuit donated by NASA in 1977. In 1978, the *New York Times* featured a photograph of David in his spacesuit and helmet. In the photo, David, attached by a thin, umbilical cord–like tube to a machine on wheels, waters the lawn with a garden hose.[26] The image is one of untroubled suburban bliss. Its caption, "Quest for Normal Life," stands in stark contradistinction to the tiny astronaut. While the photograph visually unites the miraculous "sci-fi kid" with space exploration, the caption represents a mundane domestic activity as an adventurer's "quest" for normalcy. David never really liked the suit, and when he outgrew it, the suit was replaced but never again worn.[27]

Repeated references to NASA and extraterrestrials also appear in *The Boy in the Plastic Bubble* to highlight Tod's alienation. Through the movie's visual comparison of Tod with his entrapped germ-free pet mouse, Cagney, and its consistent use of space imagery in his characterization, Tod is made alien. The Habitrail System of multicolored plastic tubes through which Cagney scurries and plays is visually likened to Tod's bubble—a veritable Human Habitrail. For example, in a scene that opens with quick-paced funky music, the camera focuses first on Cagney, running tirelessly in his tiny wheel. Zooming outward, the same shot reveals Tod, dancing alongside the running mouse, with colored lights in the background that blink to the beat of the music. Initially the scene seems to celebrate Tod's youth, much like other later famous film sequences featuring rebellious dancing teenagers in Travolta's own *Saturday Night Fever* (1977) and *Grease* (1978). However, Tod's dance is likened to the endless running of a mouse in its wheel, visualizing the movie's perception of the bubble as a hindrance to Tod's development. Just as the mouse (or lab rat?) scampers forward without moving an inch, Tod will forever be dancing in place in his glass tank.

In addition to marking Tod as somehow otherworldly, the movie's repeated use of outer space imagery also positions the medical technology of the bubble within another narrative of celebratory technological progress and imperial conquest: that of NASA astronauts landing on the moon. Following the above sequence, the camera pans to the right, showing

Cagney as he crawls through his Habitrail tube, while Tod simultaneously ducks through a tube-like passage to another section of his room to prepare a snack. A news report about NASA Skylab drones from Tod's television, announcing that American astronauts docked their command module and enjoyed their first outer space meal. Tod eats while watching the report, and the journalistic voice narrates the likenesses of Tod's routine to those of the space travelers. Buzz Aldrin's cameo appearance in *The Boy in the Plastic Bubble* to dub Tod "Champion Spaceman on Earth" and likewise, David Vetter's voyage to the outer space of Texas suburbia participated in an ongoing cultural fascination with NASA and space travel as an emblem of American national progress and pride.

In 1961, President John F. Kennedy issued his famous directive to land a man on the moon and return him safely to earth before the end of the decade. The "one giant leap for mankind" bolstered a celebratory discourse of technological innovation and nationalism, not only centered on NASA but also emblematized by sci-fi images of space travel, as they proliferated in popular culture of the 1960s and 1970s. Amid reportage of NASA and its moon mission, a genre of television that Lynn Spigel has dubbed the "fantastic family sitcom" emerged. A "hybrid genre" that was an admixture of the common suburban sitcom and "New Frontier," the fantastic family sitcom utilized space-aged imagery to "question the 'naturalness' of [the] middle-class" American family.[28]

Amidst a spate of American fantastic family sitcoms, including *Lost in Space* (1965–1968), *My Favorite Martian* (1963–1966), and *The Jetsons* (1962–1968), perhaps no cultural representation better captured this celebration of technological progress than the hit cult TV series *Star Trek* (1966–1969). Constance Penley argues that NASA became "a repository for utopian meanings" of American nationalism, technological advancement, and engaged citizenship, in part, through the organization's "symbolic merging" with the fictional *Star Trek* universe.[29] Penley shows that a discursive refashioning of "NASA" into the "slash" formation "NASA/Trek" occurred when President Gerald Ford, prompted by a massive Trekkie letter-writing campaign, demanded that NASA change its shuttle's name from *Constitution* to *Enterprise*. NASA even recruited members of *Star Trek*'s cast to various shuttle-related events to sediment the association between NASA and Starfleet.[30] Penley uses NASA's "self-conscious *Star Trek* makeover" to show how scientific knowledge and institutions become discursively refracted by cultural representation to form "popular science," or "the collectively elaborated story that weaves together science and science fiction."[31] Merging the efforts of scientists and science fiction fans to generate support for technological and scientific advancement, popular science does important cultural work, in part, by occasioning utopian visions of futuristic technology and its world-making potential to form a better galaxy still to come. With respect to David, Ted, and the fictional Tod, NASA iconography invoked the manly heroism of boys' exploring their outer space and reaffirmed a celebratory utopian vision of medical technological advancement. The bubble and the spacesuits not only constructed the boys' disabled bodies as alien but also cast medical technology as both futuristic and benevolent.

However, while a host of exciting technological innovations emerged in the postwar period, this celebratory attitude toward scientific advancement also coexisted with a cultural anxiety about new technologies and medical power. By the mid-1960s, there was a growing belief among activists, scientists, politicians, and ordinary citizens that rapidly developing technologies required new assessment mechanisms with which to judge their costs to humanity as well as their benefits. By the early 1970s, a variety of activists, including feminists, black nationalists, and disability rights activists, offered critiques of medical authority and prejudices that impeded access to health care, and they endorsed individual and health empowerment as crucial to progressive movements for social justice and equality. On the federal level, cultural anxieties about technology fueled the rise of technological assessment (TA) by the 1970s. First introduced during deliberations of the Committee on Science and Astronautics of the U.S. House of Representatives in 1965, TA was an attempt to imagine the critical societal role of evolving technology and its potential for damaging, unintended consequences.[32] Ideally, TA would also provide indispensable "translation" of technological data to policy makers untrained in the sciences, so they could make informed decisions in drafting regulatory policies for new technologies. The Office of Technology Assessment (OTA) was founded in 1972.

Concurrent with the development of general TA, a more specific substratum of TA also developed in 1975: health technology assessment (HTA). The National Research Council, the principal operating agency of the National Academy of Sciences and the National Academy of Engineering in providing services to the government, the public, and the scientific and engineering communities, conducted TAs on in-vitro fertilization, predetermination of the sex of children, and behavioral modification by neurosurgical, electrical, or pharmaceutical means. Since its inception, HTA has been animated by the emergence and proliferation of health technologies that have incited social, ethical, legal, and political concerns, including contraceptives, organ transplantation, artificial organs, life-sustaining technologies for critically or terminally ill patients, and in more recent history, genetic testing and therapy and stem cell research. Private-sector opponents of TA argued that anticipating in advance all of the consequences of new technology was impossible, and in the meantime, TA's lengthy assessment process risked stymieing crucial innovation.

With respect to David's case, Texas Children's Hospital formally discussed the ethics of David's prolonged isolation only once, nearly three and a half years after his birth. Nearly thirty doctors, theologians, and other concerned parties attended the meeting, which was initiated by the hospital's chaplain, Rev. Raymond J. Lawrence, who later publicly criticized David's doctors. Lawrence argued that the doctors coaxed David's parents into conceiving him so they would have a ready test subject for research in immunology—a charge that David's doctors have denied vehemently. This illustrates the significant disjuncture between the conversations about technology that were occurring on the federal level and the uneven ways oversight was being managed on the ground. Although TA offered a regulatory promise from policy makers while feminists, patients' rights activists, black nationalists, and the disability rights movement expressed revolutionary desires for greater access to better health care and critiques of medical power, hospital-based ethics committees still remained rare throughout the 1970s.

Just as the growth of technological assessment exposed fissures within triumphant nationalist depictions of technological innovation, images of tantrums in the bubble clashed with the news media's dominant narrative of David's and Ted's contentment in isolation. The question of tantrums, and whether or not the boys ever had them, cropped up in each of the stories as a marker of the boys' transition from childhood to adulthood and as a measure of their normality. David's psychiatrists remarked that he had "never banged on the bubble in rage or screamed to be let out"; instead, he was noted as being extremely respectful and gracious to the staff that cared for him.[33] In contrast to rebellious Ted, the media nearly always depicted David as the well-behaved son of loving parents and the willing patient of his doctors. By contrast, Ted's parents were rarely quoted in the press (most likely due to his father's very public position at NIH and relationship to the scandal of his son's confinement), so news coverage rarely revolved around Ted's relationship to his parents in the way they emphasized David's mother-son bond. However, when depictions of Ted's tantrums appeared in stories about his life, journalists and doctors read them as indicators of immaturity rather than expressions of resistance or dissatisfaction. For instance, Ted's pediatric oncologist, Dr. Pizzo, remarked that when Ted was a "youngster," he "resented the confinement" and "threw 'temper tantrums,'" but as he matured, he "thought less and less about getting out, and more about living in his sterile sanctuary . . . on living day to day. In order to deal with it, he stopped thinking about it."[34] Here, Ted's fantasy of escape, manifested in "temper tantrums," may have characterized his days as an immature "youngster," but as a mature "young man," he outgrew this type of childish resistance.

Yet controversial accounts of David's depression and defiance emerged well after his death, highlighting potentially disturbing silences in the public account of his life. One *Houston Press* article claims that David's psychologist, Dr. Mary Murphy, had planned to publish a critical firsthand account of David's confinement in 1995, entitled *Was It Worth It? The True Story of David the Bubble Boy*.[35] However, after receiving threats of a lawsuit from David's parents and Baylor officials, Murphy's publisher decided against publishing the manuscript. Murphy describes a despondent and fearful David, one who had recurring nightmares about a "King of Germs" who besieged the bubble with thousands of his evil wives. She recalls how David once smeared his own feces all over his bubble's walls upon hearing of his doctor's heart attack and describes frequent "explosive rages" followed by a pronounced fear that abandonment might be a punishment for bad behavior. She also says that David manifested nervous tics as well as a "preoccupation with death and fascination with fire," exhibited in violent drawings of angry flames immolating the hospital or his home, which he would pretend to "extinguish" by urinating on the paper. Also, as he entered puberty, David engaged in public masturbation, which "embarrassed" his caregivers. While not explicitly corroborating Murphy's account of David's feelings of depression and hopelessness, the PBS *American Experience* documentary *The Boy in the Bubble* (2003) certainly questioned the doctors' intentions and treatment decisions.

Just as Murphy's account highlighted feelings of anger and desperation that were absent in journalistic accounts of David's life, Elizabeth DeVita-Raeburn's memoir, drawn from the archive of Ted's medical records and personal journal, also reveals an entirely different story. Ted's medical files described him as "periodically depressed and withdrawn," "alternatively hostile, angry, and cheery," and "a bit of a disciplinary problem," and the papers describe how nurses cruelly removed all toys from The Room to punish Ted for not going to bed on time or not complying with medical procedures— a massive undertaking, given the lengthy sterilization process required to reintroduce them into his environment.[36] At age ten, Ted described himself as "the lost prisoner of Alcatraz," and after relating how a doctor had been offended by him, Ted writes angrily, "I am an American. I have the right to say anything I feel without being punished."[37] DeVita-Raeburn also describes Ted's penchant for resisting medical authority, alternately by throwing everything out of his room in a fury or by hiding unconsumed pills that remained undiscovered for weeks, until thousands of them cascaded from a hidden hole in the wall during a repairman's visit.

In newspaper accounts of the boys' lives, tantrums both confirmed and contradicted the assiduously cultivated image of "normal" development. Namely, the progressive narrative of the boys' development into autonomous manhood was often at odds with the progressive discourse of medical and technological triumphalism it was narratively meant to reaffirm. David's and Ted's tantrums or crankiness, dismissed as normal childish behavior, could be read as crip resistance—a pointed disruption of medical authority and its management of their bodies. However, regardless of the source of anger driving the tantrums, journalists and the boys' doctors alternately dismissed or ignored them, or they engaged in an anxious reconsolidation of the boys' well-being by using mild "crankiness" as an indicator of normality (i.e., every boy, whether in a bubble or not, gets moody or acts out from time to time). Thus, stories about David and Ted's lives manifest an implicit belief that the boys resigned themselves to confinement. Moreover, the stories subtly affirm that the boys' acquiescence not only implied consent but also evidenced their maturity and unconditional gratitude for miraculous technology and medical authority.

While reportage about scientific knowledge in popular media may have manifested a celebratory attitude toward technological innovation and American nationalism, the growth of TA, the emergence of popular science, and ongoing social movements about accessibility to health care and patient dignity in the same period revealed tensions about the cultural meaning of (and class-, disability-, and race-based differences in levels of access to) scientific advancements and their relationship to national identity and American life. The formation of TA on the federal level evidenced a desire for increased oversight, regulation, and ethical assessment of technology, whether or not this desire was operationalized in long-term policy making. Likewise, popular science in the media, whether created in disease-of-the-week television or negotiated in science journalists' accounts of Vetter and DeVita's lives, also served as a crucial analytic for critiquing national and cultural investments in technological triumphalism because they encouraged science to assess its impact on the "inner space" of the nation and its people. NASA iconography functioned in *The Boy in the Plastic Bubble* to draw key linkages among sexual exploration and technological progress and their relationship to coming of age.

The Bubble and the Tube

While the press offered images of normality and contentment for the lives of the "boys" in bubbles, *The Boy in the Plastic Bubble* approached the ethical question posed by a Baylor University medical professor to a *New York Times* reporter in one of the earliest articles written about David Vetter: "When do you decide you're not going to grow up in a plastic package?"[38] As discussed previously, the celebratory discourse of medical and technological progress could not always successfully align itself with the discourse of progress to manhood in the tale of the bubble. Representations of the bubble further complicated this alignment when they affirmed autonomy, the ability to exert control over one's life and environment, as the measure of adulthood. This liberal individualist definition of maturity, one that rests on absolute independence and insularity, is an ableist one—one that disability rights activists in the independent living movement were already challenging by the early 1970s, when they redefined "independence" as the quality of one's life with accommodations and a truly accessible society. However, another developmental milestone that was typically associated with coming of age by the 1970s remained conspicuously absent in news accounts of David Vetter and Ted DeVita: sex. Although it could be argued that cultural fantasies about childhood sexual innocence might preclude journalists from considering David a sexual being, the avoidance of this issue is particularly striking in Ted's case, since he was seventeen upon his death and had a girlfriend. *The Boy in the Plastic Bubble* would take up questions of sex and sexuality on individual and national levels by linking sexual exploration with space travel, so that the only exploratory mission worth dying for, within the movie, was sex.[39]

As journalists clamored to cover the story of a "sci-fi kid come to life" who could not be kissed by his mother, the movie adapted this mother-son pathos into a romance between a bubble teen and the nondisabled girl next door. In so doing, the movie provided one potential answer to an oft-elided (but truly unavoidable) question: When does a bubble boy become a man? *The Boy in the Plastic Bubble* reveals the inextricable linkages between fully realized manhood and the able-bodied, heterosexual requirements of "liberation." Although journalists and cultural producers generally avoided the complicated bioethical underpinnings of this question, all participated in constructing a discourse of autonomy, bravery, and manhood for the patients by transitioning them from the passive identity of "experiment" to the active identity of "explorer"—in different and equally significant ways. The significance of this transition moved from individual to national through its constant proximity to NASA iconography.

However, two potential and competing ways of achieving manhood were established through the bubble boy as a cultural figure. The first was disabled martyrdom. This option reaffirmed what Lee Edelman named "reproductive futurism."[40] Edelman argues in *No Future* that reproductive futurism, a normalizing discourse that equates the Child with the future, is a cornerstone of all politics, and ultimately bolsters the heteronormativity of all politics (because they are ultimately all future-oriented). However, reproductive futurism also bolsters (and is bolstered by) compulsory able-bodiedness, because "the Child" is generally figured as a "healthy" child who forms the promise and reward of heterosexual partnerships and future-oriented politics. When we consider how the potential eugenic applications of prenatal screening technologies affect the disabled Child's futurity, technologies such as amniocentesis, a new procedure in the late 1960s that had diagnosed David with SCID in-utero, further entangle "reproductive futurism" and reproductive control with compulsory able-bodiedness. Thus, one way of a bubble boy's achieving manhood lay in bravely martyring himself to medical technology to shore up a national investment in technological triumphalism that would also bolster reproductive futurity—"our" collective investment in and technological management of a better future for "our" children. This is the narrative presented by newspaper accounts of David's and Ted's self-sacrificial deaths. However, the movie offered an alternate solution to the question of achieving manhood. Namely, the movie attempted to resolve the bioethical dilemma of the bubble "man," or in effect, to present a Jamesonian "symbolic resolution to a concrete historical situation" by imagining another, more individualistic and liberatory way of achieving manhood and self-reliance.[41] This second path to manhood was sexual liberation.

By the time *The Boy in the Plastic Bubble* aired, John Travolta had already become a household name as the handsome, wisecracking Vinnie Barbarino in *Welcome Back, Kotter* (1975–1979). A prime-time heartthrob, Travolta had also already filmed *Saturday Night Fever*, the sexually charged movie that would catapult him into superstardom upon its 1977 release. Although the *Washington Post* television critic Tom Shales's review of the movie, "Life and Love in a Bubble," mocked the "tearjerker," he conceded that it was a "step up in quality for the season's ABC's Friday Night Movies" that "momentarily liberate[d] able actor John Travolta from the weekly caricature of 'Welcome Back, Kotter.'"[42] Classified as a "weepie" and cult classic, *The Boy in the Plastic Bubble* is often noted as the first film to demonstrate Travolta's dramatic range. The movie begins in 1959 at the home of John (Robert Reed) and Mickey Lubitch (Diana Hyland). Upon discovering she is pregnant, Mickey expresses fear that their unborn son will be born without an immune system like their first son, but John insists that they will not lose the baby this time because "[t]hey know how to save these children now" and "God knows . . . [t]here were never two people in this world more meant to be parents than you and me." In spite of their optimism, Tod is born without an immune system, and Dr. Ernie Gunther (Ralph Bellamy) tells them that he must remain in a sterilized environment until a cure is found or until his immunities develop. The majority of the movie chronicles the seventeen-year-old Tod's love affair with his neighbor, Gina Biggs (Glynnis O'Connor).

The Boy in the Plastic Bubble aired during the heyday of made-for-TV movies, which infiltrated prime-time schedules in the late 1960s. NBC's Project 120 series (1964) was the first made-for-TV movie, but ABC's prime-time Movie of the Week, which began in 1969, is perhaps the most famous of the genre.[43] Made-for-TV movies provided an economically appealing way of drawing larger audiences, given the high licensing costs for broadcasting and racier material of theatrical releases. Although ABC followed NBC's lead in establishing this genre, ABC innovated by scheduling 90-minute as opposed to 120-minute movies to cut back on production costs. At times, as with The Boy in the Plastic Bubble, made-for-TV movies dramatized major news events. NBC's TV movies predominantly offered action-adventure and suspense stories, while ABC offered comedic and social issue narratives that often featured sexual subject matter, which acknowledged "a society affected by such phenomena as women's liberation, sexual promiscuity, and divorce."[44] Moreover, this therapeutic longing for "socially responsible" and "authentic" popular culture—a transition occurring simultaneously within and across multiple mediums and in relation to teens specifically— also reflected widespread disillusionment with parental and governmental authority and deceit that was hypostatized in cultural responses to Watergate and the Vietnam War.

While The Boy in the Plastic Bubble and, as the next chapter will describe, ABC's After School Specials (1972–1994) formed part of an industry transition toward made-for-TV movies and the sexually themed programming they promulgated, both were also part of a growing trend toward "disease-of-the-week" narratives.[45] Shales noted this tendency with sarcasm when he wrote that "[t]elevision dramatists, having finally run out of terminal diseases to inflict on innocent characters, [we]re turning to more sophisticated gimmicks" with The Boy in the Plastic Bubble.[46] A term coined by the television industry itself, "disease-of-the-week" shows were either dramatic made-for-TV movies or single, self-enclosed episodes of series television that focused on characters' experiences with a disease or disability. In episodic television, rather than having a series' regular character develop a disease or disability (which could extend the plotline over multiple episodes), usually this role went to a guest star in a single episode. Thus, rather than a staple feature of a series, the disease-of-the-week plotline serves as the exclusive focus of a single episode and is resolved within the confines of a single episode.

While such dramas aimed for "realism" (i.e., medical or journalistic accuracy or educational value), disease-of-the-week shows did not highlight social and political difficulties faced by people with diseases or disabilities. In her work on popular representations of HIV/AIDS, Paula Treichler argues that disease-of-the-week shows spotlighted "the human face" of disease as a "more tolerable" alternative for television audiences than its "political face."[47] Dealing in death, pathos, and chronic illness enabled the television industry to claim that commercial entertainment programming had a "serious social edge" without offering any destabilizing or controversial social critique that might threaten ratings. Additionally, disease-of-the-week shows also overwhelmingly featured white male protagonists, operating through the evacuation or displacement of race (or occasionally by spotlighting racism as a "problem" akin to disability or disease). Disease-of-the-week television became one way in which the general public came to understand disability, illness, medical knowledge, and technology, and as a novel form of televisual representation, it also acted as a media form that tacitly staged ethical critiques of technology and its relationship to embodiment, gender, and sexuality.

Early in the movie, baby Tod is transported from the hospital to his home in a Life Island—a gurney covered in a plastic enclosure and supplied with air through portable ventilators. As the family pulls into the driveway, a mob of reporters fire questions at them as they struggle to reach their front door. After unsuccessful attempts to dissuade the reporters from taking pictures of his son, John screams, "My son is not a freak!" While David and Ted were consistently hailed as "medical miracles" and their normality anxiously asserted in news accounts of their lives, Tod Lubitch is automatically constructed not as miracle but as freak.

In fact, television critics unilaterally interpreted Tod's "freakiness"—and his disability—as a metaphor for his teen angst, alienation, and generational conflict. The *New York Times* critic John J. O'Connor lambasted the movie for its "startling . . . attitude toward age and ageing."[48] While other critics focused on Tod's "innocence" as a character "inflicted" with a terminal disease, O'Connor's review censured Tod's "mocking" behavior toward adults as epitomizing "the righteous scorn of youth." Shales described the film as "an adolescent masochist fantasy along the lines of 'Tommy,'" and said that "[a]ny teen-ager who feels isolated, picked on, or odd should be able to identify with Travolta."[49] Rather than a story of disability and treatment, *The Boy in the Plastic Bubble* was immediately understood as a teen coming-of-age story, in that critics presumed teenaged alienation and awkwardness to be emblematized by Tod's disability and his "righteous scorn" toward his captors, his parents and doctors. Tod, cast as a petulant teenager, was less sympathetic to television critics than the innocent and compliant David Vetter was to journalists, and television critics recounted *The Boy in the Bubble* not as an inspirational or tragic story of disability but rather a tale of the inherent narcissism or masochism of "adolescence." Critics seamlessly transformed Tod's disability into a metaphor for teenaged isolation. Rather than understanding his skirmishes with his caretakers as resistance to a medical model of disability that imagined his life only in the myopic terms of cure, critics simply saw generational conflict.

Although *The Boy in the Plastic Bubble* hybridized details from the public (and not-so-public) lives of David and Ted, journalistic accounts of their lives also differed markedly from the movie version when it came to standards for what constituted manhood. News coverage of David and Ted valorized their sacrifice for scientific knowledge, their role as valuable experiments, and their masculine stoicism in the face of death. Thus, their submission to medical authority and their bravery in the face of death evidenced their maturity. For instance, reporters asserted with disturbing matter-of-factness that "the 3-year old [Vetter was] a valuable research tool."[50] The NIH officials celebrated Ted's "ma[king] medical history" as the longest-surviving patient with aplastic anemia and mistakenly reported that Ted, rather than David, spent the most time in a germ-free environment. Rather than focusing on their resistiveness—a quality noted repeatedly in Ted's sister's memoirs and Mary Murphy's account of David's confinement—news media highlighted their docile adaptation to medical power as an inspiring (and scientifically valuable) performance.

This tendency was nowhere more clearly evidenced than in the repeated celebration of David's and Ted's stoicism and bravery in the face of death. In David's case especially, the press constructed his "choice" to leave the bubble as a "noble" entrance into manhood. One elegiac *Washington Post* op-ed piece written by William McPherson about David upon his death reflected explicitly on the issue of burgeoning manhood. McPherson, whose bildungsroman *Testing the Current* (1984) was published to critical acclaim in the same year, wrote that "[o]n the scale of great events" David's "isolated death . . . was not momentous," but questioned why this small event in the annals of history "should touch us so."[51] After positioning David's death on a global scale, McPherson answered his initial rhetorical question:

"Less for the pity, perhaps, than for its solitary grandeur." Rather than constructing the familiar mother-son pathos to invoke pity, McPherson mythologized David, saying that "[Franz] Kafka might have done . . . justice" to David's story of isolation, likening David to the banished cockroach-man of *Metamorphosis*. Although he concedes that David's isolation was "pitiable," McPherson argues that "it goes beyond pity"; rather, "it was in fact awesome and terrible—terrible in the classic Aristotelian sense—as was his choice, and it is his choice [to leave the bubble and undergo a bone marrow transplant] that arouses our pity, our terror and that leaves us cleansed and somehow a little more noble than we were." Again, just as Ted's value was in his inspiration to his nondisabled doctors, David's importance lay in his cathartic value to "us," the healthy onlookers, who are invited to imagine David's brave autonomy rather than his submission to the forces of research funding and medical power. McPherson noted that although "we" (presumably adults) usually associate "[n]either greatness nor nobility" with a twelve-year-old boy, David made a heroic "choice" to "craw[l] out of his cell into a world fraught with tremendous dangers and almost certain quick death." As McPherson put it, "David chose the world—the world with its filth and glory—over a long, slow death alone in his antiseptic solitary cell." In venturing out of his bubble and "choosing the world," McPherson wrote solemnly, David "chose to be a man," and in so doing, "the boy who could not himself be touched, profoundly touched us all." McPherson transformed David Vetter's treatment into a quest for manhood, emblematized by his "choosing" the "almost certain death" of a world filled with "filth and glory" over solitude, safety, and sterility. David grew up by choosing to move from passive experiment to manly explorer, or in other words, by overcoming disability and "choosing" compulsory able-bodiedness. However, given the many forces—immunological, financial, medical, and parental—that circumscribed David's autonomy, McPherson's coming-of-age narrative (and the logic of compulsory able-bodiedness it bolsters) functions, in McRuer's words, by "covering over, with the appearance of a choice, a system in which there actually is no choice."[52]

The discourses of disability present in 1970s culture for teens revealed the thin line between exploration and experimentation. However, by valorizing exploration in the form of the disabled martyr's individual overcoming, journalists collapsed the conflict between the progressive narratives of coming of age and technological advancement. Although NASA was certainly fueled (and funded) by a Cold War contest for geopolitical dominance, space exploration was rarely viewed as a participant in war or social violence, although its ascension was inseparable from American imperialist military projects prior to and during the Vietnam War (a futuristic imagining that would become more explicit in the era of military accumulation that would characterize the transition from "NASA/Trek" to the more imperial "NASA/*Star Wars*"). Likewise, the disabled bubble boy who became a man by sacrificing himself for scientific progress functioned in tandem with the self-sacrificial manhood of another contemporaneous figure on the bubble's margins: the disabled Vietnam veteran. The boys' choice of noble self-sacrifice in service to the nation—a sacrifice that became coded as their growth into adult men—resonated powerfully with imagery of "sacrifices" to the nation made by dead or disabled young veterans. As Elaine Scarry argues in *The Body in Pain*, war ultimately exists to injure the bodies and minds of the enemy, to create victims.[53] The image of boys sacrificing their bodies in service to the nation was a pervasive one in American culture during and after Vietnam, and the narrative recoding of David and Ted as manly explorers, rather than soldiers, displaced or transmuted the violence of experimentation on their bodies into an image of manly self-sacrifice, akin to that of the disabled or dead veteran. Rather than victims of military or scientific violation, boys became men, self-actualized as national citizens through their martyrdom.

However, *The Boy in the Plastic Bubble* engaged the question of disabled martyrdom in a much different way than journalists did. While stoic submission to medical knowledge gathering evidenced emotional maturity and manhood for David Vetter and Ted DeVita, *The Boy in the Plastic Bubble* imagined *resistance* to medical authority and parental protectionism as emblematizing Tod's maturity. This perspective is driven home by the movie's most significant departure from David's and Ted's stories: Tod's choice to escape the bubble and reject medical authority to pursue sexual intimacy with Gina. In its representation of coming of age, *The Boy in the Plastic Bubble* asserted the partnership of heterosexuality and physical ability as the markers of masculinity and citizenship. Thus, liberation not only *from* the bubble (and from the medical progress narrative it bolstered) but also *into* (hetero)sexuality becomes the mark of adulthood, especially because it might culminate in death.

The film ruminates on self-actualization and manhood by depicting Tod's "choice" to grow up or remain a boy based on his relationship with the outside world, a question that is posed in sexualized terms early in *The Boy in the Plastic Bubble*. The movie introduces the teenaged Tod as he is looking down at his teen neighbors from his window using a pair of binoculars. Two boys and a girl in a bikini sneak a cigarette, occasionally stealing paranoid backward glances. While smoking, they talk about how "weird" it must be for Gina to live next door to Tod. Gina concurs with her friends' assessment and adds that every time she looks up at his window, he's already looking down at her. "Like I'm surprised he's not looking at us right now," she says. Not only does the scene establish his isolation from the rest the world, but it also aligns Tod's gaze with the supervising eyes of "old people" who might catch them smoking. Throughout the movie, Tod is often shown peering through windows, or, when he attends classes at the high school via closed-circuit television, scanning the camera around the room, pausing to zoom in on Gina. Tod's voyeuristic viewing relationship with his peers, which occurs through multiple overlapping lenses (the window, the binoculars, or the surveillance camera), accentuates his detachment from the outside world.

After this visual introduction to the teenaged peeping Tod, Dr. Gunther challenges him to "grow up" and be a man. Gunther excitedly informs Tod of a new experimental treatment that "might" enable him to leave his bubble someday. Tod feigns indifference to conceal his fear of having his hopes dashed by "another [failed] treatment." Perturbed by Tod's apathetic response, Gunther grumbles that Tod has "really got it made . . . because [he] got the best excuse ever devised by anybody to avoid growing up." Tod retorts that he is growing up, to which Gunther replies, "Yes. Sometimes you're like an old man. And other times you're like a newborn baby." In saying that Tod is both an "old man" and a "newborn baby," Gunther alleges that Tod is simultaneously jaded and naive, an inexperienced boy and a cynical old man. However, this either-or categorization also serves as further evidence of Tod's nonsexuality, which was established through his sexual voyeurism in the previous scene. Tod's rejection of a potential cure disarms Gunther, because, like David's and Ted's tantrums, this rejection represents "immature" resistance to the progressive discourse of medical advancement. Although Gunther believes that Tod should man up and fight for a cure, it becomes clear that Tod becomes a man by fighting for love, by defying doctors' orders and parental rules to leave his bubble-haven and pursue an intimate relationship with Gina. However, within the story's logic, "adulthood" becomes realized only as the partnership of heterosexuality and ability, or in other words, the pursuance of normativity in a struggle to the death.

The movie establishes the romantic and sexual conflict in Tod's first trip outside his home to attend a Fourth of July beach party, where Gina accepts a dare from male friends to hold Tod's hand during the fireworks, a scene briefly discussed in this book's introduction. When she runs away from the isolator as the fireworks conclude, Tod playfully entreats her to return to his side. Instead, she joins in Tom's and Bruce's boisterous laughter, saying,

"You didn't think I was serious, did you?" and revealing that their hand-holding fulfilled a dare rather than her desire. Dramatic piano crescendo accentuates Tod's devastation as he angrily beats his bubble's walls in a tantrum induced by his sexual betrayal. That Tod's failure with Gina occurs on the Fourth of July underscores the movie's perception of his entrapment as emasculating dependence—on his parents, his doctors, and the technology that is keeping him alive. Tod's naïveté on the beach is "infantile citizenship" incarnate, and his Life Island becomes more like an incubator than a window onto the world. Various forms of literal and figurative prophylaxis will always impede his growth. Equating able-bodiedness with heterosexuality and autonomy, the movie imagines Tod's infantilizing disability as potentially *always* interfering with getting the girl—the main measure of his progress toward manhood. Through his proximity to and isolation from participating in national celebrations of independent citizenship, Tod's ability to achieve full adult citizenship without heterosexual fulfillment is called into question, and the rest of the movie seeks to remedy the problem of Tod's disabled sexuality.

When Tod discusses sex with Roy, a fellow isolated teen hospital patient, the movie further sediments its linkage of disability and problematic sexuality. A frustrated Roy explains that his doctors discovered his tumor when he was "too young for girls." He groans, "Now, I'm old enough, and I can't do anything about it!" and bangs his hands angrily on the bike's handles at the thought of "all of [his] friends out there, going to drive-ins and making out, and gettin' all that action." Roy vows resolutely, "The first thing I'm gonna do when I get out of here is get myself a hooker!" A surprised Tod, pedaling away on his exercise bike, asks whether or not Roy would fear germs, prompting Roy to laughingly reply, "Germs? I want the germs! I want to be dirty! Really dirty, you know?! . . . I wanna make it with everything that walks!" Their conversation comes to an abrupt halt when Tod asks tentatively, "Do you ever? Um . . . do you ever? . . . you know," to which a smiling Roy replies, "All the time." Tod smiles and says, "Me too."

The queerness of this scene is hard to overlook. Veritably two corners of Eve Sedgwick's "homosocial triangle," Tod and Roy revel in their heterosexuality but also demonstrate that their main form of sexual expression is—and perhaps ever will be—masturbation rather than heterosexual sex. Within the logic of heteronormativity, Tod's inability to touch queers him by rendering him unable to engage in the able-bodied regime of touch on which compulsory heterosexuality (and by proxy, sexual liberation) relies. Pedaling away on stationary bikes during this conversation, Roy and Tod will never move forward, and their queered sexuality harks back to the rat's endless running in the wheel. Tod's liberation can occur *only* when he meets the challenge of "growing up": defy doctors' orders, overcome disability, and leave the bubble to kiss the girl—or die trying. Thus technological progress, enshrined in the disabled-martyrdom-for-science narrative, is at odds with coming of age, as the bubble that was meant to benevolently protect Tod from germs now shields him from truly "growing up" into a full-fledged heterosexual.

After Gina kisses him sensuously through his Life Island's thin plastic wall, Tod designs a spacesuit so he can go to school to win her affections. Attending classes in his spacesuit, Tod embarks on his first-ever bout of teenaged delinquency when he ditches class to accompany Gina and her friends to the school football field, where they smoke marijuana. Tod's stoned companions begin laughing at his suit. To redirect their laughter, he jokes that, as an alien from Themopolis, he is "ten times stronger than earthlings." Vying for Gina's affections, Tod challenges his romantic rival, Tom, to a clap push-up contest and bets Tom ten dollars that he is the stronger man. By competing for Gina's affections, Tod demonstrates his heterosexual viability by establishing his masculine potency via his super-able-bodiedness and his rebellion against school authority.

The rest of the film shows Tod's attempt to negotiate his status as simultaneously a "cripple" and a heterosexual man and to inhabit both identities at the same time. Although Tod is victorious, the push-up contest nearly kills him when his oxygen levels deplete; he barely makes it back safely to his classroom bubble. Later, Gina reprimands Tod for "flexing his muscles" like the rest of the unenlightened normal boys. Tod desperately defends his intentions:

> I was just doing it so you'd see that I'm not a cripple. And that there's nothing wrong with me except that I can't get out of here until they tell me it's okay. . . . I'm so sick of feeling like a hospital case. Like some weirdo kid who can't even breathe normal air because he might get sick and die. I just wanna be like a man. Someone that you could care about, and not feel sorry for.

Tod's assertion of manhood continues throughout the film, and the film equates his virile heterosexuality with his overcoming of his disability. For one brief moment, the film imagines that one can, in fact, be a "cripple" and a "man," by transgressively exploring Tod's sexuality *within* the bubble. In his spacesuit, a veritable walking condom, he begins to have a sexual relationship with Gina. He goes on his first date, holding hands as he runs along the beach flying a kite with Gina. Accentuated by the exultant, horn-driven score, the scene of liberated love is punctured by Tod's father's yelling that only five minutes remain on Tod's air tank. However, as Tod's father drives home, Tod and Gina make out on the floor of the van. Gina sensuously kisses Tod's face through the thin layer of plastic, and his orange-gloved hands greedily work their way down her back as they kiss. As opposed to the perpetually unfulfilled "quest for normal" embodied by David's watering the lawn, this steamy spacesuit scene momentarily celebrates Tod's crip/queer sexuality.

Disability studies scholarship has critiqued the infantilization and desexualizing of disabled people—two problematic and mutually reinforcing attributes that continue to circumscribe disabled people's bodies and lives. In opposition to these stereotypes, the movie encourages Tod's hot crip sexuality. Gina's and Tod's sexual and romantic attraction *deepens* in his bubble and spacesuit, both of which become incorporated into rather than interfere with their sexual encounters. The scene of the spacesuit kiss does not invite pity or inspiration. It is pure pleasure. In contrast to news accounts of Vetter's and DeVita's heroic "choice" of martyrdom for science, the movie addresses Tod's sexuality *within* the bubble rather than requiring that he venture outside it.

Yet the narrative ultimately disciplines this brief possibility of queer/crip sexuality through its doctrine that "protected sex" will always be insufficient—a remarkable take on the issue of teenaged sexuality in a post–sexual liberation era defined by contestation over youth exposure to sex education and sexually themed television fare.[54] *The Boy in the Plastic Bubble* imagines adulthood as coterminous with compulsory able-bodiedness. Thus only in leaving the bubble, in spite of probable death, can Tod fully meet Dr. Gunther's challenge to "grow up." Near the end of the movie, Tod chooses to leave the bubble early one morning, in spite of Gunther's uncertainty about his chances of survival in the outside world. Briefly pausing in his sleeping parents' doorway, Tod continues outside to Gina, establishing his filial relationship as secondary to his romantic one. As opposed to the sterile, artificial, and mechanized bubble, the outside world is filled with trees. To emphasize the naturalness of Tod's "choice" to vacate his plastic enclosure, the movie links him to nature as he exits his house to touch the trees, feel the breeze on his face, and inhale a breath of fresh air. In a stark white shirt, symbolizing his rebirth, he is surrounded by greenery as he approaches Gina and her white horse. Tod touches her face, which is "so much softer than he ever imagined," and kisses her. This sylvan scene, as well as Tod's "authentic" unmediated touching, accentuates the association of heterosexuality and able-bodiedness with nature. Tod and Gina ride off together on a white horse, a symbol traditionally associated with female rescue. However, the movie's final line forecloses the possibility of reading Tod as a feminized figure, because when Gina asks where they should go, Tod replies exuberantly, "To Themopolis!" his fictional home planet in which he would be stronger than mere mortals.

The ambiguous ending does not foreclose either reading—that Tod had developed sufficient immunities and would "live long and prosper" or that, as the movie's tagline asserts, he chose "one day of love over a lifetime of loneliness" even if it meant death. While Tod's ending may be uncertain, Paul Williams's song "What Would They Say?" plays over the final scene and features the moaning refrain, "What would they say if we up and ran away? . . . Would they carry on when they realized we were gone. . . . Leave us alone, we'd make it just fine." These lyrics cast Tod's disabled overcoming as generational conflict, a defiant escape from parental, medical, and societal clutches.

The Boy in the Plastic Bubble reimagines and reinvents the story of a boy with immune-deficiency, isolated from his mother's kiss, into a coming-of-age story of emerging and achieved teen heterosexuality. This ending opens up some interesting possibilities. Tod's resistance to medical management via sexual liberation offered a subtle ethical and sexual-political critique of American technological triumphalism—suggesting some transgressive possibilities for "disease of the week" as a television genre. At a time when ethical critiques of medical power like hospital-based ethics boards, patients' and disability rights movements, and TA were nascent and largely invisible, disease of the week emphasized the emotional ramifications of medical treatments and technologies. Read in this way, sexual desire trumps the need for and technology of cure—a valuable critique of a medical model of disability that, in its quest to "fix" a body perceived as broken, neglects crip pleasures, desires, and emotional needs. Ultimately, *The Boy in the Plastic Bubble* advocates against keeping teen boys locked up from the "germs" of sex, because then they might not develop into proper heterosexual men. However, by rendering Tod's physical intimacy in the bubble insufficient, the narrative also disciplines the possibility of crip sexuality. Namely, the movie problematically suggests that, as a disabled person, Tod will never truly be heterosexual or a man; instead, he will be frozen in time and in the bubble.

On the one hand, the ending shores up the convergence of heteronormativity and able-bodiedness, and although it plays slightly with non-normative gender roles, it ultimately shores up traditional ones. Tod's decision to pursue love at the risk of death recuperates noble self-sacrificial manhood, albeit in a different way from the narrative of disabled martyrdom for science and the nation. True growth into manhood requires Tod's liberation from his disability and his dependence on the bubble and his parents. The song answers its own self-doubt about defying parental and societal expectations with the imperative: "Leave us alone, we'd make it just fine." In essence, rather than martyring himself in service to patriotic narratives of scientific progress, Tod martyrs himself for heteronormativity and adulthood.

Finally, and more importantly, *The Boy in the Plastic Bubble*'s narrative reconsolidation of compulsory able-bodiedness also makes visible a crisis in sexual liberation, which is also endemic to the regime of compulsory heterosexuality. Patrick White explains that, after institutions systematically discouraged blind children's sexuality for generations, cultural anxieties about blind children's "proper" development of appropriate gender roles and intimate behaviors fueled the emergence of sex education literature for the blind in the 1970s.[55] However, White argues that these anxieties displayed heterosexuality's contingency rather than its essentialism in revealing heterosexuality's profound dependence on sightedness. Post–sexual liberation efforts to liberate the blind from their repressive sexual past relied upon new notions of sexuality as the ultimate expression of autonomy and individuality. However, these same efforts exacted new means of normalization and control, rehabilitating the blind by assimilating them into the heterosexual matrix and rendering them identical to sighted heterosexuals. In this framework, the blind are both disabled *and* queer, since performances of gender and sexuality that reinforce heteronormativity, such as grooming or mannerisms, are culturally understood in visual terms.

The Boy in the Plastic Bubble shows that heterosexuality does not just presume sightedness; rather it also depends on certain forms of touching. Just as blindness poses a crisis to a heterosexual matrix that is wholly reliant on the visual, Tod's disability, specifically his inability to touch or to be touched, presents a similar crisis to a heteronormativity based on specific forms of unmediated sexual contact. That is, Tod can only touch himself, and therefore, cannot be sexually liberated until he frees himself from the bubble to touch someone else. In the bubble, he remains queer in spite of his obvious interest in Gina, as he is unable to engage in the regime of touch on which compulsory heterosexuality and, by proxy, sexual liberation rely. Tod's disabled sexuality and masculinity are unintelligible as heterosexual (or adult) until he can be assimilated into a nondisabled world of unmediated touch. Until then, the teenaged Tod remains a "developmental failure." McRuer argues that heterosexuality and able-bodiedness pass as the unmarked "natural order of things," but in bolstering one another, they betray their own inherent instability as hard-won "impressive achievement[s]" that are "never really guaranteed."[56] *The Boy in the Plastic Bubble* stages an implicit critique of heteronormativity by revealing that heterosexuality and normative masculinity, far from being as natural as the breeze on Tod's skin, are actually the result of struggle and sacrifice.

Overcoming Repression, Overcoming Disability

I spotlight this tension, between a sexuality that is "natural" and one that is compulsorily and artificially produced, as a way of critiquing liberation's investment in overcoming. By resituating the history of the bubble boy from the domain of medical ethics, this chapter has endeavored to consider its sexual politics. The bubble became a felicitous metaphor for protected children passing into the potentially deviant sexual and social world of adolescence. As such, *The Boy in the Plastic Bubble* triangulated concerns about masculinity, sexuality, and disability in a cultural moment when Americans grappled with the complex sexual and gender politics of a post–sexual liberation world. It revealed that sexual liberation in the 1970s existed in a paradoxical space.

On the one hand, the sexual awareness that was the culmination of "liberation" was perceived as natural and prediscursive—or as Adrienne Rich argued, "compulsory."[57] On the other hand, heterosexuality, as implicated in a coming-of-age narrative, became the hard-won achievement of a long struggle to overcome sexual repression. The cultural idea of repression played a central role in imagining teen sexual education and sexual awareness as a liberatory remedy to an imagined repressive past. Amid the first soundings of the disability rights movement in the 1970s, narratives of overcoming repression were likened to and made visible through narratives of disabled overcoming—an understudied aspect of sexual liberation's legacy in media and popular culture. This narrative substitution bolsters an ableist desexualization of disability, rendering disability and repression as aligned and undesirable. Thus, sexual liberation was also a rehabilitative narrative, one that recuperated gender and sexuality from an unhealthy, repressive past. However, sexual liberation, as it became compulsory, still could not imagine disabled subjects as sexual beings. The movie could not imagine a fully heterosexual teen boy without liberating him into the "adult" world of able-bodied touch. Thus, examining the linkage of liberation to a legacy of disabled overcoming incites a critical contemplation of liberation's essentialized place in compulsory heterosexuality.

This chapter has also critiqued the narrative of disabled martyrdom offered by news coverage of the "real" bubble boy to fulfill disability studies' dual commitment, on the one hand, to visualizing actual disabled lives (even while acknowledging David's and Ted's lives as unrecoverable) and, on the other, to tracing the cultural work of discourses of disability within diverse cultural locations of technology, violence, medical power, sexual liberation, and coming of age. By reimagining experimentation as exploration, the news media and the movie recoded the boys' submission to science into a national masculine heroism in two different but intimately related ways. Bubble boys became men through the struggle of exploring the "filth and glory" of the world and overcoming their own frailty. For David and Ted, their coming of age took the form of disabled martyrdom for a national pride emblematized by the miracle and wonder of scientific progress. Tod's "liberation" occurs when he meets the challenge of "growing up" by overcoming his disability and queerness (i.e., his insufficient heterosexuality) by leaving the bubble to touch Gina. *The Boy in the Plastic Bubble* shows that achieving sexually liberated heterosexuality and masculinity, far from being naturally assured in advance, is actually hard (and perhaps even fatal!) work. Thus, the movie questioned the "naturalness" and autonomy offered by heteronormativity as well as technological progress. Through the linkage of space exploration and sexual discovery, *The Boy in the Plastic Bubble* positioned these debates about teenaged sexual exploration against a triumphal narrative of technological progress. Rather than being martyred to science like David Vetter and Ted DeVita, Tod resists medical authority in pursuit of romantic and sexual fulfillment—in other words, his sexual liberation—a problematically heroic choice that makes him not a "cripple" but a man and reaffirms the mutual exclusivity of these two categories. In order to truly come of age, Tod must "choose" able-bodied heterosexual fulfillment even though it might mean death.

Finally, *The Boy in the Plastic Bubble* existed at the convergence of a 1970s rise in sex-themed programming and disease-of-the-week narratives. While scholars have remarked upon the emergence of each type, they have not acknowledged their historic and thematic convergences outside sexually transmitted disease stories, especially AIDS, many of which occurred much later in the history of made-for-TV movies than *The Boy in the Plastic Bubble* or ABC's *After School Specials*. Issue-based television specifically for teens newly emerged in this period as edutainment that incorporated the progressive politics of various post-1968 liberation movements but also carefully regulated them. Made-for-TV movies like *The Boy in the Plastic Bubble* and, as I will discuss in the chapter that follows, ABC's *After School Specials* formed a new approach to socially responsible programming that Todd Gitlin famously named TV's "turn toward relevance."[58] However, rather than social consciousness being achieved by pointed satire within thematic content, as in the Norman Lear adult programming Gitlin discusses, teen shows of the era connected national citizenship with mutually reinforcing narratives of achieving heterosexuality and overcoming disability in their dramatic narrative structure—a structure that would become regularized and forever impact teen programming when it became a staple of the *After School Specials*. In an era of sex-themed television, as teenaged television viewers were increasingly imagined as distinct from child viewers (both as audience members and as market segments), the "bubble" participated in a legacy of protective television and protected sex, in addition to its thematic emphasis on disability.

Issues of disability and sexuality figured predominantly in representations of teen coming of age in fledgling "teen television" of the seventies, especially in relation to two intimately related progressive discourses at work within rehabilitative edutainment. The first was a discourse of technological progress that imagined national pride and developing citizenship as inextricable from evolving technologies, including media. The mobilization of NASA and other patriotic emblems in the content of television for and about teenagers formed part of this discourse of technological triumphalism. However, this celebration of technology coexisted with a growing concern, offered by cultural producers, regulatory policy makers, and parents, that cultivating healthy teen TV viewing relationships by regulating television as a powerful technology was imperative in the production of good citizenship, as the next chapter will show.

The second progressive discourse within rehabilitative edutainment was a coming-of-age narrative that represented "healthy" adult citizenship, the partnership of able-bodiedness and heterosexuality, as the reward for overcoming disabling adolescence. Coming-of-age stories increasingly featured disabled protagonists, and disability became a pervasive and embodied metaphor for adolescence. This post–sexual liberation narrative of overcoming repression, likened to overcoming disability, was indispensable to imagining adolescent sexual development in this period. Indeed, the disabled body, being rehabilitated by heterosexual romance, provided one form of sexual liberation's enfleshment as healthy and natural. Teenagers, as recipients of this increasingly familiar narrative, were newly hailed as sexual citizens in the post–sexual liberation era, and socially relevant television, imagined as pedagogical and healthy, transformed heteronormativity and able-bodiedness into lessons, or disciplines, of good citizenship. In this context, Paul

Simon's musical portrait of the bubble formed a symptom (or expression) of this articulation, offering an ambivalent countercultural critique of modern technologies of warfare, media, and medicine through the figure of the disabled martyr in an age of receding government and advancing governmentality. The cultural figure of the teenager, as a malleable and incomplete proto-citizen, became a vehicle not only for uniting progressive discourses of technology and sexuality but also for naturalizing self-surveillance and rehabilitative citizenship—"the way the camera follows us in slow-mo" *and* "the way we look to us all."

2

After School Special Education

Sex, Tolerance, and Rehabilitative Television

I got to thinkin' about what you were sayin' about handicaps. . . .
Well, I was thinkin' I don't have to be a good talker to be able to
skate.
—Tucker "Tuck" Faraday (Stewart Peterson), in "The Ice Skating
Rink," ABC's *After School Specials* (1975)

In an era when ABC's *Happy Days* (1974–1984) and its nostalgic vision of
1950s life reigned supreme on prime time, there was little television programming that acknowledged the not-so-happy elements of teen existence.
Although young adult "problem novels" such as *The Outsiders* (1967) had
become a thriving market by the 1970s, the bulk of the era's network programming seldom "acknowledged that there was more to adolescence than
sock hops."[1] ABC's *After School Specials* (1972–1995) were a significant exception. Engaging difficult topics such as teen and adult alcoholism, homosexuality, teen pregnancy, racism, drug abuse, domestic violence, sexually
transmitted diseases, teen suicide, and child molestation, the *Specials* advised
adolescents, without the imperative of parental intervention or oversight, on
how they might begin to cope with such dilemmas.[2] In so doing, this series
reaffirmed a broader discourse of adolescence-as-problem—as a developmental "stage" defined by exposure to and weathering of dysfunction. Many
people remember watching episodes in health or driver's education classes
as educators began incorporating television into the classroom as an educational tool. But in spite of the series' wide viewership and cult classic status,
virtually no scholarly attention has been paid to the *Specials*.

As adolescence routinely became conceptualized as problem-filled—as a
"crisis"—it also increasingly became portrayed in made-for-TV movies like
the *Specials* through the metaphoric vehicle of overcoming disability. As
the disease-of-the-week formula that characterized *The Boy in the Plastic
Bubble* began populating prime-time offerings, the *Specials* also featured
a preponderance of storylines about physical and cognitive disabilities.

Functioning as a form of rehabilitative citizenship training or "*Special* education" for teenagers, the *Specials'* enforcement of disability in the teen body perpetually offered the promise of eventual normalcy through endless rehabilitation and packaged it as "coming of age." The *Specials*, as rehabilitative edutainment, culturally transmitted medical knowledge and narratives of disability for public consumption, entertainment, and education. In shows ranging from "It's a Mile from Here to Glory" (1978), about a temporarily disabled teen track star, to "The Kid Who Wouldn't Quit: The Brad Silverman Story" (1987), a semi-biographical story about a mainstreamed student with Down syndrome, the *Specials* transformed stories of disability into stories of growing up, overcoming disability, and getting the girl (or boy).

In tracing coming-of-age narratives in the *Specials*, I am not arguing that they, or any other form of rehabilitative edutainment, are illustrative texts of a "real" psychological developmental process. Rather, I argue that they are constitutive texts in a cultural process, one that produces the figure of the teenager as a developing citizen.[3] The *Specials'* ableist approach operates by mapping "immaturity" onto disability and "maturity" onto rehabilitation, a problematic association that continues to limit the ways disability and disabled people are culturally represented. ABC's *After School Specials* cast teenagers as proto- or "infantile" citizens, who were temporarily disabled by their own adolescence, sexually at risk, and in need of rehabilitation. This new "rehabilitative" approach to teen citizenship and to teen television programming fused the impulses of social consciousness, educational, and sexually themed programming of the era with the values of an emergent self-help culture. In so doing, it created a new, hybridized approach to television content and narrative structure that would address teenagers *proactively* rather than protectively. This mode of address found cultural and political traction because it imagined an impressionable and angst-ridden teen audience whose exposure to the "problems" of disability, disease, and death—even if only in a fictional universe—would instantiate emotional growth into a stable and responsible adulthood.

This rehabilitative logic was built at the intersection of several sites. An interview with the *Specials'* creator, Martin Tahse, reveals some of the intricacies of the development of the *Specials*, their intended audience, and the series' preoccupation with disability narratives. While I argue that the content and narrative structure of the *Specials* contained a rehabilitative logic with respect to teen characters and viewers, debates about the value of the programming itself also actively participated in bolstering this logic. As television increasingly became part of American lives, the *Specials* emerged amid the exponential growth of children's programming and concomitant debates about television's potential role in youth education. Amid pervasive accusations of its sexual immorality and vapidity, the television industry reformed its own reputation through this representational mode by offering socially conscious storylines and by asserting that television was a valuable instructional tool for teen viewers. In this context, the *Specials* were also negotiating shifting post–sexual liberation ideas about teen sexuality and cultural responses to increased sexually themed programming on television. In contrast to a well-documented 1950s-era discourse of television as a "threat" to children, rehabilitative edutainment emerged as a new way of "domesticating" the television to make it suitable and perhaps even healthy for a young viewing audience.[4] As television began to address teens as a new audience segment, ABC's *After School Specials* were among the earliest programming to target a predominantly teenaged audience rather than subsuming them within a family or children's audience. Rather than censuring television as damaging to young people, rehabilitative edutainment like *The Boy in the Plastic Bubble* and the *Specials* participated in debates over the educational value of television by configuring commercial shows—not just public television—as having "edutainment" value for viewers.[5] Finally, by closely examining two episodes of ABC's *After School Specials*, "The Ice Skating Rink" (1975) and "Heartbreak Winner" (1980), this chapter shows the complex and surprisingly intricate ways the logics of protection and rehabilitation played out in the content of a series that was, at the same time, groundbreaking in its attention to teen sexuality.

Contestation over television's educational value affected 1970s television offerings and was formative of television's rehabilitative approach. Assailed for its violent content in the 1950s and 1960s, television had come under fire again by the 1970s for its increasing sexual explicitness. In the context of the era's new family dynamics, including increased divorces, working parents, and latchkey kids, teens were considered at risk in historically specific ways, and with parents increasingly out of the home, youth television viewing practices were less supervised. Earlier television regulations had assumed that parents would be the primary regulators of children's television intake. However, this era witnessed a new approach to teen television that presumed absent parents who would not oversee their children's relationship with television. Thus, the *Specials* assumed a role as educator that was formerly imagined to be the province of parents, and episodes reflected this shift by depicting mainly divorced, absentee, or otherwise incapacitated parental figures. Although it is tempting to read rehabilitative edutainment's cultural impulses toward sex education and sexual television programming as inherently progressive or liberalizing, I argue that these cultural impulses toward sexual education, both in the classroom and on television, form a novel rehabilitative—that is to say, a productive and disciplinary—approach to teen sexuality and teen bodies. By combining social consciousness, educational, and sexually themed programming of the era, the new teen TV redefined teen engagement with popular culture as productive rather than damaging.

Disability Dramas and the *After School* Audience

In their twenty-three-year run, ABC's *After School Specials* won numerous awards and prizes, including eighteen Emmys, three Blue Ribbons in the American Film Festival, and the prestigious Peabody Award, among others.[6] The *Specials* debuted in 1972 amid bitter controversy over a perceived lack of quality in children's programming and a simultaneous war over the heightened visibility of sexuality on television (and in culture more generally). Viewers often remember the shows as much for their hokey didacticism as for their unique mode of address. According to National Public Radio (NPR)'s Sarah Lemanczyk, ABC's *After School Specials* addressed teenagers "not as children or adults, but as something in between" in their serious treatment of relevant teen issues.[7] NPR's retrospective piece coincided with the DVD release of select *Specials* episodes and featured man-on-the-street–style interviews with adults who had watched the series as teenagers. One man recalled that he was "forced" to watch the *Specials* in health class and remembered "Scott Baio freaking out on drugs and getting hit over the head in the water."[8] Another man laughingly reminisced about a *Special* involving an illiterate basketball player and the unlikely chain of events that constituted the story's dramatic climax: "somehow I think it was his little brother burnt his eyes with some bleach and this basketball player couldn't read [*laughter*] the back of the bottle to get him some help . . . and I think Kareem Abdul Jabar was somehow a guest star on it."[9]

Now infamous for their unabashed preaching and often hyperbolic approach to teen problems, the shows were usually dramas but also occasionally featured straight comedies or "dramedies." According to the *Specials'* producer, Martin Tahse, the series explicitly targeted teenagers and was pitched initially as a way "to cover the distance between the Saturday morning ghetto for kids and prime time" because "teenagers were not being addressed" in either venue.[10] The network intended the shows to be viewed when teens returned home from school, usually around 4 p.m. Although the *Specials* are now considered overly moralistic, Tahse said he and other creators never intended to "wa[g] fingers" but rather to approach "topics that normally were not being done at all." "And we were being entertaining," he added.

Drawing storylines from the era's young adult problem novels, the *Specials* generally devoted each episode to a single dilemma facing teenagers. To stay abreast of emerging teen literature, Tahse subscribed to *Publishers Weekly*, sought advice from the American Library Association (ALA), courted new young adult authors, and negotiated with publishers to buy the rights to novels he felt would make timely *Specials*. Storylines often featured first-time young adult novelists, because for Tahse, they "present[ed] different problems with a reality to it" and used "realistic dialogue." However, Tahse also admitted that reliance on novels formed part of a strategy for managing and minimizing potential network reticence to tackle sensitive issues, because "walking in [to ABC] with a book lent credence to the story you wanted to tell." Noting the scarcity of shows addressing "serious" issues in the 1970s, Tahse argued that soap operas were one of the few venues that dealt with "drunk driving, homosexuality, [and] pregnancy" and added that they were "getting away with murder" in comparison to more staid adult-oriented prime-time shows, whose content was not nearly as racy.

When asked whether or not the *Specials* had a "formula," Tahse responded that he was "very interested in kids getting out of ghettos." This did not necessarily mean "a black ghetto," he clarified; rather, such a ghetto might be "living in a farm" and imagining "how . . . you get from the farm to college and see another kind of a life than what your father has been doing, . . . [to show] kids who were trying to become something that they weren't."[11] Indeed, many of the *Specials*, especially those devoted to young boys, reaffirmed a "metronormative" narrative of sexual coming of age by spotlighting tensions between "conservative" provincialism, mapped onto rural spaces like farms or rough urban neighborhoods, and "liberal" cosmopolitanism, signified by boys' choices for artistic careers like figure skating or ballet (which were configured as potentially feminizing).[12] In other words, teen coming-of-age stories were at the center of the series. The *Specials* imagined coming of age as a process of developing liberal individualism by offering lessons in tolerance to citizens-in-development, often by emphasizing the tolerance of gender nonnormativity or racial otherness in narratives of overcoming disability. Lessons in tolerance rehabilitated individuals—prejudiced or cruel teenagers— into liberal open-minded adult citizens, even as such lessons generally elided the large-scale social and political reality of structural inequities wrought by systemic racism, sexism, and ableism.

Dolores Morris, then ABC's East Coast director of children's programming, also asserted another important guideline: "The protagonists are always young people, and in almost every instance, the problems in question are solved by the young people themselves."[13] Tahse recalled "very few rules and regulations" apart from the directive that "adult[s] can't solve the problem" facing the teen protagonists. For example, "A Very Delicate Matter" (1982), an episode that dealt with gonorrhea in a romantic relationship, featured two teens getting testing and treatment without involving adults. Additionally, episodes about parental alcoholism showed a transition from a teen's enabling and covering for an alcoholic parent to his/her seizing control of life by attending Alateen or, in one extreme case, a girl's staging a fire drill and descending a rope ladder from her bedroom window to be prepared for a potential house fire caused by her drunken mother's dangerous habit of smoking in bed.[14]

Problems and solutions were gender-specific, and the solution to such problems often presented itself through heterosexual partnering. All of the teens with alcoholic parents in the above examples were female, and in all of the examples, the female protagonist began taking charge of her life only after meeting a boy who also had an alcoholic parent and who dutifully showed the girl how to deal with it. While it is certainly true that problems were often solved by teens themselves in the *Specials*, it is notable that male protagonists often actively solved problems without assistance from female peers, whereas girls often cared for and sought assistance and advice from their male and female peers. Thus even as they dealt with teen sexuality in novel and frank ways, the *Specials* reinforced fairly traditional masculine and feminine roles and enforced heterosexual relationships, not only as desirable but also perhaps even necessary to facilitate coming of age.

The *Specials'* issue-driven narrative strategy circulated within and reinforced emerging theories of psychosocial development, most notably Erikson's universalizing notion of "identity crisis" as a staple feature of adolescence.[15] Ideally, rehabilitative edutainment invited teen viewers to actively participate in their own citizenship training by channeling their emotional and behavioral responses to various crises into "healthy" choices. Thus, an empathetic teen viewer, trained to react in appropriately liberal and cosmopolitan ways to the episode, would experience viewership as part of his/her development into a "good citizen": a heterosexual, able-bodied, normatively gendered, and emotionally stable adult. The *Specials* participated in configuring the resolution of teen crisis as a cultural process that was simultaneously personal, national, and emotional.

Disability was not always considered a problem in need of rehabilitation like other social problems on the series, though characters with disabilities were a mainstay especially of the early *Specials*. However, the series always presumed a middle-class white (and likely suburban) audience of "normal"—able-bodied and heterosexual—youth viewers. More often than not, the *Specials'* disabled characters were white teen boys rather than teen girls.[16] Such emphasis on male protagonists, at least in the earliest *Specials*, occurred partially by design, because, in Tahse's words, "the idea was that the boys would watch a boy show but not a girl show, whereas a girl would like a boy show too."[17] Again, assumptions about gendered behavior and development were at work, even behind the scenes.

Disability figured into the content of the *Specials* in a variety of ways. It was sometimes presented as a penalty for "bad behavior." For example, in "A Mile from Here to Glory" (1978), Early MacLaren's (Steve Shaw) all-consuming desire to break school track records rather than be a team player leads him to injury. Early sulks after failing to break the school's record, and as he returns to the bus, a car hits him and breaks both of his legs. The show depicts the accident as a penalty for Early's selfishness: had he boarded the bus with the rest of the team rather than brooding, he would have avoided the accident. While learning how to walk again, he learns the value of teamwork rather than only personal investment.

Furthermore, in a formulation typical of many teen dramas about sexually transmitted diseases (STDs), disease functioned as a penalty for "promiscuous" sex. The earliest *Specials* about STDs—the majority of which were about gonorrhea—often featured a teen cheating on his or her long-term significant other and then infecting their unsuspecting partner, who is configured as the innocent party in the infection. "A Very Delicate Matter" (1982) highlighted female sexuality as exceptionally dangerous when a female doctor argued that boys were "lucky" in manifesting physical symptoms of gonorrhea, as opposed to a girl, who could "spread gonorrhea without ever knowing that she has it."[18] The narratives construct sexually active teen girls as endangering unsuspecting boys, rather than endangered by asymptomatic diseases.

Finally, at least three episodes dealt with cognitive disability: "Sara's Summer of Swans" (1974), "Hewitt's Just Different" (1977), and the semi-biographical "Kid Who Wouldn't Quit: The Brad Silverman Story" (1987). The *New York Times* television reviewer John J. O'Connor criticized "Sara's Summer of Swans," a television adaptation of a Newberry Award–winning Betsy Byars novel featuring a cognitively disabled boy, for downplaying the character's disability. He argued that the episode portrayed the boy as "little more than extremely shy," although his disability was "the real reason for the book's Newberry award."[19] In the other two aforementioned episodes, Hewitt Calder and Brad Silverman appeared as teenagers with cognitive disabilities.[20] Notably, although sexuality is generally either avoided or pathologized in narratives of cognitive disability, the *Specials* emphasized Hewitt's and Brad's teenaged heterosexual desires for able-bodied women and used them to evidence their similarity to "normal" teenaged boys.[21] However, all of the episodes about cognitive disability featured white able-bodied actors playing disabled characters rather than casting disabled actors in the roles.

As detailed in the previous chapter, this growing televisual focus on disease and disability narratives—or what television critics have named "disease-of-the-week" shows—was significant for several reasons. First, it demonstrates that disability was a predominant cultural concern and a cultural language not only for addressing and entertaining teen viewers but also as advice for channeling teens into good American adult citizenship—which is to say, traditionally gendered, heterosexual, able-bodied, and white. While many episodes used disability to teach empathy and tolerance of difference by gently castigating able-bodied youths who teased or exploited disabled protagonists, disability also entered rehabilitative edutainment as a metaphoric language for educating teens about overcoming adversity. This narrative use of disability often presumed that occupying a state of disability was both natural and pathological for developing teens until they "came of age" into able-bodied heterosexual adults. As David T. Mitchell and Sharon L. Snyder argue, physical or cognitive anomalies, used as textual signifiers for "individual or social collapse," become the "materiality of metaphor" by providing a tangible body for the "textual abstraction" of metaphor.[22] Rehabilitative edutainment corporealized the intangible psychological process of coming of age through the physically disabled body and its overcoming. In multiple cultural locations both on-screen and off, teen proto-citizens were increasingly constructed and addressed as always-already under development, as disabled subjects in need of rehabilitation. While imagining teens as constantly "in the process" of resolving their inherent disabilities, rehabilitative edutainment, infused with emergent self-help philosophies, placed the responsibility for "treatment" squarely in the hands of teenagers themselves.

Second, the series premiered in a watershed year of the disability rights movement. Through a combination of deinstitutionalization efforts, the passage of significant federal legislation (especially Section 504 of the Rehabilitation Act [1973] and the Education for All Handicapped Children Act [1975]), and highly visible political protests in San Francisco, New York, and Washington, DC, disability emerged as a politicized identity in the 1970s.

Although generally not included in traditional histories of youth political activism, the disability rights movement and its campaign for autonomy and self-determination for disabled people formed within 1960s youth political activism that galvanized young citizens and fundamentally redefined the contested category of "youth." At the University of California–Berkeley, fiery critiques of the *in loco parentis* policy launched by the free speech movement cross-pollinated with the independent living movement in leveraging distinct but interrelated critiques of paternalism. Thus, the rehabilitative approach I trace in the *Specials* was part of a wider cultural redefinition not only of disability but also of the boundaries between "child" and "adult," inflected by youth activism of the 1960s and 1970s, including the disability rights movement. Disabled people were becoming culturally visible in new ways—as political actors, as returning Vietnam veterans, as young people demanding access to education and public space—while disability narratives increasingly emerged on television in the *Specials* and elsewhere.

In the context of new conceptions and images of disability, the *Specials*, and rehabilitative edutainment more broadly, operated under fundamentally ableist assumptions. Functioning pedagogically to train teen proto-citizens, the *Specials* presented overcoming disability as a metaphor for coming of age. However, this rehabilitative logic relied on the problematic infantilization of disabled people by equating adulthood with able-bodiedness and heterosexuality, even as it challenged paternalism by addressing teenagers as self-actualizing citizens. Through its overcoming narratives, the *After School Specials* produced a discourse of rehabilitative citizenship through the linkage of "compulsory able-bodiedness" with "compulsory heterosexuality" as the equivalent of "growing up."

"Required TV"? "Video-Guided Vegetables" and the Birth of Edutainment

In order to properly analyze the series' rehabilitative approach, we need to situate the *Specials* within multiple issues of television regulation, in general, and children's broadcasting, in particular. The shows were fundamentally shaped by contestation over what constituted "educational" television, while journalists, educators, and parents constructed television alternately as a technology in need of rehabilitation or with rehabilitative potential for young, impressionable viewers. Debates over the new sexual culture of the 1970s were often staged on and in relationship to television programming, and cultural debates about the educational value of commercial programming emerged alongside and within this context.

Parents, lawmakers, and media producers all shaped the discourse about youth, television, and sexuality in the Cold War era. Grassroots efforts through petitions to the FCC threatened to bring more regulation into children's broadcasting to combat sex-themed programming, entertainment without educational value, and overabundant advertising. Meanwhile, networks took evasive action with new regulations and new socially conscious programming, such as Norman Lear's adult fare, *All in the Family* (1971–1979), *The Jeffersons* (1975–1985), and *Sanford and Son* (1972–1977). Alongside television producers, lawmakers also responded to concerns about youth television intake. Broadcasters and policy makers codified television's role in national educational reform efforts during the Cold War.[23] Specifically, Title VII of the National Defense Education Act (1958) funded the promotion of the educational use of media, which made the use of audiovisual media coterminous with educational reform.[24] William Harley, then-president of the National Association of Educational Broadcasters (NAEB), firmly linked educational and media reform to America's geopolitical position when he hoped that Russia would "not have to launch the equivalent of a sputnik in the use of television for educational purposes in order to bring the breakthrough which American education so desperately needs if it is again to seize a position of world leadership in education."[25] Cold War anxieties heightened television's stake in affecting the nation's youth and effecting educational reform, and in this milieu, commercial television was assailed as a "vast wasteland."[26]

As Cold War educational bills increasingly linked television to American national educational reform, journalists, educators, politicians, and concerned parents configured the embattled medium as a crisis necessitating intervention. Amid the thrust to repair its deficient educational system, the nation also began to debate the place of sex in education, both in schools and on television, as the public imagined television's potential role in providing sexual instruction for young people in the wake of sexual liberation movements of the 1960s. There were two primary targets for regulation: first, commercial programming that was either "wallowing in sex" or reveling in violence, and second, advertising during children's programming. These threats materialized as imperiling to all young viewers, although teenagers were increasingly addressed as distinct from child or family viewers in this period, both in regulatory discourses and in an economic trend toward niche market segmentation.[27]

Positioned as an unavoidable and potentially indispensable element in a developing youth citizenry, television was implicated in national crises over citizenship and the youth in whose name regulatory efforts were undertaken.

Concerns over youth passivity surfaced amid familiar debates about certain youth activity, namely, the dangers posed by exposure to mediated violence. While a 1972 *Science Digest* article asked, "Does video violence make Johnny hit back?," *Time* reported the link between "TV violence" and the "national nightmare" of rising "teen-age violence."[28] This linkage sparked a national panic and a plethora of studies, including a $1.8 million five-volume report from the Surgeon General entitled *Television and Growing Up: The Impact of Televised Violence* (1972), a study that emphasized a causal relationship between increased televisual and teenaged criminal violence and contained concerns about the sexual content of shows, commercials, and even scantily-clad talk show guests.[29]

Amid a multipronged disparagement of commercial television, edutainment became a method by which various networks could market their own programming as having educational value, thus refuting the charge that they were turning young viewers into violent or sexualized beings. ABC's *After School Specials* arrived on the television scene amid a flurry of edutainment offered as a healthier alternative to Saturday morning cartoons, including the launch of shows such as *Mister Rogers' Neighborhood* (PBS, 1968), *Sesame Street* (PBS, 1969), *The Electric Company* (PBS, 1971), *Schoolhouse Rock* (ABC, 1973), *CBS Library* (CBS, 1979), *3-2-1 Contact* (PBS, 1980), *Mr. Wizard's World* (Nickelodeon, 1983), and *Reading Rainbow* (PBS, 1983), and also the rise of cable networks specifically targeting a youth audience, such as Viacom's Nickelodeon (1979) and MTV (1981). Allison Perlman argues that educational television, by coaxing the viewer to "be active, striving, achieving, trying to better himself, participating in social interaction and public affairs," carved out its own identity in opposition to commercial television.[30] ABC's *After School Specials*, as a new mode of rehabilitative edutainment geared nearly exclusively to teenagers, represented a complex negotiation between educational broadcasting (imagined as culturally uplifting and socially responsible) and commercial programming (imagined as vacuous and irresponsible).

While newspapers and grassroots organizations repeatedly asserted that children's television intake was problematic, a new cultural construction of television as potential "teacher" presaged the incorporation of television in school as an acceptable teaching tool. In his 1978 article entitled "Required TV for Students," which featured a cartoon of a television feeding an eager child viewer, the *Washington Post* writer Larry Cuban questioned the wholesale vilification of television. Since "the short- or long-term impact of TV" on youth was "self-evident," rather than "damning the tube or calling it a drug," Cuban asked, "why not mandate home viewing for children as a teacher

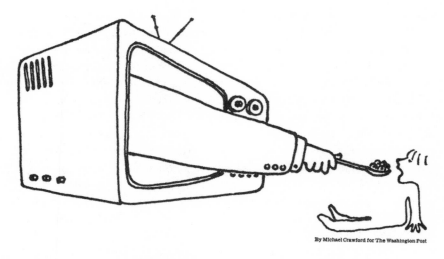

By Michael Crawford for The Washington Post

Figure 2.1. This cartoon by Michael Crawford appeared in the *Washington Post* in 1978. Reproduced courtesy of the artist.

second to school and make it accountable?" Instead of "required reading," Cuban noted that many commercial and noncommercial television shows might already fit into a "required television" curriculum for youth.

The *Specials* represented one such possibility. In contrast to what he termed the "rotten eggs" that constituted Saturday-morning children's programming, the *New York Times* television critic John J. O'Connor praised the *Specials*, saying that "[o]nly ABC has made a serious and impressive effort to venture a bit further than typical series for young people," and lamented that such quality programming appeared only once or twice a month.[31] O'Connor noted that the *Specials* formed with "remarkable speed" to address the many "loud" complaints leveraged by the grassroots Action for Children's Television (ACT) "about cartoon gluts and violence overdoses" in programming for young people.[32] While the resounding discourse of television reform, especially children's programming of the late 1960s and early 1970s, took issue with televised violence and sexuality as they related to teen viewers, educational television's importance—in both devoted educational programming and commercial television that had "turned toward relevance"—was a method of disciplining the technology by managing its content in order to make it safe for youth consumption. Television negotiated its own disciplinary role for teen viewers through its rehabilitative approach to proto-citizens on-screen as well as in off-screen regulatory debates.

Specialized Sexual Liberation

A growing debate over sexual education in schools began to boil alongside and within concerns over sex on TV. The role of television in relation to young people shifted within a new sexual culture defined by a conflict over sexual openness and sexual education, changing gender norms, and evolving ideas about "young people" and their place as participatory national citizens in the new post–sexual revolution culture of the 1970s. The *Specials* thus emerged out of contestations over the management of teen bodies, as sexual and increasingly sexualized, and the role of television in mediating such debates in a rehabilitative way for young viewers.

Although television historians often lump children and teenagers together within moral panics over culture and media effects, children and teens were clearly not the same audience within post–sexual liberation regulatory discourses or in the understanding of television content producers, both of which increasingly addressed teens in this period as sexual subjects and potential political actors. Thus, while children needed protecting, teens were approached as proto-citizens who needed proactive programming to help them safely navigate the path to healthy citizenship and normative adulthood. In the new social and sexual milieu of the 1970s, the "viewer" himself or herself—that is, the viewer in need of television regulation—was redefined. Although television studies has often framed the prototypical television viewer in whose name regulatory efforts are undertaken as an innocent child or as a "youth," this catchall designation largely elides age-specific issues in television regulatory efforts. TV regulation and programming of the 1970s manifested a subtle bifurcation in its configuration of the viewer in need of protection.[33] When the problem of television was configured in terms of "growing up," the conjured subject of studies about media's relationship to violent behavior (and of the government policies and industry regulations that often relied on such studies) was increasingly a teenager rather than a child.

Additionally, regulatory discourses were always implicitly gendered. The problem of "teenage violence" was always "Johnny's" rather than Jane's, as such studies gendered media-induced violent behavior as male, even while the target audience of regulation fell under the supposedly gender-neutral generational designation "youth." Finally, while representations of violence and sexuality were certainly imagined as threatening to children and teenagers alike, teenagers were explicitly addressed as sexual subjects in the *Specials* and their clones. The impossibility of childhood sexuality stood in stark contrast to the threatening inevitability of teen sexuality, and commercial television content sought both to profit from a teen market and to be perceived as responsive to public concern.

By the 1970s, public discourses about media and sexuality were deeply fraught. While some commentators trumpeted commercial television's educational value, others turned their attention to media as a different kind of "educational" tool. A January 1964 *Time* cover story proclaimed (and lamented) the arrival of a "second sexual revolution" characterized by increasingly common public discussions and representations of sex in the media and in society.[34] The late 1960s and early 1970s witnessed the proliferation of contraceptive pills and premarital sex as well as an increase in divorce rates and dual-income households. Dr. David Reuben's controversial *Everything You Always Wanted to Know about Sex, but Were Afraid to Ask* was published in 1970, followed quickly by the famous *Joy of Sex* (1972) and *Our Bodies, Ourselves* (1973). Moreover, teen magazines like *16* and *Tiger Beat* emerged in the mid-sixties to titillate "teenybopper" girls (ages ten to nineteen) with romantic and sexual fantasy. Ilana Nash argues that although the "general tone" of the articles in these magazines "trained girls' imaginations along traditionally heterosexual, romantic lines," the magazines gradually incorporated feminist principles and encouraged sexual fantasy, often including "kissable color pinups" that displayed shirtless or swimsuit-clad teen idols.[35] Nash notes that "*16* and *Tiger Beat* served a similar function for [girls] that *Playboy* did for boys," with "the most privileged photographic space" reserved for the centerfold.[36] Meanwhile, myriad articles about sex education surfaced in publications as diverse as *Christianity Today, Ebony,* and the *New York Times Magazine.*[37] Article titles posed provocative questions, such as "Sex in the Schools: Education or Titillation?," configured sex education as a "powder keg" or an "invad[er] of the schoolhouse," and even begged to "[b]ring back the stork!"[38]

Sex education discourse configured youth sexuality as simultaneously natural and threatening and represented an undisciplined or uneducated teen sexuality as dangerous to the stability of the nation. Janice M. Irvine argues that the rise of sex education debates in the late 1960s and 1970s inexorably challenged the Romantic ideal of nonsexual childhood. Furthermore, as mentioned in the previous chapter, similar sex education initiatives were also taking place among disabled students in the 1970s, when sex-education-for-the-blind campaigns proliferated to address "a persistent, implicit anxiety among the educators of the blind that the blind were insufficiently heterosexual and that their 'restrictive' environment was to blame."[39] Cultural anxieties about sex education for able-bodied and disabled teenagers alike pervaded American society.

Two seemingly opposing impulses characterized seventies commercial television as it mediated cultural conflicts over teen sexuality and tensions between commercial and educational programming. On one hand, commercial television engaged in virtuous "social consciousness" programming, which purported to tackle controversial racial, sexual, and gender issues. On the other hand, it spurred on profitable and racy sex-themed television, perceived to be degraded in contrast to more "serious" socially conscious television. Addressed predominantly to adult audiences, television's "turn toward relevance" featured frank language and challenges to traditional family structures and sexual norms, while "jiggle television" and soap operas challenged notions of sexual propriety.[40]

Elana Levine argues that made-for-TV movies and regulatory debates about television content constructed a "discourse of youth sexual endangerment," with both sites working in tandem to produce a moral panic about the dangers of sexual liberalization engendered by the sexual revolution. This panic over sexual pleasure and danger depicted in myriad made-for-TV movies not only struck fear into viewers but also titillated them with salacious content. Meanwhile, television's role as educator to sexually endangered youth tempered accusations of its exploitativeness. Indeed, teen sexuality was a loaded prime-time issue, evidenced by the controversy over a notorious 1978 episode of NBC's hit series *James at 15* entitled "The Gift," in which James (Lance Kerwin) lost his virginity at a local brothel. Hotly debated was the show's use of the word "responsible" as code for protected sex; a *Washington Post* article, "The Initiation of James: Network Brouhaha over Teen-Age Virtue," reported sardonically that "James [wa]s not going to lose his virginity without a fight."[41] The show's creator, Dan Wakefield, removed his name from the episode and threatened to quit the show because of the changes he was forced to make by NBC's network executives. Wakefield argued that the brothel idea was outdated and instead suggested that James should lose his virginity to a love interest, "act responsibly," and discuss birth control. NBC rejected Wakefield's version, insisting that the teens not use birth control and, if they had sex at all, that it be a moment of "spontaneous passion," after which a pregnancy scare would ensure that James and she would regret their actions. In the rewritten version, James was punished for having sex when he fears having contracted a venereal disease. Wakefield eventually resigned from the series in protest, and the show's title changed to *James at 16* to mark the protagonist's sexual coming of age.

In contrast to Wakefield's battle over sexual politics, Tahse remembered very few skirmishes with the network about what was fit to air on ABC, in spite of the *Specials'* often racy subject matter, although he acknowledged that other producers "had a bad time with ABC." Tahse said he "enjoyed a position that other producers didn't enjoy" due to the success of his shows, and he recalled seeing "mostly . . . eye to eye" with Squire Rushnell, an ABC executive in children's programming. Tahse did recall one disagreement with Rushnell about a *Special* based on Mildred Lee's book about teen pregnancy, *Sycamore Year* (1974). Tahse recalled that the network "started making all these stupid suggestions about changing the script." Some were so ridiculous, Tahse joked, that they practically wanted the boy in the story to be the one who was pregnant. When ABC demanded too many changes, Tahse refused to do the adaptation of Lee's story, prompting Rushnell to joke that ABC—not its producers—was supposed to be the one refusing to do stories. This skirmish epitomizes the fine line the *Specials* walked between edgy sexualized programming and the network's disciplinary power, yet it also indicates the *Specials'* relative freedom to explore controversial material.

Sexy television incited many regulations meant to properly channel youth television intake, such as the 1975 implementation of "family viewing" time as the first hour of prime time. Levine notes that such measures lacked teeth, offering "no specific definition of 'family viewing' and leaving the onus for regulating children to the networks themselves rather than the FCC."[42] Just one short year later, the family hour policy was removed from the National Association of Broadcasters (NAB) TV Code, though networks assured onlookers that they would continue to self-police and protect young viewers from obscene content. Rehabilitative edutainment's implicit regulatory promise went further: that TV would responsibly manage and channel teen sexuality into proper heterosexuality—albeit heterosexual exploration that did not culminate in either reproduction or sexually transmitted diseases.

A combination of educational value and sexual titillation, ABC's *After School Specials* combined two dominant impulses of 1970s TV—"relevance" and sex-themed programming—by simultaneously offering moral lessons about sexual responsibility and profiting from the incitement of teen sexual desire. However, while the *After School Specials* certainly fit into this growth of sex-themed programming, they did not configure teens, on- or off-screen, as always inherently "endangered" by their own sexuality. Undertaking a new rehabilitative approach to teen sexuality and to teen television programming, the *Specials* offered a "responsible" vision of sexual liberation for teens while extolling their own value as entertaining education. Although multiple episodes emphasized the perils of STDs and teen pregnancy, the *Specials* also attempted to negotiate rather than repress the complex terrain of young adult sexuality in sexually liberalized times, encouraging sexual exploration while channeling teen sexuality into heteronormativity and able-bodiedness.

Finally, the series participated in a critical refinement of the boundaries between "youth" and "adult," providing provocative sexualized content for teen viewers while simultaneously disciplining their sexual desire into commercialized "sex edutainment." Populating television screens with *Tiger Beat*'s latest alluring teen centerfolds, the *Specials* encouraged sexual identification with their protagonists but carefully managed that sexuality within the series' characteristic moral didacticism and its staunch policing of nonnormative genders, sexualities, and behaviors. Thus, the regulatory power of the era, as transmitted through the *After School Specials*, produced visions of teen sexual containment rather than solely sexual endangerment.

Skating toward Normal

As a historically specific mode of addressing teenagers, the *After School Specials* employed a rehabilitative logic, which combined emergent "flexible" gender roles espoused by the feminist movement with a frankness in sexual education in the wake of sexual liberation. Rehabilitative citizenship depended on an anxiety over a perceived "loss" and a belief that it could be masked or repaired. Commercial television, according to its harshest critics, had apparently corrupted or perhaps even "disabled" teenagers by adversely impacting their development. While this betrayed nostalgia for a teen untouched by the dangers of television or of a new, sexualized culture, rehabilitative edutainment proposed rehabilitation as a middle ground, a disciplinary project that would incorporate difference while productively (re)making teens identical with the desired citizen-image of the 1970s—one characterized by flexible, heterosexual, able-bodied patriotism and tolerance. This "enforcement of normalcy," to borrow Lennard Davis's term, occurred by policing gender and sexual norms through the linkage of compulsory heterosexuality with compulsory able-bodiedness.

"The Ice Skating Rink" (1975) and "Heartbreak Winner" (also known as "The Gold Test") (1980), two stories about ice skating that feature a male and female protagonist, respectively, illustrate the sexual and gender politics at work within disability narratives. "The Ice Skating Rink" deals with a boy's stuttering problem, while "Heartbreak Winner" explores juvenile rheumatoid arthritis (JRA) in a female athlete. Both critically acclaimed episodes earned awards for Martin Tahse Productions. "The Ice Skating Rink" won the Institute for Education by Radio and Television's Ohio State Award and a Christopher Award, while "Heartbreak Winner" snagged an Emmy for best cinematography. While there are obvious differences between JRA and a stutter, the episodes (and television review articles about them) collapse the distinction, describing both as "handicaps" that impede coming of age. Rehabilitative citizenship's logic of effacement collapses differences among disabilities, molding their specificities into interchangeable metaphors for developmental challenges, or "overcoming" the disabling condition of adolescence itself.[43]

Described as "the story of a teenage boy who rises above the handicap of his stuttering," "The Ice Skating Rink" (1975), one of ABC's earliest *After School Specials*, meditates on issues of proper heterosexual development and disability.[44] Set in a small midwestern farming town, this "icy tale with a happy ending" follows the teenaged Tucker "Tuck" Faraday (Stewart Peterson) in a coming-of-age story about overcoming teen awkwardness and earning paternal respect.[45] Although Tahse never noticed that so many of his *Specials* focused on characters with disabilities, he said that this storyline fit into his desire to depict stories about kids "getting out of a ghetto" or "kids who have a dream of wanting to do something and are held back by their parents' prejudice or lack of understanding." When asked about shows featuring disability, he immediately referred to "The Ice Skating Rink," saying that Tuck's stutter "is not that dangerous—it's not multiple sclerosis," but he argued that his focus on disability was "without question" a "teaching tool" so that "other kids watching with slight disabilities could identify with it and see that somebody could overcome it." Tahse hoped viewers would identify with Tuck even if they did not stutter and realize their similarities to Tuck: "'I don't stutter, but I have a limp' or 'I wear glasses but [Tuck] got over it and became something.'" The *After School Specials* used disability as "the materiality of metaphor" and as a "teaching tool," but scarcely imagined "severely" disabled viewers as audience members.

A *New York Times* "Recommended Viewing" program, "The Ice Skating Rink" centered on Tuck, "a cornflake-faced country kid, tousle-headed and snubnosed, with a Colgate smile," as he was described in the *Washington Post*.[46] Although the show focused on Tuck's hardships with girls, the review noted his sex appeal. Tuck may look "like the kind of golden boy for whom life is a breeze," the review states, but although "all the girls should like him," Tuck's stutter renders him "an alltime loser." Synopses of the story do not describe "The Ice Skating Rink" as a story of overcoming a "handicap" or disability; rather, they summarize the plot with such phrases as "overcoming shyness" or "a gawky lad learns to skate."[47] Thus, the narrative presents Tuck's stutter as an explicit "handicap," and the stutter signifies adolescence itself. It is at once a "normal" indicator of teenaged awkwardness and an unnatural condition, a disability induced by the trauma of witnessing his mother's drowning in a flood when he was a child.

Tuck's disability functions narratively as an impediment to his development of heterosexuality and manhood. The narrative not only shows that Tuck's overcoming disability and achieving heterosexuality rely on one another but also indicates that his individual overcoming has broader significance to national health. In one scene, Tuck's teacher calls on him to answer a question about President Franklin Roosevelt. Apparently uniquely positioned as a stutterer to speak about the disabled president, Tuck is symbolically and visually linked with Roosevelt. The camera focuses on him while his elderly teacher, Mrs. Bayliss (Molly Dodd), recounts Roosevelt's heroic stewardship of the country through the Depression and World War II, adding that "the amazing thing about this man was that in spite of the fact that both his legs were paralyzed, he was able to rise above this affliction to become one of our greatest presidents." Focusing on Mrs. Bayliss from a low angle, the camera replicates the attentive students' perspective and aligns the viewer's gaze with those of the students. Throughout her lesson, the camera continuously crosscuts from her to Tuck, as he concentrates diligently on her words while his peers' attention wanes. When the camera cuts to a pretty blonde girl, Elva (Cindy Eilbacher), she smiles at an unnerved Tuck, who fails to return the gesture. In the shot's foreground, a book on the teacher's desk clearly reads *Voices of a Nation*, implying that the "voices" are meant to be the students'. After waxing poetic about Roosevelt's virtuous overcoming of polio to assume strong leadership over a nation in crisis, Mrs. Bayliss asks Tuck to provide more historical insight into this national hero. As Elva eyes him amorously, Tuck stands and stutters nervously that he did not complete his homework assignment, a lie meant to help him avoid talking in class more than is absolutely necessary. Tuck's voice comes out haltingly, while the students' vicious laughter drowns out the teacher's futile scolding. The scene's final image is of Elva, laughing mercilessly as a defeated Tuck takes his seat.

This *After School Special* immediately establishes its narrative preoccupation with disability, sexuality, and masculinity through Tuck's and Roosevelt's overlapping overcoming narratives. Roosevelt's story, a famous national overcoming narrative, provides an idealized image of powerful masculinity "in spite of" the presence of disability. The scene also links Tuck's disability to heterosexual failure and emasculation, in that Elva's initial interest devolves into laugher at his stutter (much as Gina's mocking laughter emasculates Tod on the beach in *The Boy in the Plastic Bubble*). Later, when he walks Elva home, he avoids talking entirely despite her teasing ("Cat got your tongue?"). While they sit together, Elva sidles up to him flirtatiously and threatens to leave if he does not speak. In a last-ditch effort to remain silent,

Tuck tries to kiss her. Screaming, "Dummy!," Elva slaps Tuck's face, revealing that she was only flirting with him to win a bet that she could make him talk and that usually she "can make boys do anything [she] want[s]." As if Elva's laughter and stinging rejection were not horrible enough, we also learn from Tuck's little sister that Elva is not the only one calling him names. Tuck does not ride the bus home, she says, because other kids "pick on him and call him dummy." Upon hearing this story, their unsympathetic father, Myron (Rance Howard), growls at Tuck, "Looks like you just can't stand to act like everybody else! Gotta be different, like you's tetched." His father's and sister's insults link Tuck's stutter to mental illness ("tetched"), inferior intellect ("dummy"), and insufficient masculinity, emblematized by his weak inability to stop the bullying, to model bravery for his little sister, or to be a viable sexual prospect for Elva.

However, Tuck's inability to conform also becomes a unique virtue, as long as it can be productively channeled within the rehabilitative norms of heteronormativity and overcoming—or in other words, into the normative expectations of healthy adulthood. Roosevelt's image links Tuck's overcoming disability to national heroism, in which a masculinist and ableist overcoming narrative leads to the development of white patriotic American citizenship. However, his sexual failure with Elva represents his disability as an obstacle to heterosexuality and adulthood. This narrative figures disability as an essential "adversity" that teen subjects must overcome to come of age as adults and citizens by equating compulsory able-bodiedness and heterosexuality with Americanness and adulthood. This narrative rendering of compulsory able-bodiedness positions Tuck within a patriotic framework of "overcoming disability," intimating that Tuck will develop his voice, while the other "voices of the nation," the student-subjects on-screen and in the audience, will learn from his struggles.

Everything begins to change for Tuck when Pete Degley (Jerry Dexter), a former professional figure skater and owner of a new ice rink, gives Tuck private skating lessons, boosting his self-confidence and transforming him into an economically productive man. Pete's immediate interest in Tuck initially seems suspicious, as if he might take advantage of a vulnerable and isolated young teen. The two are often completely unsupervised, as Pete gives Tuck a tour of the rink and encourages him to try skating. When Tuck says that he cannot skate, Pete quickly offers to give him his first skating lesson at night, if he comes back alone. Tuck, ashamed, tells him that he cannot afford to pay for lessons, but Pete insists, "Nobody said anything about paying, . . . but listen, keep it under your hat, huh? I wouldn't want anyone knowing I was giving lessons before the rink opened, especially not for free . . . right?" At nightfall, Tuck sneaks from his house to the rink. Pete skates over to Tuck, puts his hand on the back of Tuck's neck, and guides him back to choose a pair of rental skates. Arguing that Tuck will be cold in his light clothes, Pete offers his own sweater to keep Tuck warm.

Pete's special attention toward Tuck proves to be innocuous, but initially seems vaguely homoerotic, since his attentions are clandestine and focused so exclusively on Tuck. Although the narrative later abruptly introduces Pete's wife, Lily (Devon Ericson), initially Pete is single, new in town, and without friends his own age. The ice rink's positioning in the middle of a rural space already serves to isolate Pete, while the contrast of Tuck's hard labor on the farm codes figure skating as a frivolous and feminine luxury activity.[48] Already queered by his emasculating stutter, Tuck tells Pete that his parents would think he was "loony" if he were found to be, in his little sister's words, "skating like a girl."[49] While a 1970s audience might have presumed Pete's heterosexuality, Tuck's and Pete's association with the feminized sport of figure skating necessitates an active narrative recoding, or "rehabilitation," of their perceived compromised (or queer) masculinity that recasts them as heterosexual, able, masculine men.

Pete divulges that he is disabled as well and offers his own overcoming as a positive example for Tuck. Discussing the knee problem that ended his professional skating career, Pete tells Tuck matter-of-factly, "It's a handicap— there's no doubt about that. I guess everyone has some sort of handicap to wrestle with. I'm lucky it's just my knee. Look at me. I got my own skating rink, right?" The narrative links Pete's and Tuck's figure skating explicitly to their respective disabilities, as they bond over their mutual status as "handicapped." Skating becomes a means not only to overcome disability but also to achieve normative heterosexuality and masculinity. Tuck eventually finds his true talent in figure skating after realizing he "do[es]n't have to be a good talker to skate."

The narrative rehabilitates Pete and Tuck into masculine men by spotlighting their participation in skating not as a passion or hobby but rather as a pathway to economic productivity and romantic relationships with women. Described by one *Washington Post* reviewer as "brave-mouthed . . . handicapped fellow[s]," Pete and Tuck, coded as queer/disabled, are both rehabilitated into "better" heterosexuals than Tuck's lackadaisical brothers, Tom (Billy Bowles) and Clete (Robert Clotworthy), or his severe father, Myron.[50] Prior to the show's climax, in which Tuck performs publicly in front of the entire town, Pete's heretofore unmentioned wife, Lily, arrives and quickly explains that Pete was her former doubles partner and that she has been caring for Pete's ailing parents in another city. Pete arranges for Lily to be Tuck's partner for the rink's opening night festivities. At the Faraday dinner table, Tom and Clete rib Tuck about looking "kinda spiffy" and ask tauntingly whether he has a date. They burst into laughter before Tuck can reply.

The rink is quickly established as a space of heterosexual courtship, as Tom and Clete playfully grope their respective girls on the ice, falling down gawkily and laughing. Their inability to function on the ice will stand in stark contrast to Tuck's nimble athletic prowess. During Tuck's and Lily's flawless performance, images of an incredulous and awestruck Myron punctuate the footage of Tuck's routine. Even Tom and Clete smile in wonderment at Tuck's hidden talent. Ecstatic over their performance, Pete says excitedly to Tuck, "I thought I was going to have to carry some of those screechin' girls out tonight! Tucker Faraday, from now on, you're going to have to beat those girls off with a club!" Introducing Pete's wife to the story resolves any vagueness about Pete's sexuality and displays Tuck's athleticism (read: able-bodiedness) and heterosexuality to the entire town. Although Tuck has been a successful singles skater throughout the narrative, he needs a female "partner" in order to demonstrate his heterosexuality, masculinity, and able-bodiedness, and in the end, he will need to beat away gaggles of determined girls rather than avoid their gazes or their ridicule.

Tuck also gains his father's respect as an economically productive and responsible family man through the narrative recoding of skating from a feminine leisure activity into a masculine "job." Pete pays Tuck one hundred dollars for his performance and offers him a teaching job at the rink. Turning most of the money over to his speechless father, Tuck tells him to buy his stepmother a coveted new stove without revealing the source of the extra cash. Just as Pete's disability is overcome by his ownership of the rink, Tuck's skating is recast as productive work rather than indulgent art. Although "prancin' around that skatin' rink with a girl" can hardly be considered "workin'," says Myron, the money is "honest" and "appreciated." Thus, Pete's and Tuck's economic productivity recodes them as masculine, while their artistic labor differentiates them from other more traditionally masculine men in the narrative.

Pete's and Tuck's masculinity is a rehabilitated version of traditional masculinity, a flexible "new masculinity" that David Savran argues became "hegemonic" in the 1970s.[51] This softer masculinity involved "a reconsolidation of the characteristics and fantasies associated with a residual, entrepreneurial masculinity combined with an avowal of certain qualities traditionally associated with femininity."[52] Rather than asserting figure skating as a masculine activity, the narrative presents rink ownership and skating lessons to legitimate skating as masculine productive work. Still, Tuck represents a healthier, more flexible masculinity than that of his father or brothers. By the end of "The Ice Skating Rink," Tuck's difference no longer means that he is "tetched" or a "dummy." Rather, Tuck will now have to "beat away" countless "screeching girls" while his new job will earn extra cash for the family. Together, these sexual and economic changes render permissible his participation in skating without compromising his heterosexuality or masculinity. In the end, Tuck's flexible masculinity and able-bodiedness are inextricably linked to his heterosexuality: he is construed as being at his healthiest and most mature when his solo skating becomes co-ed pairs skating. While skating *like* a girl might have feminized Tuck, skating *with* a girl masculinizes him by making him a heterosexual man and by replacing his stutter, the primary element of his characterization, with athleticism, economic productivity, and overcoming.

Five years later, the *After School Specials* broadcast "Heartbreak Winner," which follows the figure skater and Olympic hopeful Maggie McDonald (Melissa Sherman) from her unbeatable performances on the ice to her diagnosis with juvenile rheumatoid arthritis (JRA). "All is not Olympic gold that glitters," states the *Washington Post*, describing the central lesson of the "'Heartbreak' tale" as "giving is more important than victory or gold."[53] Comparison of the ice skating episodes highlights how the *Specials'* representations of coming of age were explicitly gendered. While Tuck's task in "The Ice Skating Rink" was to become an appropriately masculine citizen by overcoming his disability and asserting his heterosexuality, Maggie's prime developmental task in "Heartbreak Winner" is to rehabilitate her femininity by disciplining her (masculine) sports ambition into normatively feminine caretaking rather than individual achievement. To do so, the narrative requires Maggie not only to secure a heterosexual pairing with a boy but also to nurture others and to "accept" rather than overcome her disability. This more passive (read: feminine) acceptance involves her focusing less on her skating career and more on her social life, specifically directing her interest toward another male figure skater, Bobby (Chris Hagan), and helping Joey Taylor (Mark James), a young African American wheelchair user with severely injured legs, to walk again. While Tuck's heteronormativity is linked to his overcoming into able-bodiedness, it is only when Maggie accepts her disability as a limitation (aided by Bobby's compassionate insight into her condition) that her heteronormative coupling can occur. In the end, the movie emphasizes Maggie's acceptance of bodily limitation and the subjugation of individual desires in favor of collective goals. Although McRuer's theory of compulsory able-bodiedness does not explicitly discuss gendered differences in its expression, juxtaposing "Heartbreak Winner" with "The Ice Skating Rink" reveals that the gender politics of compulsory able-bodiedness work to construct normative "adult" masculinity in terms of economic productivity and individualistic pursuits while it constructs femininity in terms of caretaking and the sacrifice of individual goals in favor of nurturing others.

The episode simultaneously valorizes and labels excessive Maggie's dedication to skating, because her rigorous practice schedule inhibits her ability to partake in traditional teenaged life events—most importantly the pursuit of boys. The narrative actively contrasts Maggie with Cindy (Tammy Taylor), a fellow figure skater who lacks Maggie's discipline and consistently chastises Maggie for being an antisocial "gold medal bore." While bad-girl Cindy skips practice, dates boys, and goes to parties, "Miss Perfect" Maggie puts in countless hours at the rink to perfect her skating routine. Cindy dons fashionable clothing and makeup and wears her hair long, while Maggie appears more masculine, with a short haircut and tomboyish dress. Maggie's mother asserts that Maggie takes after her father "with her drive and determination," while Maggie's father jokingly advises her not to "marry an attorney" like himself. In spite of Maggie's obvious dedication to skating, her mother establishes "drive and determination" as masculine qualities shared by her father, while her father emphasizes her inevitable marriage rather than her career. Both parents implicitly reaffirm heteronormativity and traditional femininity as ideals. Moreover, though the narrative valorizes Maggie's commitment to her sport by constantly comparing it to Cindy's poor work ethic (which Maggie earnestly helps to improve), it also subtly critiques Maggie's myopic pursuit of the gold medal at the expense of a "normal" teen girl's life, even before her JRA is discovered. Indeed, this *Special*'s early establishment of some "unhealthy" masculine aspects in Maggie's personality helps to set up a somewhat surprising, if utterly characteristic, narrative operation: Disability, represented as a developmental obstacle, not only incites Maggie's process of coming of age but also rehabilitates her, as she is forced to shift her priorities from a focus on herself (i.e., the advancement of her skating career) to a focus on caring for others, as she assumes the roles of romantic partner, mother figure, and mentor.

During a skating competition, Maggie's knee buckles during a crucial jump and sends her crashing to the ice. When Bobby offers help, Maggie indignantly yanks her arm from his grasp. Courageously finishing the routine, Maggie wins the competition in spite of her fall. Standing in the middle of the ice amid resounding applause, she collapses and is rushed to the hospital. Maggie continually lies to doctors and her parents about her pain level and vehemently denies her disabled status. One evening she sneaks out to skate against the doctor's orders. Her transgression lands her back in the hospital with a flare-up, and she snarls at the nurses, "I hate hospitals! They're for people with something wrong with them. Sick people. Not me." Before and after her diagnosis, Maggie expresses contempt for other disabled patients and exhibits "bad patient" behavior, constantly undermining medical authority and resisting rehabilitation.

Her inability to "get well," the story tells viewers, stems from her selfish inability to identify as sick and submit to the care and management of her body by male doctors and her blossoming love interest, Bobby. Maggie's acceptance of JRA occurs through her relationship with two boys in the story: Bobby, who becomes a quasi-boyfriend, and Joey, an African American disabled child and fellow patient. Becoming a girlfriend to Bobby and a symbolic mother to Joey facilitates Maggie's rehabilitation. Rehabilitation productively channels her competitive energy into her mentoring of others rather than into more "selfish" individualistic pursuits, such as skating for pleasure or glory or resisting medical authority.

At first, Joey's hopeful "can-do" attitude, emblematized by his post-recovery plans to play for the New York Knicks, positions him as the ideal patient, in contrast to the pessimistic, self-hating Maggie. When Joey tries to cheer Maggie up, she dismisses him from the room and snarls that she and Joey are "losers" and "failures" who will never be able to fulfill their professional athletic dreams. However, Nurse Pearl argues that Joey's optimism is just "slick street talk" to "cover" his fear that an upcoming operation will not fix his legs. Pearl tells Maggie that Joey "do[es]n't need the wheelchair" and that the doctors have high hopes that Joey will walk again. As Pearl speaks, Maggie is visually linked to another woman, who stands in the foreground. The woman is never introduced to Maggie or the audience, but she and Maggie share the same hair color and style and wear nearly identical hospital robes. Nurse Pearl and this woman conduct a conversation in ASL, and the deaf woman not only enjoys a positive relationship with the nurse but also "cleans up" after Maggie by wheeling her empty wheelchair back into the hospital. Maggie's linkage with a deaf woman, who seems compliant and conversational with the medical staff, foreshadows Maggie's eventual acquiescence to medical authority—and her resultant happiness and maturity.

However, until the doctors' machinations succeed in allying them, Maggie and Joey's unruly resistance to rehabilitation exasperates the doctors. The doctors are puzzled that, although they have been "medically successful" with Joey's and Maggie's bodies, the patients have not been emotionally responsive to or participatory in their rehabilitation. Joey "still won't try to walk," and even though Maggie heals from her recent flare-up of JRA, she will not "accept that she'll never compete again." Rather than a failure of medicine, their failure to rehabilitate reflects a failure of will. The doctors develop an alternative strategy—enlisting Maggie's help with Joey's rehabilitation in the hopes that it will spur both of them to rehabilitate themselves.

Before Maggie can participate in this plan, she must first accept, with Bobby's assistance, that she "ha[s] JRA" and "learn how to live with it." In other words, the narrative depicts rehabilitation as the admixture of heteronormative romance and female passivity. Armed with a bouquet of flowers and a night's reading about JRA, Bobby sneaks up flirtatiously on a sulking Maggie and pleads that JRA "doesn't mean that . . . life is over or that you can't teach somebody else to be the best skater in the world. It just means it won't be you, Maggie." Maggie screams, "Why don't you go and kick some other cripple when they're down! . . . I hate being a failure, and I can't stand being a cripple!" to which Bobby replies, "Then stop being one!" Positioning disability as antithetical to achievement and overcoming as a mere matter of willpower, the series' rehabilitative logic shows that, just as teens can willingly inhabit rehabilitative citizenship, they can also actively "cripple" themselves.

It is only after being picked up and kissed by Bobby after she crashes to the ground that she accepts her diagnosis. In her choice to "stop being" a cripple, she also actively distances herself from other disabled people, who are construed as at fault for their failure to achieve rehabilitation, as she says triumphantly, "I'm not a cripple, and I'm not a failure. . . . I've got JRA, and I've gotta learn to live with it." Maggie's budding relationship with Bobby links heterosexual love with the hospital's rehabilitation efforts, a narrative formula that quickly became a staple of 1980s young adult literature about illness, as the next chapter will show. Although the logic of compulsory able-bodiedness required Tuck to overcome his disability and challenge patriarchal authority by asserting his masculinity and heterosexuality, Maggie must submit to medical and patriarchal authority in order to rehabilitate herself.

While overcoming narratives like "The Ice Skating Rink" proclaim individual triumph over disability rather than interdependence, "Heartbreak Winner" valorizes interdependence, but only through a reassertion of heteronormativity and a traditional femininity characterized by passivity and nurturance. Maggie's coming of age occurs not only through her acceptance of her disability, the help of male doctors and peers, and her own physical and emotional rehabilitation, but also through her participation in the rehabilitation of others—namely, Cindy and Joey. In Maggie's case, this overcoming narrative also transforms her body and her JRA into an object of knowledge for Bobby, like the doctors, to "figure out" as her friend and

potential love interest. Finally, Maggie secures lackadaisical Cindy's rehabilitation as well. Cindy commits to practicing hard with Maggie as her
coach. In keeping with gendered differences in the operation of compulsory
able-bodiedness, Joey is expected to overcome disability, while Maggie is
encouraged to accept hers while sublimating her individual desire to assist
in the rehabilitation of others.

The scene in which Joey walks for the first time evokes the visual iconography of Christian faith healers and the American telethon, as crowds
of people chant encouragingly to a nervous Joey to "get up out of that chair."
A scene of multicultural solidarity, Joey's struggle to walk provides a liberalizing rallying point for racial harmony and heterogeneity, as white, African
American, Asian Indian, and other Asian American hospital kids become
his cheering section. In spite of Nurse Pearl's coaxing that "[c]rutches are
better than a wheelchair any day," Joey crashes to the ground in a heap.
Everyone falls silent except Maggie, who emerges from her room to encourage Joey's persistence. Once resistant to medical authority, Joey and Maggie now not only represent the ultimate rehabilitating-citizen-subjects but
also embody the triumph of liberal antiracism. They yield to the will of the
doctors, partner across the color line, and provide inspiration to able-bodied people around them. Finally, in this scene, the narrative also signals the
transcendence of racial difference through the materialized metaphor of disability. Here, disability, as what Mitchell and Snyder call "narrative prosthesis," works to depoliticize racial and gender differences as well as differences
in ability by emphasizing a shared humanity, fully realized in overcoming.[54]
Thus, Maggie's mentoring relationship with Joey reconstructs her, through
her own volition, as more feminine—docile, maternal, and less ambitious—
while Joey and the rest of the nonwhite crowd in "Heartbreak Winner"
appear as an emblem of racial harmony achieved through individual will to
overcome disability.

Tolerance and Rehabilitative Citizenship

The *After School Specials'* demise is generally blamed on the rise of syndi-
cated talk shows coupled with the proliferation of teen issue–based edutainment in movies and 1990s prime-time teen TV series, such as *Beverly Hills,
90210* (1990–2000).[55] Although Disney discontinued the *Specials* upon its
purchase of the ABC network, their didactic, issue-driven formula lives on
in traces today, for instance, in the issue-driven "very special episode" format of contemporary teen television dramas. Comedy Central's *Strangers
with Candy* (1999–2000) was a satirical take on the *Specials*, and its nostalgic

humor indicates that some 1970s teen viewers likely resisted the *Specials'* earnest rehabilitative narratives. In spite of its status as a contemporary object of ridicule, the series' place in television history in addressing teens as a serious audience distinct from children, its innovative educational format, and its lasting legacy on teen programming should not be understated. As rehabilitative edutainment, "instructive" television programming traded on and reshaped cultural conceptions of television as a medium as well as ideas about audiences and the ideological work of narratives.

Intervening in our views of television's role in society, rehabilitative edutainment endeavored to train teens into proactive, responsible citizens via racy commercial fare. Although emerging contemporaneously with educational television, the *Specials* and other shows of their ilk represented unprecedented departure from educational TV and its objective to democratize access to high art by offering televised theater and opera to "uplift" adult viewers.[56] Its edutainment approach was an invention of the commercial market rather than something desired solely by industry professionals or activists proclaiming the virtue of educational television. As television continued to negotiate its place in the American family in tumultuous times, this rehabilitative logic toward teens not only expected to mold teen viewers, as subjects, through progressive edutainment but also hoped to reform commercial programming's image from damaging and frivolous to healthy and educational.

By trading on and shaping our views of teenagers, ABC's *After School Specials* were an entirely new television offering for a brand new audience segment, and it is important to analyze and historicize the specificities of teen viewership rather than considering audiences solely in the binaristic terms of "child" versus "adult" or subsumed within the catchall "youth." Specifically geared toward teens rather than adults, this rehabilitative model dramatized teen coming of age in disability narratives and positioned them in relation to national iconography, transforming coming-of-age stories into rehabilitative citizenship stories. In the television content of the 1970s and its biopolitical engagement with teen bodies both on- and off-screen, this was never a relationship of total submission. Rather, televisual rehabilitative edutainment invited and required the participation of teenagers in their own overcoming or acceptance, encouraging liberatory "exploration" rather than submission to authority figures, even while assimilation to traditional norms of gender, sexuality, and ability evidenced an adulthood achieved through struggle rather than assured in advance. With their bittersweet and incomplete endings, the *Specials* indicated that a teen's ability to solve a given problem was not a permanent cure. Rather, the series presented coming of age as a constant negotiation, a self-surveilling construction process, while teen sexual exploration was both encouraged and safely contained within romantic, heteronormative love or within the danger of imminent sexually transmitted disease. Rehabilitative logics, while ableist and oppressive, opened up possibilities for sexual openness regarding teen sexuality and constructed a new active rather than passive teen television viewer and proto-citizen.

Finally, by incorporating rather than stigmatizing difference, the *Specials* relied on a universal human resonance of their developmental narrative of overcoming while granting center stage to white, middle-class, able-bodied teens, who stood in as universal developmental imperatives. In representing and redefining heteronormativity and able-bodiedness as central and related objectives for American citizens, the *Specials* spotlighted difference to use it ideologically and pedagogically. Yet the *Specials* also eschewed structural critiques of the prejudices and problems they presented by containing difference within overcoming narratives that promoted the transformative power of individual will. Furthermore, by locating extreme prejudice in rural spaces and people, like Tuck's farmer father, the series largely failed to implicate its middle-class white audience in the problems of racism, ableism, sexism, or homophobia.

The *Specials* mobilized narratives of overcoming or accepting disability as a teaching tool. This narrative strategy did important and unacknowledged historical and cultural work in conceptualizing adolescence and citizenship and in establishing a rehabilitative promise of tolerance. Wendy Brown argues that although tolerance has been constructed as a "transcendent virtue," it is instead a "historically protean . . . vehicle for producing and organizing subjects" that had become a dominant mode of governmentality in the United States by the 1980s.[57] Likewise, McRuer refers to the celebration of "flexible" able-bodied and heterosexual individuals, who "are visible and spectacularly tolerant" of disabled and queer others, as a primary effect of neoliberalism.[58] The acquisition of tolerance is used as a developmental milestone in coming-of-age narratives because tolerance is future-oriented: tolerance depoliticizes identity and effaces difference by emphasizing empathy and "betoken[ing] a vision of the good society yet to come."[59] Scholars of media and cultural history would do well to historicize tolerance's emergence as edutainment, its *a priori* good in the emotional and political realms of citizenship, and its role in normalizing visions of teen crisis and "healthy" development.

Popular culture has long been a venue to teach tolerance to children and teenagers. However, it is also important to consider how disability narratives and teen subjects have been employed in service to this emotional and political vision of good citizenship and its recuperative powers. Although Brown and others consider the important historical and cultural work of tolerance in constituting identity, we should also think about its emergence and role, historically, as a mediator of various forms of identity crisis—both generational and political. Such crises point to the centrality of adolescence and disability in rehabilitative visions of the individual and the nation. Rehabilitative edutainment, as a method of biopolitically producing and managing citizens, emphasized tolerance's rehabilitative role in emotional growth by mapping overcoming disability onto coming of age and casting coming of age as, among other things, becoming tolerant of otherness and questioning (but, crucially, without altering) existent hierarchies—or, in the tidy summation of one review of "The Ice Skating Rink," by demonstrating that "grit and natural-born goodness win out [and] everybody is worthy, in his way."[60] In this way, tolerance and rehabilitation emerge historically and cooperatively, through figurations of adolescence and disability, as modes of governmentality within the media and cultural history of neoliberalism.

3

Cryin' and Dyin' in the Age of Aliteracy

Romancing Teen Sick-Lit

The one thing that Dawn Rochelle remembered most about her four-
teenth birthday was that she was still alive. In her diary she wrote: . . .
*Today at school I heard that Jake Macka is moving. I wonder what it
would be like to have him kiss me. I wonder if any "normal" boy will
ever kiss me.*
—Lurlene McDaniel, *I Want to Live*

Nothing feels as real as a Lurlene McDaniel book.
—From a printable bookmark, www.lurlenemcdaniel.net

In 1989 a literary time capsule was buried in the Library of Congress in
Washington, DC, a treasure to be unearthed in the year 2089. In partnership with Pizza Hut's "Reading Is FUN-damental" program and the Barbara
Bush Foundation for Family Literacy, the Library of Congress's Center for
the Book invited schoolchildren to participate in an essay contest and nomi-
nate their favorite books and authors for inclusion in the capsule, which was
meant to be a repository of the nation's youth reading heritage.[1] Among its
other selections, the capsule housed the most-nominated book in the competition, *Six Months to Live* (1985), the first of the popular Dawn Rochelle
series, which describes thirteen-year-old Dawn Rochelle's diagnosis and
treatment for leukemia. Penned by the young adult/"inspirational" novelist
Lurlene McDaniel, the book sold half a million copies through book fairs and
clubs from its initial publication through the late 1990s.[2] To date, McDaniel
has authored over fifty young adult (YA) novels, virtually all with the same
melodramatic formula: after being diagnosed with a potentially fatal chronic
illness, a girl falls in love with a boy. However, *Six Months to Live*'s placement
in the Library of Congress's time capsule, a symbol of American reading culture, made this immensely popular YA formula nationally significant. The
rehabilitative underpinnings of this romantic illness narrative infuse its content, as these stories perennially link their illness plotlines to their romantic

ones and also, through their pedagogical impulse, to the nationally "fit" reading publics that policy makers, parents, and authors imagined producing when they encouraged reading "healthy" literature.

By the 1970s, realistic YA "problem novels" had emerged as a predominant literary form for teenagers. Meanwhile, made-for-TV movies and series like ABC's *After School Specials* capitalized on this popularity, often drawing their inspiration from the problem-filled pages of YA literature. However, by the 1980s, the problem novel's contours began expanding to include what I term "teen sick-lit."[3] Often called "ten-hankie-novels" or "tearjerkers," teen sick-lit utilizes a characteristic formula that combines an illness plotline with a romance plotline. The illness plot begins with a white teen girl's manifesting unexplained bruises or fatigue, which end up being symptoms of a chronic illness, such as cancer.[4] During her treatment, the obligatory romance plotline begins, in which the ill girl's pursuit of a boy parallels and positively affects her process of "getting well." Generally, the sanctioned object of the ill girl's affections is a "normal" boy, which is to say, nondisabled and not ill.[5] This second narrative strand subtly differentiates teen sick-lit from problem novels, which do not always involve a love story. "Disease-of-the-week" narratives had already become a staple of daytime and prime-time television when teen sick-lit emerged and targeted a young female audience. It blended the didacticism of the problem novel with the melodrama of the paperback romance novel, which was becoming a booming market predominantly for female readers in the 1980s. Teen sick-lit certainly falls within a longer genealogy of classic sentimental illness literature by and about women, which has been scrutinized by literary scholars and historians.[6] However, while teen sick-lit has built on and expanded the popularity of this genre, popular illness narratives about teens dealing with disease and disability, as they proliferated from the late 1970s through the 1990s, also incorporated and refashioned new literary tropes of paperback romance novels for women and problem novels for teenagers.

This chapter surveys various works of teen sick-lit about cancer, including Lurlene McDaniel's Dawn Rochelle series (*Six Months to Live* [1985], *I Want to Live* [1987], *So Much to Live For* [1991], and *No Time to Cry* [1993]) and Jean Ferris's *Invincible Summer* (1987). I choose to focus on McDaniel because she is arguably the most prolific teen sick-lit author in American literary history, although many of her contemporaries, including Judy Blume, Isabelle Holland, Jean Ferris, Cynthia Voigt, the pseudonymous Elizabeth Benning, and Lois Lowry, also penned individual books that fall within a timeworn tradition of illness narratives by and about women.[7] McDaniel's series chronicles thirteen-year-old Dawn Rochelle's diagnosis with leukemia in *Six Months*; her near-death experience with chemotherapy and a bone marrow transplant in *I Want to Live*; her experiences at cancer camp with other girls, many of whom eventually die; and finally, her budding romantic relationships with both able-bodied boys and boys with cancer.[8] *Invincible Summer* follows Robin and Rick, who both have acute lymphocytic leukemia, through their diagnoses, brief recoveries, and Rick's death. McDaniel has published most prolifically in this subgenre and achieved recognition in national reading programs of the era, while Ferris's award-winning novel demonstrates a few significant variations on the usual teen sick-lit formula in its affirming representation of teen sexuality. Although McDaniel's texts often depicted conservative and tragic images of illness—whose rehabilitation was dependent on traditional, heteronormative relationships—Ferris offers resistive, sexy images of hospital spaces and ill bodies.

As the previous two chapters have shown, made-for-television movies of the 1970s, as well as the problem novels on which they were often based, offered progressive ideas about race, gender, and sexuality informed by a variety of post-1968 social movements. However, by the 1980s, the political climate in the United States had begun to change. Amid the rise of the New Right and compassionate conservatism, teen sick-lit reflected a far less tenacious embrace of the sexual and gender politics underpinning liberal progressive social movements than its problem novel predecessors, and instead reaffirmed conservative political and sexual values. Among its other strategies, teen sick-lit often endorsed rigorously gender-differentiated roles for its characters while it also maintained the co-constitutive relationship between compulsory able-bodiedness and heterosexuality. Ill boys demonstrate their athleticism and virility "in spite of" their illness or during their remission, while ill girls endlessly cultivate their normality by rehabilitating physical beauty in a largely "female world of love and ritual."[9] A "normal" boy, who has never been ill, however, is usually depicted as the ill girl's most treasured prize. Thus, the novels' linkage of illness and romance plotlines manifests how the logics of heteronormativity and able-bodiedness materialize as disciplinary frameworks within teen sick-lit.[10]

Teen sick-lit's content operated narratively to establish cultural meanings about teen coming of age, sexuality, and disability, but the genre also played a role in broader conversations about the cultural value of literary realism and YA literature. Snyder and Mitchell demonstrate literature's "discursive dependency" on disability as a metaphorical device and method of characterization, and by doing so, they reveal storytelling to be a prosthetic practice, as stories aspire to be "whole" or complete.[11] Building on their work, I argue that disability narratives also have been instrumental in configuring the emotional practice of *reading* as prosthetic, as an imagined *a priori* "good" in the production of healthy citizens. Thus, this chapter also excavates teen sick-lit's legacy within broader discussions about individual and national health as it is tied to reading and the emotional disciplines of citizenship. By contextualizing teen sick-lit within national reading initiatives of the era, this chapter maps out a relationship between youth reading and national health, as it was being established in the 1980s, in order to consider the role of sadness in the production of citizens. Thus, building on theories of affect, this chapter reflects on the role of sadness in the interdependent constitution of literary realism as socially valuable; of "normal" teen subjectivity as angst-ridden; of disability as tragedy; and of coming of age as a gradual process of rehabilitative emotional management. Although an "affective turn" has characterized recent cultural studies scholarship, scholars have presumed (and privileged) adult, able-bodied, and neurotypical subjects in their analyses of affect.[12]

To analyze teen sick-lit and its cultural production of sadness, I use Deborah Gould's term "emotional habitus" to describe social groupings' collective (and only partly conscious) "emotional dispositions . . . or inclinations toward certain feelings and ways of emoting" that partly inform political discourses and establish cultural norms.[13] An emotional habitus delimits what is emotionally possible at a given moment—defining certain emotions as preferable or appropriate while dismissing or disciplining others. Cultural debates about the medicinal value of literary realism—or more specifically, "sad stories"—emplotted YA literature itself into a coming-of-age narrative of development by configuring the reading of emotionally difficult stories as an indispensable step in teen maturation. Teen sick-lit's manipulation of sadness, a form of "affective labor," gained new cultural value as a palliative for a new crisis, "aliteracy," a neologism created in 1984 by the Library of Congress to describe a rapidly spreading disease: a systemic American unwillingness to read. This cultural desire for teen sadness shored up a powerful cultural fantasy that an emotionally stable, healthy, empathic, reading-enthusiastic adult citizen-subject would (inevitably) emerge after the storms (or illness) of adolescence.[14] Thus, conversations about literary realism triangulated concerns over national health and fears of apathetic citizenship and sought the remedy to these problems in the virtuous consumption of emotionally evocative stories about teen illness. As so-called sad books collided with initiatives to dispel teen ennui and encourage reading, policy makers, parents, and literary critics reaffirmed a normative developmental (read: teenaged) identity by linking individual emotional responses of teen readers (who were imagined as always-already emotionally excessive) to the national and pedagogical project of citizenship training. What materializes in such descriptions are the various "structures of feeling" that form an emotional habitus—specifically, one that imagines emotional volatility as prediscursively inevitable for evolving teenagers and empathy as characteristic of mature adulthood.[15] This production of sadness depended on disease and disability, and in this emotional economy, sadness was good for you. As I discuss in the conclusion, this particular image of teens gained traction as it developed within a post-Fordist economy that increasingly commodified emotion. Whether or not adult "ex-teens" believed that teen sadness was biologically essential to adolescence or culturally produced, "typical teenagers"—YA readers and its characters—persistently appeared alternately as emotionally excessive or apathetic proto-citizens in need of various rehabilitative projects to cultivate empathic citizenship. Problem-driven popular culture was one such treatment regimen for the condition of adolescence and one to which disease and disability were central.

The story of how a book like *Six Months to Live* came to be in a literary time capsule is a complicated one—one that interweaves shifting publishing markets; cultural fears about a dying book culture, strangled by television and new media; the emergence of literary realism as a valued component of youth sentimental education; an ongoing relationship among disabled overcoming and adolescent emotional and sexual coming of age; and an ascendant emotional style of labor, as it emerged amid a post-Fordist economic shift away from industrial jobs and toward new white-collar "service" labor that required "emotional intelligence." While teen sick-lit wove tragic pedagogical tales of love and rehabilitation, both sadness and reading itself began to have rehabilitative functions in relation to a phantasm of a largely non-reading (and thus apathetic) public sphere. In an era in which young people's individual reading practices were being construed as a litmus test for the health of democracy, teen sick-lit's tragic images of ill girls on the verge of their first kiss formed a linkage among healthy citizenship, sadness, and literary realism.

Rehabilitative Realism

In 1963, *Time* magazine lamented the limited selection of literature for teens as compared to the "barrowfuls of fresh and forgettable picture epics" for "under-sixes."[16] "Teenagers," *Time* reported in ableist language, "unless they have been permanently crippled by early years with Dick and Jane, can begin to forage for their literary fare cheek by jowl with their parents. But how does one bridge the gap between, say, Pooh and [J. D.] Salinger?" A dearth of age-appropriate reading fare for teenagers, especially white middle-class "Dicks and Janes" combined with federal initiatives that constructed reading as central to any Great Society, created a market opportunity upon which publishers seized voraciously.

By the early 1970s, conditions were ripe for the proliferation of young adult literature, when government policy and the publishing industry seized upon a new market segment of the reading public. In 1965, President Lyndon Johnson's Elementary and Secondary Education Act (ESEA), part of the "war on poverty," along with the Head Start program, vowed to enhance the nation's schools and libraries by pouring federal dollars into the growth of school libraries for the purchase of nonconsumable instructional materials. This investment in libraries encouraged publishers not only to reissue children's literature classics but also to begin publishing new literary fare for adolescents, which constituted a virtually untapped literature market.[17] Moreover, paperback books had become firmly entrenched as a more profitable publishing market in the sixties, making YA titles cheaper to produce.[18] Amid a proliferation of YA literature in the 1970s, a new literary genre, the "YA problem novel," emerged for teens and quickly became YA literature's most recognizable form.[19] Accounts of the YA problem novel's point of origin vary. Literary historians alternately cite Holden Caulfield's adolescent angst in J. D. Salinger's *Catcher in the Rye* (1951), Louise Fitzhugh's *Harriet the Spy* (1964), or S. E. Hinton's *Outsiders* (1965) as the earliest problem novel prototypes, although *Catcher* was not written for an adolescent audience.

YA literature itself is a projection of an adult fantasy of childhood and coming of age, or in the words of Jacqueline Rose, "[t]here is no child behind the category 'children's fiction,' other than the one which the category itself sets in place."[20] Thus, literary offerings for youth are only partially a reflection of what children actually want or need from literature. Rather, YA literature discursively produces an imagined teenager, constituted at the nexus of publishing market demand, adults' nostalgia about their own teen experiences, and cultural hopes and expectations of what a "healthy" reading experience might produce in teen readers as proto-citizens. Thus, disciplinarity is inherent in the very form, function, and category of fiction for children and so-called young adults, for "building an image of the child inside of the book," argues Jacqueline Rose, "secure[s] the child who is outside the book, the one who does not come so easily within its grasp."[21] Albeit less explicitly, this process of "securing the child" also secures "the adult," discursively constituting adults as emotionally managed, empathic, and coherent subjects in opposition to emotionally volatile and developing teen readers and protagonists.[22]

This disciplinary operation of securing is readily apparent in YA problem novels, as their formula drew from popular psychological notions of identity crisis as they circulated in the late 1960s. Generic characteristics of problem novels include a teenaged protagonist; events that revolve around the protagonist's struggle to resolve conflict; and a story told from the viewpoint and voice of a teenager. While the novels offer insight through characters' experiences, endings never offer happiness, safety, or security for readers or protagonists, an aspect of problem novels that most distinguishes them from children's books. Parents are generally absent or at odds with teenagers in these novels, and themes address so-called coming-of-age issues, including sexuality, drugs, death, or illness. Their structure and prose as well as their character and plot development are secondary to the chosen social problem that forms their core. Although the problem novel continues to be a dominant YA literature format, critics of the genre note its formulaic approach to storytelling and stock characters while bemoaning its general lack of literary merit and preachy tone. Simultaneously didactic and entertaining, problem novels are prescriptive. By detailing the problems faced by teen protagonists, problem novels also conjure impressionable teen readers to regulate "how their readers will think and act" after completing the books.[23] Thus, these novels were part of a broader turn toward "literary realism" for teenagers.

Just as in the era's turn toward socially responsible television programming (which often drew its storylines from popular YA problem novels), the pedagogical project of rehabilitative citizenship is inherent in the problem novel, of which "teen sick-lit" is one variety. Over sixty YA novels that span over two decades constitute Lurlene McDaniel's oeuvre, which overwhelmingly narrates tales of love and loss in the face of life-threatening illness. Her novels have appeared on several best-seller lists, including *Publishers Weekly*'s, and she received a RITA Award from the Romance Writers of America in 1992, while three of her novels were selected by children as International Reading Association (IRA) and Children's Book (IRA/CBC) Children's Choices in 1989 and 1990.[24] McDaniel's target market has been girls aged twelve to fifteen, but she once remarked that she had "always been amazed" that "guys read these books and seem to enjoy them."[25] Although many YA novelists and film and television writers have occasionally featured illness or disability as one problem among many from which to draw their storylines, McDaniel's work focuses nearly exclusively on disease and disability.

Although my analysis will certainly not end with a wholesale indictment of this literature, perhaps it should begin with one. Teen sick-lit indulges in some of the most egregious and patronizing of cultural stereotypes of disease and disability. Alana Kumbier argues that these books avow the most "insidious dominant cultural ideas we have about sick people," portraying them as objects of "inspiration . . . and pity"; tragic and innocent; "narcissistic" and duplicitous figures in need of medical and parental surveillance; and most importantly, "vehicles for others' emotional growth and sentimental education."[26] In these texts, disabled people function as what Elizabeth V. Spelman describes as "spiritual bellhops," or "carriers of experience from which others can benefit." Teen sick-lit's ill girls serve as inspirational and educational figures for a teen audience, largely presumed to be nondisabled.[27] For example, McDaniel cites her own experience raising boys as giving her special insight into the reality of teen male subjectivity: "I try and make the boys talk like guys, sound like guys and react like guys. [Characters] say, 'Well, you know, she's got cystic fibrosis, and that grosses me out.' You've got to be realistic."[28] While offensive ableist remarks such as this might reflect "realistic" dialogue and prejudicial cultural perceptions about disability, they also work to further distance and distinguish able-bodied characters (as well as an imagined nondisabled audience of readers) from "gross" disabled characters. Nevertheless, it is insufficient to simply critique the ableism of sentimental stories about disability and romance without examining, historically and critically, their pervasiveness and cultural work. To excavate this work is not to excuse or ignore its ableism but rather to show how ableist stories about disability opened up opportunities for discussing (and enforcing) cultural norms of teen (hetero)sexuality, healthy embodiment, and appropriate modes of emotional expression and cultural consumption.

Blending the didacticism of the problem novel with the melodrama of the extraordinarily popular Harlequin paperback romance novel, teen sick-lit generally features female protagonists on the sexual precipice between childhood and adolescence, and the prevalence of a third-person, partially omniscient narrator means that the sick girl rarely gets to speak for herself.[29] As Sheila Egoff argues, the young adult problem novel spotlights young people "defined by the terminology of pain," and teen sick-lit manifests an obsession with physical pain, recounting symptoms and procedures in excruciating detail.[30] Teen sick-lit revolves around diagnosis of and treatment for chronic illness, often enlisting readers to participate in diagnosing the protagonist's mysterious symptoms. The books usually conclude with the remission or death of the main or supporting characters. Although the novels may, in some ways, encourage teens' understanding of illness or death, the texts continually emphasize the undesirability of disabled bodies, juxtaposing the grotesqueness of the diseased body and its medical management against healthy, natural, and attractive (able) bodies. All of these perceptions of illness are presented as "realistic" and intrinsic to illness, rather than constructed through ableist, sexist, ageist, racist, or classist cultural norms.

Teen sick-lit also espouses rehabilitative edutainment's belief that the resolution of problems (in this case, disease or disability) is mainly up to the protagonists themselves. Over and over, ill girls in teen sick-lit are told "the 'will to live' has a scientific basis" and that a positive attitude "enhances [their] chance of recovery" and "improve[s their] life's quality."[31] In some ways, this reflects a liberal progressive desire for individual health empowerment and agency, one that was being promoted by post-1968 depathologizing movements that critiqued medical authority. However, such an individualist approach to recovery also functions as a form of discipline and dismissal, implying that a failure to rehabilitate reflects a failure of will, or that structural political issues, such as economic disparities or ongoing racial, ableist, homophobic, or sexist prejudices that impede access to privatized health care and other forms of support, are irrelevant so long as one possesses the individual determination to overcome illness. In McDaniel's novels, disease itself (rather than damaging cultural perceptions of disease or depersonalizing medical treatments) immediately and only dehumanizes, as Dawn in *Six Months to Live* imagines herself upon diagnosis with leukemia as "a white rat trapped in a science experiment . . . caught in a maze . . . with no exit, . . . a rat with no future" (7).

Teen sick-lit's narratological operations are dependent on the novels' adherence to the valued conventions of YA literary realism. Blurring the distinction between "real victims" and the novels' own fictional characters, McDaniel consistently notes how important it is for her texts to convey a "medical reality."[32] She often cites her own exposure to illness, such as her son's juvenile diabetes and her own treatment for breast cancer, as her primary inspiration for stories, because "writing about the trauma . . . and effects" was "therapeutic."[33] McDaniel's Random House website notes that she ensures "medical accuracy" in her fiction by "conduct[ing] extensive research," consisting of interviews with health care professionals and work with medical groups and hospice organizations, such as the Tennessee Organ Donor Services. McDaniel also dedicates her novels to "real people"—"the human element"—who are fighting or living with cancer, including doctors, patients, volunteers, or the families of people with cancer. For instance, Dawn Rochelle's last name derives from Rochelle Lynn Dove, to whom *Six Months to Live* is "lovingly dedicated," while *Till Death Do Us Part*'s (1997) dedication reads like a tombstone: "This book is lovingly dedicated to Jennifer Dailey, a victim of cystic fibrosis, a lovely flower, plucked up by the angels after fourteen years on this earth, March 12, 1997. *Dear Jennifer, your family and friends will miss you. May your walk in heaven be joyous!"*[34] By including this information, McDaniel postures her fiction as both activist and memorial, inviting readers to associate characters with real people living with illness.

In-depth descriptions of procedures and treatments and didactic explanations of medical jargon further bolster teen sick-lit's seeming authenticity. In recounting treatments and procedures, especially in Lurlene McDaniel's work, the novels use precise medical terminology and explain up-to-date treatments while detailing the physical ravages of chemotherapy. For example, *Six Months to Live* features in-depth descriptions of spinal taps, "imaging" strategies, and chemotherapy, as well as patients' resultant vomiting and hair loss.[35] *Invincible Summer* describes the vomiting, weight loss, and canker sores that occur after chemotherapy. Overall, McDaniel's "real" firsthand experience with illness and experience with health professionals, combined with the medical jargon that fills out the pages, are all part of the packaging—a form of expertise that undergirds the stories' literary realism.

McDaniel's brand of literary realism is also central to the stories' pedagogical function. Didactically recounting exhaustive lists of symptoms and treatments, the novels emphasize the vulnerability of the body.[36] In so doing, the novels encourage a diagnostic gaze, so that while engaging in sympathy for the ill protagonists, readers participate in the diagnosis of symptoms and the brutal side-effects of chemotherapy or other treatments, described in lurid detail, which cultivates a feeling of *schadenfreude*, or pleasure derived from observing the misfortune of others. For example, Dawn Rochelle "look[s] down self-consciously at her legs" at the "huge, angry-looking bruises glar[ing] back at her," the same bruises that had been a "road sign that had said Cancer" to her doctor (*Six Months* 5). *Invincible Summer*'s Robin ventures to the library to research unexplained bruises on her arms and "wished she still thought her fever and lingering fatigue were the results of the flu" (32). Symptoms are "road signs" that the reader is meant to decode, and avid readers of this genre improve their own diagnostic skills from book to book. Moreover, if contemporary readers need additional information, they can always consult the "Health Resources" tab on McDaniel's Random House website, which provides links for health-related organizations focused on cancer, organ transplantation, depression, and suicide. While the teen sick-lit's objectification of the body may produce fear or sympathy in the reader, it also provokes fascination, combining the clinical gaze of symptom analysis with an idolizing gaze of romantic intrigue. Either way, by fostering this diagnostic gaze, the books also encourage readers' hyperawareness of their *own* bodies in relation to the ill textual bodies whose symptoms they are compelled to read.

Romance, Recovery, and Reconsolidation

Likening realism to the characteristic skin blemishes of adolescence, Robert Lipsyte noted sardonically that, prior to the 1970s, "few pimples of realism marred the bland face of juvenile fiction."[37] However, as Julia Mickenberg describes, during and after the Cold War, children's literature provided fertile ground for articulating popular front struggles against racism, fascism, and economic injustice, and it was also partially responsible for initiating the broadly countercultural politics of the 1960s and 1970s New Left.[38] Historically, the YA problem novel emerged amid (and indeed actively participated in) the faltering of the Cold War consensus that occurred in the wake of the Cuban missile crisis, the Kennedy assassination, Birmingham, Berkeley's free speech movement, the Watts riot, and ongoing protests over U.S. involvement in Vietnam, a volatile cultural moment in which writers "embraced a new realism for a young adult audience" to account for the fact that children could not (and perhaps should not) always be insulated from the dangers of "real" (read: adult) life and responsibilities.[39] The YA problem novel, as opposed to "children's books," enacted a fundamental redefinition of the divide between childhood and adolescence. Although they encouraged an "adult posture" toward the world, problem novels also reflect a profound mistrust of parental authority that historians have come to associate with 1960s radicalism, after which "came the deluge" of problem novels in which adults no longer act as "keeper of the moral universe for children" and instead expose children to "the untidy realities of the adult world with no moral judgment attached."[40] Rather than reflecting the diversity of teen literature offerings, the "problem novel" and "YA literature" often seamlessly implied one another from the 1970s onward, in that what differentiated "YA" from "children's" literatures (and likewise, children from teenagers), for literary critics and publishers alike, were the problems themselves.[41] Teen sick-lit was in plentiful company, as the expanding young adult publishing and television broadcasting trend, as rehabilitative edutainment, broadly emphasized issue-driven pedagogical approaches to their readers, and as realism gained cultural relevance and value as a preferred mode of emotional citizenship training for developing teenagers.

While many children's literature scholars, advocates, and literary critics celebrated the problem novel's turn toward frankness even as they lamented its dreadful aesthetics, still others nostalgically mourned the loss of innocence signaled by the problem novel's existence and perceived necessity. Barbara Feinberg criticized the growing cultural embrace of literary realism, or "grim books" that "made children cry, as if this were the pinnacle of something to be desired."[42] Feinberg's scathing critique of literary realism's "bec[oming] synonymous with progress" is political and cultural rather than simply aesthetic. She asks provocatively, "How had trauma—endless stories of childhood trauma—managed to garner the cachet of multiculturalism, and hence the protection" of the "strict, humorless watchdog of Political Correctness?"[43] Five years after her book's initial publication, Feinberg remained critical of the *New York Times Book Review* and other reading recommendation lists that "confuse social issues with literature."[44]

However, this concern with social issues was a vital catalyst for the diversification of YA literary offerings. In the post–civil rights era, young adult publishing increasingly sought out African American and Latino/a writers and featured nonwhite protagonists. Lipsyte's landmark novel *The Contender* (1967), the story of Alfred Brooks, an African American boxer who resists the peer pressure of an inner-city gang, first disrupted YA literature's overwhelming focus on white middle-class families. Other award-winning YA books, penned by Maya Angelou, Sandra Cisneros, and Walter Dean Myers, soon followed in its wake to describe nonwhite, non–middle-class protagonists in urban centers like Harlem and Philadelphia. Protagonists in these novels, such as the thirteen-year-old heroin-addicted Benjie Johnson of Alice Childress's *A Hero Ain't Nothin' but a Sandwich* (1973) or the reluctant twelve-year-old gang member Jamal of Myers's Newberry Award–winning *Scorpions* (1990), confronted racism, sex, drug addiction, poverty, incarceration, and gang violence.

However, until the 1990s, not only did YA novels featuring white middle-class protagonists vastly outnumber those featuring nonwhite protagonists, but also, so-called multicultural problem novels barely ever featured disease and disability narratives. When they did so, a white character generally appeared as a disabled friend of the nonwhite protagonist, so the pair could bond over a shared "outsider status." For example, Bruce Brooks's Newberry Award–winning novel *The Moves Make the Man* (1985), set in Massachusetts in 1961, describes the unlikely friendship between Jerome Foxworthy, the only African American boy in an integrated school, and Braxton "Bix" Rivers III, a white teenaged basketball player with mental illness and an institutionalized mentally ill mother. Likewise, Robert C. Lee's *It's a Mile from Here to Glory* (1972), which was adapted as an ABC *After School Special* sharing the same title, likened the marginalizing effects of racism to the social isolation produced by disablement in its account of the friendship between Early MacLaren, a white runner who is partially paralyzed in an accident, and his nondisabled African American teammate, Billy Patnell. Perhaps this lack of representation of disability derived from the problem novel's pedagogical formula. Namely, if race or racism often appeared as the problem with which "multicultural" YA literature grappled, the problem novel's single-issue approach left little room for a discussion of other "problems" of embodiment and identity, like disability or illness. In teen sick-lit, black characters, when present at all, often appear either on the periphery, as sidekicks or hospital nurses caring for ill white girls, or at the center, as grateful recipients of white charitable giving, for example in missionary outreach to Africa or volunteer caregiving work (in the case of *Baby Alicia Is Dying* [1995], volunteer work at a home for abandoned HIV-positive babies). Teen sick-lit overwhelmingly focused on white girls with chronic illness, and in this respect, the books have maintained "a possessive investment in whiteness."[45] Disability functions in these narratives as a way to queer whiteness, marking difference and outsider status in white bodies and presenting this difference through an economy of suffering and sadness.

Thus, Feinberg's equation of "trauma" with "the cachet of multiculturalism" and the protective growl of the "humorless watchdog of Political Correctness," however, is much more than a call for fewer sad books. It also reveals a nostalgic longing for a return to a pre–civil rights moment that was somehow more innocent and less "traumatic" than the too-honest (or too-racially diverse?) present. Without engaging explicitly with the "problem" of race, as many problem novels did, teen sick-lit conjured a vision of suffering white protagonists that is historically and politically significant. YA problem novels emerged alongside and within 1970s U.S. white ethnic pride revivals, which, according to Matthew Frye Jacobsen, articulated a new (white) identity politics of ethnicity, "Ellis Island whiteness," which highlighted similarities between ethnic prejudice encountered by white ethnics, such as Italian Americans or Jewish Americans, and racial prejudice experienced by African Americans and Latinos.[46] Through this post–civil rights vision of Ellis Island whiteness, Jacobsen argues, white ethnic pride movements reframed cultural debates about the hardships of slavery and the era of Jim Crow by establishing U.S. white ethnic immigration history as a parallel and equal hardship, a historical reimagining that enabled white ethnics to disavow their white privilege. The American disability rights movement also began amid these white ethnic revivals. Historians of the disability rights movement often have invoked its relationship to civil rights rhetoric and protest strategies even while eliding how disability issues of accessibility to public space and health care are (and always have been) further exacerbated by racism and classism. As Chris Bell notes, in its emphasis on a shared disability meta-identity that supersedes other differences (or in the words of Lennard Davis, the idea that disability, as a less stable category than "traditional identities," can "*transcend* the problems of identity politics"[47]), the field of disability studies has often failed "to engage issues of race and ethnicity in a substantive capacity, thereby entrenching whiteness as its constitutive underpinning."[48] Attendant to Bell's claim, we must consider how the emergence of increasingly white problem novels about disease and disability might not only be an effect of shifting attitudes toward disability engendered by the disability rights movement but also a reaction to an increasingly multicultural young adult publishing industry. In the latter case, stories of ill white girls marshaled the sympathy of readers to represent (and indeed, to rehabilitate) a form of traumatized whiteness in a post–civil rights moment. Thus, ableist storytelling conventions in teen sick-lit did not simply elide race by focusing nearly exclusively on white protagonists; rather, they reconsolidated a version of whiteness-without-white-privilege by narrativizing, through disability, a post–civil rights image of white middle-class suffering.

Although it may have capitalized on (and partly produced) the same market as the liberal problem novel—namely, impressionable teen reader-citizens who might benefit from the bitter pill of literary realism—teen sick-lit often assiduously reconsolidated traditional gender roles, heteronormativity, and whiteness through its conjoined narrative of romance and recovery. As a direct response to seventies feminist and queer (re)imaginings of gender and sexuality, teen sick-lit reconsolidated traditional gender and sexual norms. For instance, in *Six Months to Live*, Dawn describes her hospital roommate and soon-to-be best friend, Sandy, as "Barbie-doll cute" with "cheeks [that] glowed with pale pink blusher" (24). Dawn is often seen putting on makeup and contemplating whether or not illness would make her undesirable to boys. She wishes that Jake, her nondisabled love interest, had kissed her before chemotherapy "ma[d]e her ugly and sick"—"[n]ow that she had cancer," neither Jake nor any other boy "would ever want to kiss her as long as she lived" (24–25). Dawn wonders whether or not a "normal boy" would ever find her desirable again. Although McDaniel's books labor to represent "authentic" depictions of illness, their covers connote illness with props and settings rather than with visibly ill teen bodies. For instance, in various reissued editions, *Six Months to Live*'s cover designs feature a brunette, curly-haired girl in a robe, sitting on a hospital bed and clutching a teddy bear. Apart from being seated on a hospital bed, these cover girls bear none of the physical signs of illness that are described in vivid detail in the books, such as weight loss, baldness, or bruising. While the book's initial cover design featured Dawn alone, many more recent editions feature a girl (positioned in the foreground) and a boy in various "couples" poses, holding hands or hugging. Others lose the hospital iconography entirely, featuring photo-graphs in natural settings or bedrooms. Most emphasize the romantic cou-pledom of the boy and girl on the cover rather than the visibility of illness. The displacement of illness from the cover parallels one of the most signifi-cant narrative operations of teen sick-lit: the female protagonist's recovery is intimately connected to romance with a nondisabled boy. Adherence to traditional gender roles combined with the pursuit of heterosexual romance becomes the central strategy of rehabilitation.

The books designate important differences between "natural" and arti-ficial feminine beauty. When both girls begin to go bald from chemother-apy and as Sandy contemplates getting rid of a box full of now "useless" combs and ribbons, Dawn's mother arrives with a hairstylist to bob the girls' hair, and they happily try on different wigs. *Six Months to Live* then transitions abruptly to a description of the "toll" chemotherapy has taken on Dawn's body:

> A fine rash covered her arms and legs. . . . her blood vessels erupted, caus-ing deep purple bruises to appear like splotches on her body. Her skin took on a blackish cast as the drugs affected the pigmentation. Scabs formed on her lips, and she could no longer bear to look at her own reflection in the mirror. (45–46)

As if to underscore the falseness of the wigs and makeup, the text jars the reader back to recognition of the "ugliness" of cancer in stark contradistinc-tion to the trappings of femininity—makeup, wigs, and beautification ritu-als—that directly precede it; meanwhile, Dawn laments, "It isn't me" as she views her emaciated reflection.

At other moments, makeup does not represent a mode of getting well or feeling better, but rather represents a potentially dangerous form of duplicity. In *I Want to Live*, after discovering that her leukemia has relapsed and while deciding whether or not to undergo a bone marrow transplant, Dawn goes to the mall with Rhonda, who is "lucky . . . to have nothing more serious to decide than what outfit to wear!" (*I Want* 202). She spends nearly her entire allowance on makeup, which she applies in the mall's bathroom, prompting Rhonda to note that such rebellion is out of character for Dawn. However, "bored and tired of being sweet little Dawn," Dawn replies flippantly that she "feel[s] like living dangerously" (203–4). Standing before the mirror, Dawn, in full makeup, observes that she "didn't look like Dawn anymore. She looked older, more grown up" (204). Rhonda and Dawn proceed to the mall pizza parlor, and observing couples sitting at other tables, Dawn wonders "what it would be like to go on a date, a real date with a guy to talk to and hold hands with. Would she think of anything to say? Or would she just sit and stare stupidly at him?" (205). The girls are titillated when two older boys take notice of them, unnerving Dawn but exciting Rhonda. One of the boys, Ricky, rests his arm on the back of the restaurant booth behind Dawn and begins to flirt with her. As she sits with Ricky, Dawn reminisces about the boys in her life, including her love interests and brother:

> She thought about Mike. "*Who wants to date a one-legged boy?*" She thought about Greg. He'd kissed her. She thought about Jake. He'd never kissed her. She thought about Rob. He loved Darcy. Who would love Dawn? She turned her face. It was inches from Ricky's. Suddenly, the thought of Ricky touching her made her skin crawl. (207–8)

When confronted with casual flirting, Dawn begins to juxtapose love with lust, and she reevaluates her relationships with Greg and Jake as being based on physical attraction rather than love. Romance might be innocent enough, but sexuality provokes feelings of guilt. Dawn jumps up abruptly and runs to the ladies' room. She questions herself internally, "*What's wrong with me? What's wrong with me?*" and feels "sick to her stomach"—but not "because of any chemotherapy" (208). In contrast to other mirror scenes throughout the series, in which Dawn is confronted with "reality" in the form of the progression of her disease, here, Dawn is confronted with the artificial and duplicitous trappings of femininity, which make her sicker than her treatments. She washes off all her makeup, careful to also "clea[n] out the sink, drying it with paper towels until no traces remained of her 'dangerous living'" (208). When safely contained in the presumed non-erotic spaces of doctors and patients, such as the hospital or cancer camp, makeovers are encouraged as a therapeutic treatment to maintain traditional gender roles by allowing ill girls to affect able-bodied norms of beauty. However, makeup becomes "dangerous living" when it is sexualized as a strategy for attracting men.

Further evidencing the series' distinction between sexuality and gender, makeup is also used as a rehabilitative strategy with the tomboyish Marlee Hodges, an unruly camper whose defiant attitude and gender nonnormativity challenge Dawn's authority as a camp counselor in *So Much to Live For*. Described as "mean and nasty" by fellow campers, Marlee consistently refuses to participate in camp activities designed to promote a sense of unity and fun among fellow campers. Dawn attempts to spruce up the cabin for the other girls, but they arrive to find the cabin trashed by Marlee. Defying feminine norms of domesticity, she purposely leaves her bunk in disarray to prevent the girls from winning the "Clean Cabin Award" and refuses to make crafts (295). She also bullies other sick teenagers at camp, heartlessly tripping a "one-armed girl" on a hike and embarrassing other girls by snatching off their headscarves "right in front of two guys" (*So Much* 292). As an unruly crip and genderqueer, Marlee resists rehabilitation.

In addition to her unwillingness to join the community, Marlee's refusal to conform to able-bodied and feminine standards of beauty is criticized because a "poor appearance" evidences her unhealthy attitude toward disease. "[P]artially bald, with wispy tufts of hair standing straight out," Marlee does not bother with headscarves. In spite of her plucky challenge to Dawn's authority, as she stares at Dawn through one glass eye, Marlee looks "more pitiful than mean" (296). Although Dawn initially describes camp as a place where "everyone felt perfectly free to 'come as they were,'" whether "on crutches . . . bald . . . with partial limbs . . . with sores and bandages . . . [and] without pretense or shame about how awful they might look or feel," Dawn, the doctors, and the book's third-person narrator all emphasize improving Marlee's poor appearance as the main strategy in a rehabilitative project—one that also has the secondary effect of facilitating a romance between Dawn and her nondisabled and non-ill assistant, Brent, the brother of her deceased friend Sandy (294).

When Dawn expresses her frustration with Marlee's intractability, Brent argues that "maybe it would help if she fixed herself up a little. . . . She could make a little effort, you know, some makeup, covering her head—stuff like that" (306). Brent links Marlee's poor attitude with her unkempt appearance: Although "most girls knew how to do that stuff [beautification rituals] from birth," Brent "bet[s] that Marlee never pulls herself together." Dawn concedes quickly but offers that Marlee might just not know how to fix herself up. Although Brent believes that Dawn's femininity comes from a natural, innate force, they believe that Marlee, an assertive tomboy, needs special assistance in cultivating desirable (i.e., healthy) femininity, which is equated with "pulling herself together" to recover from disease.

Dawn and the other girls try to lure "party pooper" Marlee into a makeover (319). After thrice resisting their demands, she storms from the tent and is pursued by Dawn, who defends the group's good intentions. Marlee repeats stubbornly that she doesn't wear makeup, which makes "anger boil" inside Dawn: "She wanted to shake the girl" because "people had bent over backwards to reach out to Marlee" without her gratitude or cooperation (320). When Dawn rises icily to leave Marlee outside the tent, Marlee confesses her true reason for not wearing makeup. Although she tried to apply eye makeup after losing her eye, "it kept watering and watering" until eye shadow and mascara ran down her face and made her "look like a freak" (320–21). Worse still, the makeup congealed her lashes and caused a painful dry eye socket.

Rather than acknowledging Marlee's emotional and disability-related reasons for not wearing makeup, Dawn presses, "There must be women who have glass eyes and know how to manage makeup" like "actresses in Hollywood" (321). Marlee asserts that she was ugly before cancer and asks why she should bother, since no amount of makeup would enhance her appearance. Dawn argues that the same hard work and determination Marlee displayed in relearning to dive with damaged depth perception could also be applied to "makeup and mascara" (320–22). Despite Marlee's physical inability to wear makeup, the book insists that Marlee only "*feel*[s] ugly" because she is not trying hard enough to maintain traditional standards of able-bodied feminine attractiveness. Dawn's efforts facilitate a celebrated "turning point" for Marlee, who allows Dawn to apply makeup and a borrowed wig and outfit— a "dramatic" improvement (324).[49] When Dawn and Brent convince Marlee that Brent finds her attractive (even though he actually wants to pursue Dawn) and simultaneously help her to cultivate her own femininity, Marlee's crip/queer resistiveness is tamed. Marlee is now a full-fledged member of camp society, and her rehabilitation is completed when she is made over from an unfeminine queer outsider into a properly gendered sexual object for Brent—a "normal" boy.

Countering myriad radical feminist and disability political critiques of and activism around cancer treatment and recovery of the last several decades, McDaniel's fiction not only naturalizes compulsory able-bodiedness but also delimits "gender-appropriate" sick role behavior as women's embodying heteronormative and ableist standards of beauty while subordinating their subjectivity, desires, and needs to the comfort of "the well."[50] In her article "Dying Teenagers in Love," *Bust* magazine's Marni Grossman details her own complex identification with teen sick-lit's protagonists:

> I envied the girls in McDaniel's books, not in spite of their ailments but because of them. Dying girls get the last laugh. They are loved and cherished, and they are, above all, good—even if they aren't. Because you can't really talk trash about a girl on her deathbed.[51]

Namely, Grossman suggests that young girl readers' "attraction" to teen sick-lit derives from a "Beth March syndrome" that has been deeply entrenched within a traditional femininity that defines "suffering [a]s a woman's most noble role" and "lends an innate goodness to the sufferer" of a terminal illness.[52] This complex identification, with and against the ill body, suggests that something deeper is occurring, particularly with respect to teen girl readers and their socialization into the norms of traditional femininity through stories of disability and suffering.

While certainly participating in the ambivalent desire for disability, suffering, and femininity that I have just described, *Invincible Summer* also resists dominant ableist and sexist bodily aesthetics by depicting the unmade-up ill body as sexy. While Rick is in a brief remission, Robin is afraid to let him see her looking like a "ghoul" and a bald "bag of bones," because she worries he will lose interest once he is surrounded by beautiful, healthy college girls (91–94). Rick reassures her that she "always look[s] beautiful to [him]," even if she would be more comfortable with his wearing a blindfold (91). Rick lies on the bed with Robin, and when he "feel[s] her bones, like twigs," he longs to join her under the blankets (103). As Rick's health worsens, Robin regrets her decision to keep Rick from seeing her while she was ill. When she recalls her own humiliation at vomiting from chemotherapy in his presence, she asks, "How could she not have understood the tenderness with which he'd held her afterwards, and the way he told her that it didn't matter?" (139–40).

As opposed to McDaniel's ill girls, who constantly dwell on their lack of curves and ugliness, Ferris describes Robin's ill body as desirable. Robin asks whether Rick wishes he were still with his ex-girlfriend, who was probably "big and healthy and sexy" in contrast to the emaciated Robin (106). Rick rejects Robin's demand that he "get a normal girlfriend" and "forget about [her]." Undeterred by his devotion, she says, "You wouldn't make love to me now . . . not on a bet," to which Rick replies, "I'd make love with you in a second if I thought you'd enjoy it" (106). Before he leaves, he rolls onto his stomach and "kisse[s Robin] *as if she were* big and healthy and sexy" (italics mine) and says, "Think that over" (107). Just as the Dawn Rochelle series rewards girls for adhering to able-bodied ideals of feminine beauty, *Invincible Summer* denies Robin any of her *own* satisfaction with her appearance and instead "proves" her attractiveness by showing that she can still serve as an object of male desire. However, in contrast to McDaniel's books, which cannot imagine an attractive ill body unless it is first made over, *Invincible Summer* shows that Robin's body is "sexy" to Rick just as it is, albeit through ableist language. The novel describes his kissing her not as an ill person but "as if she were big and healthy and sexy."

Though heterosexual romance is a central feature in teen sick-lit, it is also a source of ambivalence. On the one hand, girls' pursuit of boys is connoted with immaturity, as the books configure casualness about dating as an indulgence of the healthy. For example, female teenaged cancer survivors throughout the Dawn Rochelle series persistently joke about girls who "seem to waste so much of their time and energy on the dumbest things," girls for whom "a Saturday night without a phone call or a date is grounds for suicide" (*Six Months* 94). However, in spite of this ambivalence about casual flirtation or dating, teen sick-lit also channels female protagonists into teen romance, representing coming of age as the ability to distinguish true love from immature infatuation. More importantly, teen sick-lit encourages heterosexual monogamy because, when combined with adherence to traditional able-bodied gender roles, it is the genre's central rehabilitative strategy.

Although McDaniel's novels include various disabled and nondisabled love interests for Dawn and other girls with cancer, the Dawn Rochelle series consistently polices the boundaries between well (and thus desirable) boys and sick ones. For instance, just before Marlee's failed makeup session, the girls ask pessimistically, "Aw, who wants to kiss a girl who's bald and barfing?" (*So Much* 316). Dawn describes her romance with Greg, a cancer survivor and her love interest from the previous summer camp, and the girls are incredulous that Dawn was kissed while she "looked all wasted from chemo." However, they also argue that kissing a "chemo geek" at camp does not count as real sexual experience: "All right, so some guy kissed you at camp. But what about a *normal* guy—one who doesn't have cancer" (*So Much* 317). Throughout the novels, Dawn's cancer consistently interrupts her unrequited love for the nondisabled Jake Macka, which augments the illness narrative as the series' only other unifying narrative strand. Although Dawn shares a first kiss with Greg, the novels mainly imagine their intimacy to be "practice" for the real thing: a romance with the nondisabled Jake.

In *Six Months to Live*, Greg's and Mike's healthy appearance stands in stark contrast to Dawn's and Sandy's baldness and skinniness (Sandy regrets appearing in a bathing suit in front of the boys without "a curve left!"). In remission and with full heads of hair, Greg and Mike are described as "vital and healthy," "firm and muscular," "tanned and lean," and "so strong and healthy" (*Six Months* 85–88). Greg's attention "made [Dawn] feel feminine and exciting," and she felt "awed pleasure" that he "was planning a full and active future" in spite of having cancer "just like her" (92). However, the books contain and discipline romance carefully. Although the four campers "spent velvet summer nights at barbecues, camp movies, and on long moonlight walks" and shared a few kisses, Greg and Mike were all at once "friend, beau, and big brother" to Dawn and Sandy, rather than solely romantic partners (94).

The novels also draw stark differences between Greg, a nondisabled competitive swimmer and Olympic hopeful, and Mike, who is "self-consciou[s]" about his prosthetic leg. Mike's disability, first hidden beneath a pair of jeans, is revealed to the girls' surprise when they all go swimming. Again, the novel reflects its persistent anxiety about how disease complicates traditional able-bodied markers of gender. Sandy invites Mike into the water, saying she "doesn't care" about Mike's leg but jokes that she *does* care about "bein' around a boy who has more hair than I" (91). The boys demonstrate their athletic prowess in the pool and horse around with the girls. Dawn "couldn't help but glance" at Mike's amputated leg beneath the water, but he quickly proves his gracefulness with "a beautiful back flip under the water" (93). While the novels linger on the question of sexual attractiveness of disabled bodies, the novel reconsolidates Mike's attractiveness through his demonstrations of physical ability in the water.

Although Mike represented a viable love interest for Sandy when she was undergoing treatment, when he demonstrates interest in Dawn the following year while she is in remission, he is no longer a viable candidate for her affections as a disabled man and cancer survivor. Mike says bitterly that "[n]ot too many girls are hot to go out with a one-legged guy" and concedes that he "know[s he's] not like Greg" ("*or Jake,*" thinks Dawn) but would still like to keep in touch with her (*I Want* 178–79, 182). Through Dawn's thoughts, the narrator commends Sandy for her embrace of Mike's disability but disciplines the possibility of his pursuing a relationship with the now-healthy Dawn. With a body incapable of ever being fully rehabilitated and always asymptomatically ill with a potential relapse, Mike would never represent a viable romantic interest for Dawn within the story's logic, as he would never be a "*normal* guy," which is to say able-bodied and entirely cancer-free "like Jake" or Brent.

Lurlene McDaniel's series also encourages heterosexual romance as a salve for cancer for its female protagonists. Heterosexual love may not cure cancer, but it certainly eases the pain of death. "Color returns to [Marlee's] cheeks" when she fantasizes about Dawn's kiss with Brent on her deathbed. Marlee tells Dawn, "I wished I could have been kissed, just once. For real. Not like in my dream. . . . You don't mind me dreaming about Brent kissing me, do you?" (*So Much* 386–87). When Marlee expresses her fears about death, Dawn "quiet[s] Marlee's fears" by saying that "another dream about Brent" might be waiting for her in her slumber. Marlee's final words are "And you tell Brent hi from me" (388). The tragedy of Marlee's premature death is compounded by her failure to truly experience heterosexuality in the form of a kiss (as opposed to *The Boy in the Plastic Bubble*'s triumphant ending, in which Tod trades his life for his lover's kiss), while her romantic fantasy acts as the comforting dream that helps her to die peacefully.

Moreover, the novel offers Dawn's fantasies about Jake as a form of holistic treatment that augments her chemotherapy. One of Dawn's visualization techniques involves rescuing Rapunzel (most likely a substitute for Sandy, who has enviable blonde hair prior to her cancer treatments) and her long, golden tresses from "the wicked witch Leukemia" (*Six Months* 53). Dawn rides on a horse with her teddy bear, Mr. Ruggers. As the bear raises his lance, Dawn "pressed herself closer to his warm bear body," but the bear suddenly morphs into Jake Macka, causing Dawn to "blus[h] and let go" because she "felt awkward hugging Jake so tightly" (*Six Months* 54). Without Jake (and especially his trusty lance), Dawn cannot rescue Sandy or herself. As mentioned previously, the blossoming romance between Dawn and Brent also helps her to rescue Marlee. Again, the novels betray conservative gender norms, configuring ill girls as imprisoned Rapunzels in need of a rescuing prince rather than self-actualized young women.

Although Dawn experiences other romances throughout the books, the series encourages her continual monogamous pursuit of Jake as paralleling (and facilitating) her survival of cancer. Her romantic object choice is configured as a choice between "two different worlds"—the world of disease and disability, inhabited by Mike, Greg, and Brent, or the world of health, inhabited by the able-bodied Jake (*No Time* 424). Following the memorial groundbreaking ceremony for the Marlee Hodges Cancer Facility, Dawn and Jake stand before a "Tree of Life" mural whose leaves bear the names of cancer survivors. Jake encourages Dawn to choose a leaf on which to write her name. "You know that old saying 'This is the first day of the rest of your life?'" Jake says. "I always thought it was corny, but now it seems to fit. What do you think, Dawn? Is that true?" (533). Jake's question prompts Dawn's internal monologue about her future plans:

> Perhaps her cancer would be permanently cured. Maybe she'd go to medical school. . . . Maybe she'd get married. And maybe she'd be able to have children someday in spite of the grim prognosis. Maybe life was for living. She said, "Yes, Jake Macka, it's true." He brushed his lips lightly across hers, then tucked her under his arm, against his side. "Then let's go live it." She hooked her arm around his waist, and together they walked down the deserted hallway toward the light streaming through the windows. (532–33)

The story of Dawn Rochelle ends with an image of romantic coupledom—reproductive futurism embodied in the promise of marriage, children, and its curative and future-giving essence. Prior to this scene, Dawn and Brent have an amicable breakup, because they realize that Sandy's memory is "the [only] glue that holds [them] together"; after he kisses her on the cheek and she looks into his face, "she knew the past was truly over" (523). Stuck in the illness of the past, Brent and Dawn could never achieve the futurity embedded in the book's image of able-bodied heterosexual romance. Although Dawn finds out that chemotherapy has rendered her infertile earlier in the novel, these thoughts are dismissed through unwavering faith in reproductive futurism's guarantee. In the shadow of an Edenic tree of life, Dawn and Jake walk toward "light streaming," not as the angelic light of death but as the life-giving sun.

In contrast to the domestic and heteronormative ideals of marriage and family offered up in the Dawn Rochelle series, *Invincible Summer*'s Robin and Rick do not wait for the promise of health and reproductive futurity in order to engage in romance and sex. Through their relationship, the novel transgressively resignifies the antiseptic hospital space into an erotically charged zone and markers of illness into sexy emblems of romantic intrigue.[53] When Robin and Rick watch *Casablanca* together in the hospital, the nurses remark crossly that a hospital is "not a nightclub," to reestablish discipline on a space that is not supposed to cultivate romantic attraction (47). Later, to commemorate their first date and first Christmas as a couple, Rick gives Robin a custom-made piece of jewelry, a silver hospital bracelet bearing her name, "Gregory, Robin." This gesture remakes a traditional symbol of illness into a romantically charged symbol of their relationship. Later, while Robin and Rick undergo tests at the hospital to determine whether or not their cancers remain in remission, Robin loses her virginity to Rick in his hospital room: "The planning, the anticipation, the motel reservation, the new nightgown, the Christmas perfume, all proved unnecessary when confronted with love and need and opportunity" (126).

After discovering that Rick's cancer has returned, Robin gives him "the kind of kiss" one should "not give an invalid in front of his mother" (140), before the couple ventures to a hotel for some privacy. Although the novel reminds us that "invalids" are not supposed to be kissed passionately, their sexual relationship continues as Rick's health worsens. He describes being "starved for touching" since he seems "contagious, or breakable, or contaminated" to his parents (152). After trying all of the lights and faucets in the hotel room, Rick says to Robin in sexual double entendre that "[e]verything works" (153). Just as Robin's ill body is described in sexualized prose, Ferris also describes Rick's body as attractive. Recalling the scene of Robin's erotic bony figure that incites Rick's sexual desire, Robin "feel[s] the heat radiating from his bones all down the length of her body" as a result of his thinness (153). They go on a date to a fancy restaurant, and Robin "observed how sharp his bones seemed, the planes of his face defined in clean angles," and "[r]ather than looking gaunt, he looked somehow purified, refined down to his framework" (158). In this case, illness has chiseled Rick into a more attractive man.

Although the novel presents eroticized ill bodies and a fulfilling sexual relationship, *Invincible Summer* also eventually contains this desire within the heteronormative dream of marriage and children. Robin wishes for marriage, and Rick suggests they "pretend" to be married, which acts as a veritable proposal, since he says that "no one else has ever had that offer from me . . . [o]r ever will" (158). The novel also charts a transition in Robin's thinking about babies that occurs as Rick's health is in decline. In the beginning of the novel, Robin describes newborns as "raw and unfinished" beings that might not grow into "real people" (38). By the end of the novel, babies "no longer loo[k] raw and unfinished" but instead "fresh and promising, a new crop of people starting out," although "[s]ome would be straight and strong and others would develop poorly, the way plants did, even in the same soil . . . a mystery" (160–61). Given pervasive and persistent cultural depictions of disability and disease as unattractive and nonsexual, *Invincible Summer*'s eroticization of ill bodies and spaces and its fostering of transformative crip sexuality are significant. This depiction differs starkly from the portrait of longing to "kiss a normal boy" offered by Lurlene McDaniel. However, Robin and Rick's relationship is also ultimately contained within a heteronormative "cycle" of marriage and reproduction, and illness is still configured as "developing poorly" in the "same soil" as "normal" healthy people. McDaniel's novels encourage the performance of heteronormativity as indispensable to recovery, while *Invincible Summer* suggests that reproductive futurity or normalcy, embodied by marriage and kids—or in the words of Rick, "survival at any cost"—might not always be the prize.

A female-dominated field of cultural production and reception, teen sick-lit of the 1980s and early 1990s often manifested an anxious disavowal of the previous decade's liberal feminist ideals in its recuperation of traditional heteronormative femininity. However, while McDaniel's texts are more conservative in their depiction of gender, sexuality, and disability than Ferris's, Marlee, an unruly crip, tears at the story's borders, challenging conventional approaches to rehabilitation and ableist ideals of feminine beauty that seek to make disabled people "identical" rather than equal to able-bodied individuals.[54] Her practical joke on the campers near the end of the story, in which she purposely pops out her glass eye onstage in front of the whole camp, is the opposite of the passive "acceptance" of disability that is so often demanded of female protagonists in teen sick-lit. Rather, this performance spotlights her disability to mock ableist pity. Although her resistance is ultimately contained within the twin fantasies of traditional femininity and heteronormativity (in her deathbed fantasy of Brent), Marlee remains a resistive queer/crip figure who embodies a transgressive "piss on pity" disability politics even in more conservative texts.[55] Meanwhile, *Invincible Summer*, although it often describes the desirability of the ill body in ableist terms, delights in a fulfilling sexual relationship between people with illness and recasts the antiseptic hospital into an erogenous zone. Even as both texts probe the cultural meanings attached to sexuality and disability, heterosexual romance had rehabilitative value for teen sick-lit's protagonists, while literary realism provided a treatment regimen for developing teen reader-citizens. Cultural ideas about the power of literary realism did not necessarily prioritize documentary-style authenticity as the most important facet of YA literature for developing citizens. However, teen sick-lit's supposed "emotional realism" gained traction in a cultural moment in which emotion began to attain unprecedented economic value.

Vanishing Readers? Sadness, Authenticity, and Apathetic Citizenship

Teen sick-lit's emergence and the cultural value of literary realism as medicinal for developing citizens said a lot about an American cultural investment in reading and its relationship to shifting economic expectations, the expansion of mass media, and a notion of participatory citizenship in a post-1968 public sphere that had been changed inexorably by progressive social movements. Meanwhile, private corporations, parents, and government organizations positioned reading as a potent, rehabilitative experience for the national body, as teen sick-lit rose in popularity and pervasiveness amid reports of a reading crisis threatening America: aliteracy.

Librarian of Congress Daniel J. Boorstin warned Congress, in his letter of transmittal accompanying the Center for the Book's congressionally authorized 1983–1984 report "Books in Our Future," that American democracy and the ability of American "citizens . . . to remain free and qualified to govern themselves" was being "threatened by the twin menaces of illiteracy [the inability to read] and aliteracy [the unwillingness to read]."[56] Newspapers avidly covered the report, which was generated by a committee of scientists, educators, and literary scholars. *New York Times* articles gasped, "They are everywhere—people who have the ability to read . . . bare essentials" like "road signs, labels on food packages, television listings, and product instructions" but "never look between the covers of a book."[57] Although "Books in

Our Future" provided few concrete statistics and no direct plan of remedy, reporters and advocates were "sure in their bones" that aliteracy was a growing national problem.[58] If the book had less than six months to live, experts feared an ongoing slow death of reading culture that threatened an American democracy epitomized by a well-read citizenry.

The vaguely menacing moniker "aliteracy" incited an explosion of new governmental and commercial initiatives to promote book culture in the 1980s. While state- and federally sponsored initiatives urged "family reading," many emergent programs emphasized youth literacy, while new forms of commercial edutainment, like YA problem novels and made-for-TV movies based on literary texts, promoted youth reading. In 1986, Public Law 99-494 officially designated 1987 as the "Year of the Reader" and encouraged efforts "to restor[e] the act of reading to a place of pre-eminence in our personal lives and in the life of our nation."[59] President Ronald Reagan further distilled the target audience for reading intervention when he named 1989 the "Year of the Young Reader" by presidential proclamation. Established by public law in 1977, the Center for the Book spearheaded a series of cultural events to encourage reading, including the assembly of the literary time capsule and the previously described "Books in Our Future" report. The following George H. W. Bush administration joined the national, state, and local organizations to form the Barbara Bush Center for Family Literacy. Meanwhile, commercial industries, including television networks and restaurants, seized on the Center for the Book's message of inter-media partnership to fuel their own profits, again, by engaging in cultural debates about the health value of commercial media for youth rehabilitative citizenship projects.

For example, in a national seminar entitled "Television, the Book, and the Classroom" (1978), Frank Stanton, the former president of CBS, expressed annoyance about the condescension embedded in the notion that "the ordinary citizen is weak-minded to the point that a few hours of television each day can turn him into a video-guided vegetable."[60] Rather than deadening intellects, Stanton argued, television stimulated people's interest in countless subjects, and he suggested that an economic and creative partnership between books and television could be mutually beneficial.[61] Beginning in the late 1970s, CBS's "Television Reading Program" provided junior high and high school students with matched-to-broadcast scripts of selected CBS specials along with supplemental reading lists and reading enrichment guides for teachers.[62] PBS developed *Reading Rainbow* (1983–2006), a television show that emphasized the importance of reading for imagination and education. Meanwhile, producers of ABC's *After School Specials*, discussed in the previous chapter, drew voraciously from emerging YA novelists.[63] In 1985, in a joint undertaking, ABC and PBS formed Project Literacy in the US (PLUS), while NBC partnered with the Center for the Book on its anti-aliteracy campaign, featuring a number of pro-reading public service announcements that featured stars from hit television shows to promote reading while promoting NBC programming. American Cablesystems even launched a campaign to promote reading that urged its 300,000 subscribers to turn off the TV for an hour of daily family reading time. Also in 1985, Pizza Hut's "Reading Is FUN-damental" campaign yielded its well-known program, "BOOK-IT!," which partnered with schools to provide educational materials and to offer incentives to students, including free personal pan pizzas, t-shirts, or holographic BOOK-IT! buttons, for meeting their reading goals.[64] Finally, while the book was allegedly dying, book "superstores," such as Barnes and Noble, proliferated in suburban shopping centers, catering to middle- and upper-class consumers by producing a salon-like browsing atmosphere, with cushy leather chairs, soft lighting, and coffee bars, in opposition to lowbrow magazine stands. Ironically, noted the *New York Times*, such bookstores opened amid the lowest average verbal SAT scores since 1980.[65]

Indolent Gen-X'er teens epitomized what the *Christian Science Monitor* named "the case of the vanishing reader," in part because they were choosing to consume other media like videogames and television.[66] Thus, cultural fears about the "vanishing reader" triangulated ongoing anxieties about new technologies, such as television, computers, and videogames, and their potential to damage engaged citizenship in the public sphere. Journalists often disparaged these media for interfering with youth reading practices. In particular, the *New York Times* spotlighted "aliterate" and "computer-crazy" Gen-X'er teens, born between 1965 and 1983, as a "different breed altogether that did not grow up valuing reading."[67] In a media-saturated world, young people were especially "[b]ombarded by . . . electronic games" and "hypnotized by a gamut of television stations" with little oversight by absent "harried single parents or in dual-income families where the habit of reading has been lost."[68] Further compromising already imperiled family values and child development in a postfeminist world populated by ever more working moms, television made the stakes of aliteracy higher for this generation's indolent and unsupervised citizens. Although reluctant readers had likely always existed, reporters argued, aliteracy was a new crisis, exacerbated by mass media in a country in which "more than 98 percent of . . . households ha[d] television sets."[69]

In spite of multiple reports of the book's imminent death, certain segments of the book publication market flourished. One report noted that popular fiction accounted for two-thirds of the total number of books bought in 1991, while half of mass-market paperbacks were romance novels, a publishing trend that doubtlessly impacted the birth of teen sick-lit.[70] However, for many, the popularity of lowbrow reading materials only served as evidence of an ongoing crisis. "Just when we needed more quality fiction [for teens]," librarians lamented, "[t]hey gave us romances and Choose-Your-Own-Adventures."[71] "Goodbye serious reading," one newspaper said sardonically, "Hello, fluff."[72] By disparaging romance novels as "fluff," journalists and literacy advocates addressed female readers as particularly predisposed to aliteracy.

As the national focus on youth aliteracy combined forces with a booming YA literature market, this coalition attempted to solve the national problem of aliteracy through the YA problem novel, equating teen desire to read "serious" (and thus, socially responsible) literature with engaged "healthy" citizenship. The aliteracy crisis for teens may have operated in gender-neutral language, but in the realm of emotional instruction, typically construed as women's work, women bore special responsibility for their complicity with the rising tide of aliteracy—especially amid increasing dual-income households in white middle-class families. The case of the vanishing reader was ultimately exacerbated by the case of the vanishing white middle-class stay-at-home mom.

If television was creating mindless apathetic drones, reading might create emotionally engaged (and thus socially responsible) citizens. While the best-selling author Allan Bloom lamented what he called "the closing of the American mind" in his 1987 book of the same title, the aliteracy crisis revealed less about reading practices and more about generalized anxieties about increasing class stratification, the operations of racial capitalism, and increasingly precarious employment as the postindustrial U.S. economy transitioned toward a global service economy by the 1980s. Journalists worried that "airport book" readers or those who "rea[d] computer screens for information and figures" would outpace the reproduction of an educated citizenry that read "great books," which, in contrast to popular literature, magazines, or computers, demanded more sophisticated "tactics of repose and concentration."[73] Two classes of people will develop, reported the *New York Times*, a "narrow elite" of readers and a large majority who would "not be bothered to read."[74] The expansion of white-collar work and college education opportunities for the white middle class were accompanied (and indeed, facilitated) by the elimination and global export of American blue-collar jobs. Racial and class inequality in U.S. schools, facilitated in part by a post-1970 middle-class white suburban flight and ongoing poverty and scarce resources in nonwhite urban neighborhoods, combined with the twin processes of welfare elimination and prison expansion to widen a racialized gap between the rich and the poor.[75]

Starting in the 1980s, the cultural and political tide turned against desegregation, as courts increasingly denied new desegregation plans and grew lax in enforcing the *Brown* decision on a federal level. Thus, journalists' fears about the possible development of two classes of Americans, which aliteracy *might* produce, required a strong disavowal of the ongoing disparities in education and opportunity for African Americans and Latinos in comparison with their white peers of all socioeconomic classes. By shifting cultural investments—of both the ideological and monetary kind—away from illiteracy, poverty, and a widening racialized achievement gap, the aliteracy crisis, like teen sick-lit itself, manifested a possessive investment in whiteness as much as it undergirded the painful impact of an economic shift toward precarious employment for all.

Although cultural panics about aliteracy mobilized an image of an uninformed public that was "increasingly unable to think for itself" and "more and more susceptible to the manipulations of the elite," the feared citizen who was truly at the heart of the epidemic was worse than uninformed.[76] S/he was *apathetic*. Debates about literary realism converged with cultural ideas about good citizenship around the issue of appropriate emotional expression and its role in childhood development. Liberal and conservative arguments about the merits or perils of literary realism manifested two shared beliefs about healthy popular culture's transformative power and its significance to the disciplines of citizenship. First, reading problem novels would (and perhaps even *should*) incite emotional upheaval, such as sadness or fear, in its readers. Second, emotional realism was a necessary growth experience for teenagers, who were conjured as problematically emotive—either emotionally excessive or apathetic—and thus in need of the emotional instruction that healthy literature might provide. Despite publishers' claims and authors' intentions, the core essence of teen sick-lit's realism does not derive from authorial experience with illness, the strategic use of medical jargon, or their pedagogical focus on problems. What made a problem novel "realistic," and in turn, what made problem novels alternately valued or vilified, were negative emotions and their evocation and manipulation. In other words, teen sick-lit's cultural capital derived from sadness itself. The cultural value of literary realism has something to do with "how we feel" and how we believe *others* should feel. The cultural belief that others need to be *taught* how to feel properly forms the essence of the rehabilitative intersection of romance and illness narratives in teen sick-lit—and likewise, their historically significant place in the commodification of emotional management as a new requirement of labor.

If aliteracy represented an indifference to reading—or worse, an indifference to democratic citizenship—teen sick-lit traded in an *excess* of feeling, an angst-ridden melodrama that presumed to incorporate the body of the reader into citizenship and growth through the visceral experience of sadness. McDaniel's titles—*Sixteen and Dying* (1992), *She Died Too Young* (1994), *Don't Die My Love* (1995)—produce the expectation of sadness for readers. Combining the affective and intellectual dimensions of immaterial labor, McDaniel's texts (and teen sick-lit more generally) also presented the deep sadness they engendered readers to feel as real. "Everyone loves a good cry, and no one delivers heartwrenching stories better than Lurlene McDaniel," reads the opening line of McDaniel's biography on her author page on the Random House website.[77] Fans often use the phrase "cryin' and dyin'" to describe McDaniel's depressing books. There are ten groups devoted to McDaniel on Facebook, and many fans praise the books for the tears they produce—or, in the decisive words of Andrea Haddad, a young fan of McDaniel's books, "Crying is the reason I prefer Lurlene's books over all the other books."[78]

Teen sick-lit's brand of literary realism operates partly through the novels' impression of medical authenticity (i.e., the text "feels real" because it seems medically accurate). However, teen sick-lit also manufactures an intense feeling of sadness and sympathy as a form of bodily involvement with reading that is somehow exceptional, because it is more authentic than other reading experiences. As a printable bookmark on Lurlene McDaniel's website says, "Nothing feels as real as a Lurlene McDaniel book." By affectively involving the reader—body and soul—in the fear-inducing process of diagnosis, the titillation of new romance, and the sadness of "real" problems like illness and death, teen readers, especially teen female readers, were newly hailed as emotionally unruly subjects, anterior to politics and "under construction." The pedagogical impulse that underpins both YA literary realism and rehabilitative citizenship functions not only to regulate behavior but to discipline feeling. This citizenship project relies intimately on tragic and inspirational stories of disease and disability, not because they *are* real but because they make us feel "real" emotions like sadness. Negative affects have been culturally sanctioned as growth-inducing emotions, although this particular incitement of sadness relied on ableist stories that continue to be damaging to people with disabilities or diseases.

This medicinal value of reading for developing teen citizens operated through the interdependent work of "authenticity" and "sadness." Various librarians, interviewed by Feinberg, touted the value of award-winning realistic fiction, because it encouraged children "to enlarge their frames of reference . . . [and see] the world from another perspective" and become more courageous in confronting their own problems.[79] The YA literature scholar Marc Aronson argues that the grimness of problem novels is something that caters naturally to teen tastes, since all teens, by nature, enjoy bleakness and crave "intense feeling" such as "bleak despair" to make a book seem "real."[80] Both assessments of transitions toward YA problem novels equate sadness with reality. Aronson's perspective even essentializes sadness, and a craving for it, as part of the biological nature of adolescence.

In an era in which the liberal pedagogical problem novel featured non-white, non–middle-class, disabled, and queer voices to teach lessons about tolerance, disease narratives became a predominant means of conveyance for emotional realism's rehabilitative power. However, as mentioned previously, teen sick-lit's recuperation of white suffering and white middle-class problems usually elided race and ignored (or actively disavowed) white privilege. Instead, teen sick-lit offered a postracial humanism predicated on life-or-death "human" struggles with disease and disability. In this respect, emotional realism, specifically sadness, became rendered not just as a shared (and unifying) feeling but also as a universal language that nonetheless continued to centralize the problems of white middle-class protagonists as universal human experiences of "growing up."

The normative cultural understanding of adolescence as an affective stage defined by the universal human experience of deep suffering and sadness— and likewise the construction of sadness as somehow more "authentic"— has been crucial to the interweaving of engaged citizenship, participatory democracy, and emotional instruction as national values. Their biopolitical mapping onto teen proto-citizens also reaffirms them as shared cultural values. While the linkage of reading with the maintenance of the public sphere is a timeworn historical theme, the pedagogical, problem-driven teen fiction that had emerged as dominant across multiple mediums by the 1970s was really a new youth cultural form—and a historically significant one when contextualized within the shifting affective economies of neoliberal consumer capitalism, as I will discuss at the end of this chapter as well as in the book's conclusion.

Egoff writes that the realistic adolescent novel "[takes] the approach that maturity can be attained only through a severe testing of soul and self . . . featur[ing] some kind of shocking 'rite of passage' such as the uprooting of a child's life by war, the death of a close friend or parent, an encounter with sex."[81] When imagined in the seemingly apolitical terms of human development, the affective labor of sadness performed by problem novels, including sick-lit, participates in the social construction of angst and "despair" as inherently characteristic of adolescence; "happiness" and "innocence" as descriptive of childhood; and an objective clinical gaze and emotional reservation as the province of adults. Teen sick-lit reifies this developmental narrative, by imagining realist stories about teen angst as epitomizing not only the genre called young adult literature but also the very condition of being a teenager. As sad stories for teens' emotional growth crossed into multiple mediums and coalesced into rehabilitative edutainment, the very first volume of a new interdisciplinary scholarly journal concerning adolescent development, the *Journal of Adolescence*, featured an essay that posed a provocative question: "Adolescent Depression: Illness or Developmental Task?"[82] The problem novel, along with parents, authors, librarians, and literary critics who endorse it as culturally valuable, construct a reassuring progressive narrative, an image of the coherent and healthy (or able) adult subject that emerges after weathering the storms (or illness) of adolescence. At their core, problem novels rehabilitate disease in their pages to rehabilitate adolescence outside of them, as reading emotionally realist texts forms healthy, emotionally managed citizens—who are most healthy when in monogamous heterosexual romantic partnerships.

However, while the novels' affective mode depends on ableist stereotypes of disability as tragedy, experiences of sadness in teen sick-lit also offer an unexpected disability political critique of the "coldness" of medicalization. Though McDaniel is not explicitly defined as a "Christian writer" in her promotional material, critics describe her as an "inspirational novelist," and her books are very popular among Christian youth and gained immense popularity amid the rise of the New Right in the 1980s. McDaniel once commented that she studied "medicine and traditional grief therapy techniques to give the novels a sense of serious medical reality" but also "studied the Bible to instill the human element—the values and ethics often overlooked by the coldness of technology."[83] Characters in her books often have spiritual discussions about fate and the afterlife. For McDaniel, medical knowledge does not always lead to salvation. McDaniel attends an Orthodox Presbyterian church and describes herself as very "'into' Calvinistic theology."[84] Indeed, with titles such as McDaniel's earliest publication, *If I Should Die before I Wake* (1983), *As I Lay Me Down to Sleep* (1991), or *Lifted Up by Angels* (1997), Christian iconography unsubtly pervades McDaniel's texts in biblical epigraphs and plotlines.[85] Jean Ferris's *Invincible Summer* also emphasizes spirituality, opting for "belief" rather than organized religion. Robin's grandmother, Libby, "thought everybody should believe in something. She didn't care what they called it, God, or Fate, or the Wind in the Trees" (29). However, as opposed to McDaniel's books, which foster a sense of resolution via faith, *Invincible Summer*'s Robin is more ambivalent about faith, rarely attending church, lampooning the twitchy "Reverend Hamster," and questioning his sermon's message that God never dishes out more difficulty than people can handle (32). However, the novel still encourages "prayers to unknown saints," not as "a life insurance policy" but as a way of realizing that "sometimes the prize is peace and rest" (151). Thus, spirituality, if not formalized religion, represents a mode of coping and resolution within a variety of teen sick-lit novels.

Although McDaniel's texts reflect conservative gender and sexual norms, their resistance to medical "coldness" or dehumanization shares much with secular disability rights movements of the twentieth century. Yet while the "human element" embodied in McDaniel's spiritual approach claims "values and ethics" as its province, such an ethical critique of medicine is achieved from the superiority and distance of third-person narration and allows "patients" to stray from medical authority only when medicine has exhausted its capabilities. However ableist and antifeminist her books may be, McDaniel's activism, as a cancer survivor and parent of a disabled child, is a form of disability activism that complicates the dominant narrative of post-1968 liberal progressive disability activism, which largely positions it as an outgrowth of secular civil rights or other liberal identitarian movements. Reading McDaniel into histories of disability and civil rights exposes some of the persistent political and racial splits within disabled communities, augmenting secular disability critiques of medicalization with theologies of suffering and redemption.

The Managed Heart of the Teen Reader

Just one year prior to the passage of the Americans with Disabilities Act (ADA), young readers chose McDaniel's love stories about chronic illness and disability as representative texts of an American youth reading community in the Library of Congress's literary time capsule. Teen sick-lit readers were encouraged to grow through reading books that had medicinal value, while fictional protagonists were forced to come of age through their relationship with disease and, oftentimes, mortality. The affective labor of teen sick-lit produced a linkage, in the words of Ann Cvetkovich, between "political and therapeutic cultures" and "political and emotional life."[86] Teen sick-lit operated as "repositories of feelings and emotions . . . encoded not only in the content of the texts themselves, but in the practices that surround their production and reception."[87] In the case of teen sick-lit, on one level, a public of readers, and on the other, a public of inherently angst-ridden (and angst-craving) "teens" themselves, were discursively produced through the affective labor of "grim" literature. Exposure to "reality" in the form of sadness and loss was meant to incite growth into adulthood, much as reading was meant to sustain democracy and citizenship.

I have argued throughout this chapter that teen sick-lit, through its conjoined romance and illness narratives, reaffirms compulsory heterosexuality and able-bodiedness as a central component of its pedagogical project of cultivating sadness. Cultural investments in defining adolescence as a transitional affective stage defined by deep suffering and incapacity (and likewise the equation of sadness with authenticity) have been crucial to the construction of American ideals of what it means to be an engaged and productive citizen. Since this developmental narrative continually animates stories of "overcoming" disability or disease, with the linkage of heteronormativity and able-bodiedness forming the "happy" ending that is healthy coming of age achieved, scholars must reevaluate the relevance of affect theory to the study of age and dis/ability as well as to the more traversed realms of gender and sexuality. Teen sick-lit remains extraordinarily popular. In its pages, heterosexuality and able-bodiedness still often connote not only happiness but also maturity—an association that bolsters heterosexist and ableist ideas about disability and queerness as infantile, narcissistic, tragic, or eliminable.

This proliferation of the problem novel, and later, of teen sick-lit, took place within a larger cultural demand for issue-based rehabilitative entertainment for young adults that began in the late 1960s. This transition to literary realism was a way of grappling with the myriad social changes wrought by sexual liberation and liberal depathologizing social movements of the 1960s and 1970s. However, by implying that getting the guy was the key to getting well, teen sick-lit represented a stubborn retrenchment into heteronormativity and traditional gender roles. In a fledgling YA literature market, teen sick-lit and other problem novels were not only popular but also were insulated from critique because of their supposed "medicinal" value. For example, while the turn toward the problem novel had expanded YA literary offerings to include nonwhite characters and authors, teen sick-lit, by contrast, represented a significant reconsolidation of whiteness, as novels rarely featured nonwhite characters as anything other than recipients of white charity or caregivers to ill white characters. Moreover, while feminists, like those who wrote *Our Bodies, Ourselves* (1971), engaged in ongoing resistance against the medicalization of the female body, teen sick-lit not only medicalized the teen body but also endorsed the selfsame traditional gender roles against which second-wave feminists had struggled.[88] In reaffirming heteronormativity, teen sick-lit formed part of the edifice of heterosexuality as an institution that lesbian feminists were critiquing within mainstream feminism and within broader U.S. culture. Even as female authors secured a central place in young adult publishing, and while authors like Judy Blume faced censorship for books like *Deenie* (1973), a narrative of disability that challenged sexual norms, teen sick-lit of the 1980s and early 1990s proliferated as a conservative alternative to more liberal problem novel offerings of the 1970s. Finally, teen sick-lit's encouragement of readers' decoding of symptoms and self-surveillance participated in a rise of a self-diagnosis market, already ongoing in the self-help industry. Teen sick-lit normalized increasingly profitable forms of medicalized self-surveillance, hypostatized in health information websites like WebMD, a longer genealogy taken up in this book's conclusion.

However, in considering *Invincible Summer* and the linkage of illness and teen romance more generally, I also want to suggest that the linkage between political and therapeutic cultures might produce something *other* than disciplined, restrained, heteronormative teen sex by suggesting an alternative form of heterosexuality outside inevitable marriage and reproduction. In a certain sense, illness suspends the rules of the timeline of teen sexual development, which often tacitly legitimates premarital sexual contact that might otherwise be discouraged. Most importantly, the linkage of romance and illness has the transgressive potential of eroticizing hospital rooms and ill bodies, which usually appear as antiseptic and nonsexual. In this sense, teen sick-lit opens up significant possibilities for desiring, rather than simply rehabilitating, disability.

Yet even as teen sick-lit often appears to operate solely at the level of individual emotional investment, I want to suggest, in conclusion, that these texts (and conversations about their pedagogical value) also engaged with a broader emotional, economic, and cultural order of the late 1970s that scholars have alternately referred to as neoliberalism, globalization, post-Fordism, or late capitalism. In 1979, Arlie Russell Hochschild profiled airplane stewardesses to characterize an emergent "emotional style" of labor that took root within post-Fordist deindustrialization, which was characterized by a transition away from manufacturing and toward a service economy.[89] Amid an increasing abstraction and dematerialization of labor, emotion became commodified as a service. New forms of affective labor gained cultural and economic currency, so that having a "managed heart" became compulsory: "Seeming to 'love the job'" became part of the job itself, while emotional performances, like happiness, ease, or concern, gained new exchange value.[90] An immaterial "caring" labor, affective labor involves the production and manipulation of affects, such as feelings of satisfaction, passion, or ease.[91] As opposed to subjectively experienced emotions, affects involve a relationship among bodies, feelings, and economies; affective labor assembles "social net-works, forms of community, and biopower."[92] In other words, affective labor dramatized the inseparability of seemingly distinct realms of the emotional, cultural, political, and economic.

Emotional management wove into the workplace while the institutional management of adolescent emotion became a formal rehabilitative citizen-ship project undertaken in the public educational landscape. The passage of the Education for All Handicapped Children Act (Public Law 94-142) in 1975 required all public schools to provide equal access to education and one free meal a day for children with physical, intellectual, or learning disabilities as well as those with emotional or behavioral problems in the "least restrictive environment" (i.e., disabled students should be educated alongside rather than segregated from their nondisabled peers). Now codified as IDEA (Indi-viduals with Disabilities Education Act), this landmark legislation, amid a broad popularization of psychology in the 1970s, helped to install school psychologists as a permanent fixture in U.S. schools. By 1988, the number of school psychologists had quadrupled from 5,000 in 1970 to more than 20,000, and by the 1990s, as discussed in the next chapter, the question of whether or not depression was essential to adolescence (illness or develop-mental task?) would be taken up in debates about direct-to-consumer phar-maceutical advertising and youth antidepressant use. The rehabilitative treat-ment of teen sadness by psychologists, cultural producers, policy makers, and health corporations would become a controversial and lucrative indus-try by the twentieth century's close.

Amid a broader transition toward affective labor, feminists also began politicizing emotion in new ways. For instance, Janice Radway's seminal *Reading the Romance* (1984) challenged canonical literary studies by consid-ering women's affective investments in reading "trashy" romance novels (teen sick-lit's close cousin)—a critical refocusing that relocated the object of liter-ary analysis from the text to the "social event" of reading and the individual and collective affective experiences it produced. Meanwhile, feminists cri-tiqued IQ testing and sexism in the classroom using newly circulating con-cepts such as "emotional IQ" or "emotional maturity."[93] They also invented "feminist standpoint theory" to problematize Western patriarchal values like rationality and objectivity by asserting the primacy of individual feelings and experiences (also an ongoing project of disability studies).

Teen sick-lit materialized within this multilayered affective order, and offered a good cry as a form of rehabilitative treatment for still-malleable teen proto-citizens. Teen sick-lit, and the attendant affective investments of parents, literary critics, publishers, and cultural producers in its social value, established regulatory emotional conventions for teens and imagined them as unfinished projects. The convergence of multiply overlapping sites—the compulsory able-bodiedness and heterosexuality dramatized in teen sick-lit's illness/romance narratives; cultural debates about the value of literary realism; and a new affective economic and political order—reaffirmed a teen emotional habitus that imagined teens as naturally predisposed toward excessive emotionality and sadness. Affective labor, the fundamental power of any emotional habitus, involves the ability not only to incite emotion but also to establish and enforce norms delineating appropriate feelings and their expression.[94] This form of power is often overlooked, perhaps because, to hark back to McDaniel's bookmark, it feels so real.

Pierre Bourdieu described habitus as a feel for the game. What "feel" was teen sick-lit offering teenagers exactly, and for what game? The emergence of the problem novel genre, filled with sad books that "felt real," bolstered an image of teen emotional excessiveness as a natural (but pathological) condition, an image that gained traction in a new affective economy and its attendant commodification of human emotion. Capitalizing on an intimate public of mainly female teen readers and asserting the affective value of reading sad literature, publishers, parents, and educators erected lucrative new publishing markets, pop-cultural pedagogical tools, and developmental imperatives regulating teen emotion, embodiment, and sexuality. Thus, I am suggesting, borrowing Berlant's term, that a teen "intimate public," cultivated by countless problem-driven stories about overcoming disability, over-emotionality, and suffering, greased the wheels of broader post-Fordist cultural, political, and economic transitions. However, Hochschild, Hardt, and Negri have mainly accounted for the cultural histories and legacies of the manipulation and exchange of *positive* emotions, or corporate core values like "service with a smile." By contrast, the "caring" affective labor of teen sick-lit, and of the problem novel more generally, was rendered through a revaluation of negative affect—a core value we might call service *through* tears.

Teen sick-lit's rehabilitation of impaired and "emotionally unmanaged" teenagers, overcoming their "disabling" adolescence, bolstered a powerful cultural fantasy: that of the stability promised by (and to) adult citizens. This promise of "the good life" would become increasingly unfulfilled in a neoliberal age characterized by "precarity," an economic, cultural, affective, and political fragility that increasingly cuts across economic classes, cultural identities, and geographical boundaries to form a "globalized or mass-homogenous class," the "precariat," which is defined by the perpetual instability of ceaseless economic crisis.[95] Global precarity has been a by-product of insecure employment, exploitative demands for workers' limitless physical and emotional flexibility, disappearing government investment in forms of social welfare, and the collapse of radical post-1968 social movements. Situating teen sick-lit as an affective engagement with the broader emotional currents and economic changes of its cultural moment reveals the ways ideas about teenagers and disability have undergirded the emotional disciplines of maturity and citizenship; the interrelationship among culture, the body, and the economy; and the affective labor of cultural production. By emphasizing the naturalness of vulnerability, self-surveillance, and emotional management, YA literary realism endeavored to give teens a dose of reality. What it gave them was a feel for the precarious game of late capitalism.

4

Crazy by Design

Neuroparenting and Crisis in the Decade of the Brain

The teenage brain may, in fact, be briefly insane. But scientists say,
it is crazy by design. The teenage brain is in flux, maddening and
muddled. And that's how it's supposed to be.
—Barbara Strauch, *The Primal Teen*

In his award-winning 2003 book, *Yes, Your Teen Is Crazy! Loving Your Kid
without Losing Your Mind*, Michael Bradley joked about the difficulty of raising teens in the twenty-first century. The joke begins with a concerned parent's arrival at a psychologist's office to ask that the psychologist evaluate his
moody thirteen-year-old son.[1] Prior to meeting the young patient, the doctor
offers the following diagnosis: "He's suffering from a transient psychosis with
an intermittent rage disorder, punctuated by episodic radical mood swings,
but his prognosis is good for a full recovery." The shocked parent asks, "How
can you say all that without even meeting him?" The doctor confidently
replies, "He's 13."

From the black leather–jacketed James Deans of the Cold War, to the post-
1968 youth counterculture freaks, to the sad sick-lit readers of the 1980s, adolescence has often been interpreted through the affective lens of emotional
crisis, a period characterized by emotional volatility or negative affects, like
depression, rage, ennui, and despair. The previous chapters have shown just
how fully representations of responsible citizenship for teenagers sutured sadness with "reality." In other words, cultural agents have broadly imagined identity crises, with their attendant emotional upheaval, as a kind of temporary
insanity, both a normal rite of passage *and* a pathological condition in need of
various forms of discipline. In many ways, the image of the "crazy teenager"
is perennial, from Progressive-era "feebleminded" and sexually wayward
youth, to the enigmatic rebel without a cause, to the always-already potentially
depressed teenager that had emerged by the late 1970s. Educators, psychologists, parents, cultural producers, and politicians have used the rhetoric of craziness to describe generational conflict and to explain rebellious behavior.

However, with the advent and ascension of adolescent neuroscience in the 1990s "Decade of the Brain," something changed. While previous generations depicted teenagers as besieged by hormones or as willful rebels, the development of adolescent neuroscience in the late twentieth century meant that a new generation rooted the emotionally tumultuous condition known as adolescence in neurophysiology for the first time in human history. From the 1990s onward, popular representations of neuroscience research in newspapers, news magazines, and parenting books spotlighted teenagers and their brains in unprecedented ways. In this cultural milieu, parenting experts, politicians, and science journalists who were concerned about issues of childhood development in the late twentieth century found a new language in which to express their fears and proffer solutions. As scientific knowledge about the brain permeated popular culture, representations of "crazy" teenagers with dangerous (and endangered) incomplete brains manifested a new image of adolescence as a form of temporary "brain damage" that required new forms of rehabilitative management. Mobilizing the rhetoric of disability and rehabilitation, experts in parenting books and news media described teenagers as "disabled" by their unfinished brains and configured coming of age as a rehabilitative journey that would culminate in "stable" adulthood and ensure national health.

What was born out of this popularization of neuroscientific knowledge about the teen was a new compassionate medicalization model for dealing with teens that I call "neuroparenting." Emerging in descriptions of teens in parenting texts, government policy, and news media, neuroparenting was premised on "neuroplasticity," the idea that the brain's wiring changes as a result of external stimuli and experience. At first a medical discovery, the concept of neuroplasticity quickly animated a new "brain culture" premised on harnessing neuroplasticity in order to optimize brain performance.[2] Teenagers were singled out as a particularly unruly group, however, and the advent of adolescent neuroscience redefined teens as "flexible," albeit in possession of (or perhaps possessed by?) "temporarily disabled" brains. While discourses of neuroplasticity often promised optimization through brain exercises, neuroparenting represented the other side of the coin. It blamed the teen's incomplete brain for "symptoms" of adolescence, such as laziness or bad decision making, and it configured teens as physiologically in need of disciplinary intervention, so that adults—parents, educators, politicians, doctors, and pharmaceutical industries—might mold the brain before its development was complete. Crucially, this approach conjured an image of "normal" adolescence as a disability, a temporary but significant neurological impairment.

Of course, this new knowledge about the teen brain was not natural-ized in a vacuum. Rather, it relied on a "preexisting condition": rehabilita-tive edutainment's representational conventions, which had corporealized the developmental process of adolescent coming of age through the meta-phoric image of overcoming disability. Thus, when they argued that normal adolescence was a neurological impairment, proponents of neuroparenting mobilized well-established discourses of disability and rehabilitation, which were already ubiquitous in teen popular literature and media. Neuroparent-ing naturalized a teen emotional habitus defined by excessive emotion and medicalized it as a physiological impairment. As this medical knowledge was taken up and translated by parenting experts, educators, policy makers, and cultural producers, adolescent neuroscience also promised to help parents rewire teen brains in "nonjudgmental" ways.

Neuroscience has offered many compelling insights about neurophysiol-ogy, teenaged and otherwise, and its effects on behavior and perception. It is not the task of this chapter to evaluate the scientific validity of this body of knowledge, but rather to analyze its cultural work. This chapter offers an analysis of the cultural stakes and knowledge-power of brain-based thinking about adolescence as it pervaded popular culture of the 1990s and beyond. In the broadest terms, to trace the cultural ascendance of neuro-science as it entered the popular consciousness is to probe the increasing inextricability of citizenship, medicine, optimization, and embodiment in the post-genomic age.[3]

Part of this story is old—another genealogical layer in ongoing debates about intersectionality, social constructionism, essentialism, and iden-tity waged in relation to cultural legacies of eugenics, scientific authority, and cultural citizenship amid rapid technological change. As the twentieth century drew to a close, the brain infused debates about multiculturalism, disability, AIDS, and mental illness. Alongside other marginalized groups such as African Americans and gay men, teen bodies and minds in particu-lar—always-already "crazy by design"—became highly visible foci of these debates. Medical anthropologists and science and technology historians have produced valuable critiques of the cultural politics of science by observing psychiatrists, neuroscientists, and geneticists and by scouring scientific jour-nals. Many have noted the unsettling ways in which specters of scientific rac-ism and sexology animate contemporary sciences of genetics and neurosci-ence by analyzing their "neoeugenic" tendencies.[4] Still others have analyzed the eugenic overtones of increasing technological control over reproduction, such as prenatal testing and genetic counseling that hold out the dream (or dystopia) of "designer babies," often by facilitating the selective abortion of disabled fetuses.[5] Likewise, cultural studies approaches to studying science and technology, emerging from disciplines as diverse as American studies, media studies, disability studies, and feminist science studies, have critiqued narratives of technological determinism that anthropomorphize technology and fail to account for the uneven, resistive, and creative ways it is culturally negotiated and understood.

Yet part of this story is also new—a story of technological intrigue comprising new imaging technologies, genetic mapping, and pharmaceutical promises of living "better than well" in the era dubbed by President George H. W. Bush as the "Decade of the Brain."[6] New discoveries like "neuroplasticity" gained cultural currency by promising that the brain would keep learning and changing, and, if its dynamism were properly harnessed, that people could continue optimizing its function and living better and longer lives. Likewise, new and controversial mood-altering pharmaceutical treatments for a variety of psychological conditions emerged, while direct-to-consumer advertising for antidepressants and other drugs on television simultaneously sparked familiar narratives of technological triumphalism and growing unease with the corporate privatization of medicine and health care. To trace the ascendance of this way of thinking about the body and citizenship through the cultural figure of "the teenager" is to show how (and how quickly) perpetual self-optimization became cast as a natural, universal, and compulsory facet of "healthy development" rather than a historical turn, steeped in the cultural and political economies of neoliberalism.

This new neuroscientific knowledge reflected a shift in cultural conceptions of health and able-bodiedness as perpetually unfinished projects. Importantly, I argue that this shift also required (and employed) a new conception of disability. By the 1990s, amid pervasive popular cultural representations of disability and a celebratory political embrace of multiculturalism and "neurodiversity," disability acquired a new discursive mobility. Through the combination of disability activism and heightened media visibility around the 1990 passage of the Americans with Disabilities Act (ADA), disability increasingly became visible as a politicized cultural identity and a claim to the entitlements of citizenship rather than solely a pathologized medical condition to be cured or rehabilitated. In essence, although disability had always *been* cultural, its cultural and political dimensions, rather than only its medical ones, became culturally legible in a post-ADA world. As previous chapters have argued, fictional representations of teen life have routinely used disability and overcoming to characterize sexual and emotional coming of age. However, in the Decade of the Brain, disability became much more than a metaphor, as it animated debates about proper parenting, antidepressants for youth, juvenile justice policies, school violence, and the origins and nature of sexual, gender, and racial difference. While news media and parenting guides represented neuroscientific insights as a way of making adolescence intelligible and manageable, the underdeveloped teen brain became construed as always-already maladjusted, threatening, and unmanageable.

Although the popular digestion of neuroscience configured all teens as disabled by their incomplete brains, this chapter shows the ways this discourse of adolescence-as-disability operated in gender-specific and racializing ways as the United States negotiated cultural changes wrought by civil rights, feminist, disability, and queer activism. This was due, in large part, to the specific context of these neuroscientific discoveries' emergence, as reportage of the inherently unstable and explosive teen brain collided with reportage of school shooting and "superpredator" epidemics of the 1990s as well as counterterrorist "information gathering" of the twentieth and twenty-first centuries.

Thus, in spotlighting the impaired adolescent brain, I aim to show how universalizing, transhistorical, and embodied notions of disability and adolescence have become increasingly *useful* to the privatizing logics of neoliberalism. Utopian dreams of engaging plasticity to cure social ills relied on essentialized notions of age (i.e., "healthy development") and disability (i.e., "overcoming disability") as mutually reinforcing discourses of depoliticization, as they were marshaled in service to a liberal humanism, bolstered by scientific knowledge and animated by the simple notion that we were all once teenagers who had overcome. Rehabilitating teens and the disabled—a seemingly apolitical good—became the preferred vehicle for a vision of a neoliberal, postracial, and postfeminist humanism that rested in physiology and individual will and actively disavowed and perpetuated structural inequality. Teens had become a species, characterized by biological risk factors. Time-worn depictions of "nurture," emblematized by external force explanations for the postwar rebel without a cause, gave way to late twentieth-century ideas about teens' fundamentally pathological "nature," as teens became patients with treatment options. Neuroparenting formed one of rehabilitative citizenship's lifelong treatment regimens for chronic youth.

New Frontiers: Temporary Insanity in the Decade of the Brain

Invoking imagery of the cosmos, *USA Today* reported in 1992 that the "new frontier" of the late twentieth and early twenty-first centuries would no longer be "the space between planets and solar systems," but rather the "trek" to the "inner space . . . between your ears."[7] While NASA may have dominated the public and popular scientific imaginations of the 1970s and 1980s, the "the gelatinous three-pound world called the brain" had replaced the moon as the great undiscovered country of the 1990s.[8] Journalists eagerly broke the brain down into its component pieces to demystify its functions, incorporating readers' very bodies into reportage of exciting neuroscientific discoveries. *Newsweek* science journalist Sharon Begley warned readers that, if they had purchased one of a thousand "test copies" of *Newsweek*, "a specially embedded microchip" would give them "a mild electric shock" while reading the article. Of course, the microchip was a fiction, but Begley continued, "Deep inside your brain, a little knob-shaped organ no bigger than a chickpea is going like gangbusters right now (at least if you're the gullible type)."[9] Readers were swept into the examining room from their living rooms as the brain arrived on the scene as a potent cultural force at the intersection of popular science, embodiment, and public policy.

On July 17, 1990, President George H. W. Bush proclaimed the 1990s the "Decade of the Brain," spurring a national initiative that was intricately linked to disability and citizenship. Linking a triumphal story of medical exploration that might lead to "improved treatments" for or "prevention" of disabilities such as paralysis, epilepsy, schizophrenia, autism, muscular dystrophy, and depression, Bush added that neuroscientific research might also aid the "war on drugs," "prevent harm done to the preborn children of pregnant women who abuse drugs and alcohol," and "enhance our understanding of Acquired Immune Deficiency Syndrome."[10] Here, a better understanding about the functions and malfunctions of the brain would not only rehabilitate diseased or disabled bodies, but also combat other national ills, such as drug abuse, bad motherhood, and AIDS.

Before the Decade of the Brain was named officially, the field of neuroscience was experiencing rapid growth but relatively low visibility. Although the presidential proclamation raised awareness of neurological disorders, it did not include actual funding for neuroscience research. Outside the laboratory, scientists and politicians lobbied for research funding by representing the Decade of the Brain, to Congress and to the American public, as a critical project for maintaining national health by curing disabilities. Dr. Lewis L. Judd, MD, chair of the Governmental and Public Affairs Committee for the Society for Neuroscience, appeared before the Senate Appropriations Subcommittee on Labor, Health, Human Services, and Education in 1994 to request government funding for neuroscience research. Invoking interlocking discourses of national, individual, and economic health, Judd warned Congress that underfunded neuroscience research would be "an

economic tragedy and detrimental for the health of the nation."[11] Reaffirming the presidential proclamation, Judd listed brain disorders among other
social problems, such as substance abuse and addiction (both "inextricably intertwined with the epidemic of violence in our society"), the "rapid
rise in suicide rate in our youth," the "mental enfeeblement" of people with
Alzheimer's disease, and the "scandal of the homeless mentally ill."[12] Judd
and others not only argued that curing brain disorders would lessen the
suffering of diseased and disabled people, but they also mobilized new post-
ADA disability political language about neuroscience's role in fostering the
autonomy and independence of American citizens "crippled" by brain disorders.[13] Dedicated neuroscientists, he argued, represented the "only real
hope" for the "tens of millions of our citizens who suffer from brain disorders" to be able "to live more productive and less disabled lives in the
future."[14] As they postured for government funding, scientists like Judd
appealed to seemingly apolitical notions of individual and national health
and the cure of disease and disability, even while the disability rights movement continued to demand that access to society, employment, and political representation, rather than cures for impairments, were its community's
"real hope" for the future.

The Decade of the Brain proclamation was also a federal response to
simultaneous reports, issued by the National Institute of Neurological Disorders and Stroke and the National Advisory Mental Health Council, which
declared neurological disorders to be among the most pervasive and costly
problems facing America in the coming decade.[15] Nine days after his Decade
of the Brain proclamation, Bush signed the ADA into law. The law created
civil rights protections for people with disabilities, including equal access
to employment, public institutions, transportation, and telephone services
for the deaf. Positioning the ADA within legacies of the Civil Rights Act of
1964, Bush portrayed the ADA, "the world's first comprehensive declaration
of equality for people with disabilities," as irrefutable evidence of American exceptionalism and of the United States' geopolitical position as global
human rights "leader."[16] Bush also highlighted the act's international rever-
berations when he suggested that other nations follow the United States'
lead in disability rights, concluding his speech with the command, "Let the
shameful wall of exclusion finally come tumbling down," a subtle invocation
of Ronald Reagan's oft-quoted 1989 directive to the Soviet leader Mikhail
Gorbachev to "tear down that wall" in Berlin, Germany.[17]

The ADA was undoubtedly a landmark victory for disabled citizens
and activists. However, it was also part of a larger neoliberal privatization
of collective struggle that coexisted with (and in some ways facilitated) a

concomitant rollback of economic, political, and cultural commitments toward welfare endorsed by conservatives and liberals. The ADA further entrenched a notion of citizenship based *not* on disability pride, interdependency, and collective care (the core tenets of the Berkeley independent living movement), but rather on enshrined able-bodied American neoliberal ideals of productivity, liberal individualism, and the free market: "more productive and less disabled lives." For instance, President George H. W. Bush responded to concerns about the potential legal and financial ramifications of the ADA with "a special word to our friends in the business community":

> This act does something important for American business. . . : You've called for new sources of workers. Well, many of our fellow citizens with disabilities are unemployed. They want to work, and they can work. . . . And remember, this is a tremendous pool of people who will bring to jobs diversity, loyalty, proven low turnover rate, and only one request: the chance to prove themselves. And when you add together Federal, State, local, and private funds, it costs almost $200 billion annually to support Americans with disabilities—in effect, to keep them dependent. Well, when given the opportunity to be independent, they will move proudly into the economic mainstream of American life, and that's what this legislation is all about.[18]

The Decade of the Brain and the ADA were a complex and interrelated neoliberal economic proposition: cures for neurological disabilities promised to stem the economic drain posed by the disabled, while access to employment would "mainstream" disabled workers into full participation in American capitalism by alleviating their dependence on costly government services. With respect to the Decade of the Brain, this emphasis on technological advancement in the (seemingly apolitical) name of health found political traction in an era of neoliberal privatization and the erosion of Great Society commitments to social welfare programs. Bush's framing of the ADA emphasizes decreasing welfare dependence, an implicit invocation of Reagan's well-publicized assault on "welfare queens." Using the image of welfare "dependency," Bush's speech subtly distinguished the worthy disabled worker from the nondisabled (and presumed nonwhite) welfare abuser. Six years after Bush's ADA speech, President William Jefferson Clinton would sign the Personal Responsibility and Work Opportunity Reconciliation Act of 1996 (PRWORA), which slashed funding for basic social programs for low-income children, families, the elderly, disabled people, and immigrants and signaled, in his words, "the end of welfare as we know it."

Thus, Judd's phrase "more productive and less disabled lives" simultaneously reinforced disability as an undesirable medicalized condition even while it invoked a vision of access to economic productivity building on the inclusion rhetoric of the ADA. It is a striking juxtaposition when we consider that, less than ten days prior to the ADA's passage, the Decade of the Brain was established, promising cures to some of those with "disorders" who had been fighting for accommodation and access to equal employment in the first place. While the Decade of the Brain sought to integrate the disabled through individuating neurological rehabilitation and cure, the ADA figured individual participation in the free market as the ultimate expression of civil rights and independence. An emphasis on individual demands for accommodation offered disabled workers autonomy and opportunity, but did so by emphasizing personal responsibility over collective struggle. As I will show, proponents of neuroparenting also capitalized on new, post-ADA universalizing discourses of disability inclusion (as an apolitical good) to emphasize personal responsibility, medical intervention, and compassion for disabling adolescence. Increasingly imagining adolescence as an individual pathology rather than a social experience, neuroparenting medicalized "normal" adolescence and downplayed educational, familial, cultural, and socioeconomic factors that affected teen lives.

While scientists emphasized cures for disabilities during the Decade of the Brain, visualizing and mapping the "normal" brain ranked among their most crucial goals. After all, maintained *Newsweek*, "[r]esearch on brain-damaged people" risked not being "representative" of "us" (the presumed-normal population).[19] For the first time in history, images of live brains began circulating widely in popular culture as entertainment, education, and objects of controversy. This proliferation of brain imagery owed in large part to the sophistication of medical imaging technologies throughout the 1980s and 1990s. Meanwhile, a concomitant development of wide-ranging "neuroinformatics" technologies centralized neurological information flows through the creation of globally accessible computer databases through the Human Brain Project (HBP). As the Internet permeated American culture and became equated with the democratization of knowledge, the HBP promised to create a "global . . . 'corporate brain,'" a computer database of brain scans and histories to act "as a central resource for researchers around the world."[20] The true power of new imaging techniques like positron emission tomography (PET), according to some journalists, was not their curative promise for ill brains but rather their voyeuristic ability "to peer inside the minds of the healthy," rather than drawing conclusions from psychiatric evaluations or dead brain tissue.[21]

PET scans began to appear in popular magazines by the early 1980s, purportedly to illustrate the difference between normality and mental illness. For example, a 1983 issue of *Vogue* featured an article entitled "High-Tech Breakthrough in Medicine: New Seeing-Eye Machines . . . [That] Look inside Your Body, Can Save Your Life." Alongside the piece, three PET scans of brains appeared with boldface, white, single-word captions describing the brain below it: "NORMAL," "SCHIZO," and "DEPRESSED."[22] Similarly, in the 1990s, *Newsweek* ran a cover story entitled "Mapping the Brain," which featured six PET images meant to establish a visual contrast between "normal" brains and disabled or unhealthy brains: a learning brain alongside a brain performing a routine; the brain of a "retarded patient" that is "much more active" than the brain of a "normal volunteer"; and a "clinically depressed person" alongside a "healthy person."[23] Reportage like this assiduously crafted a unified population of "healthy" brains in contrast to unhealthy ones.

These images not only were sources of cultural fascination but also wielded immense cultural power in debates about social constructionism and essentialism as they related to the origins of identity and social inequality. Begley described the persistent invocation of the brain to "prove" a host of cultural differences—such as gender, race, sexuality, criminality, and eventually, generational conflict between adolescents and adults—as the indisputable "triumph of materialism."[24] Brain scan imagery and biochemical explanations for behavior and identity pervaded American culture throughout the 1990s, as journalists avidly engaged in rhetorical dissections of gray matter, reporting evidence of a "gay brain," a "lesbian ear," and gendered differences in corpus callosum size that might map the location of "female intuition."

The biologist and feminist science historian Anne Fausto-Sterling described an explosion of newspaper and magazine coverage of new discoveries about the corpus callosum, a bundle of nerve fibers connecting the right- and left-brain hemispheres, in 1992. Scientists had found that the organ was larger and more bulbous in women's brains than in men's, seemingly substantiating the titular phrase of the best-selling *Men Are from Mars, Women Are from Venus* of the same year.[25] *Newsweek* and *Time* ran parallel feature stories about gender differences and brain anatomy, as journalists, scientists, and readers surmised that the corpus callosum might be "the basis of woman's intuition" or provide an explanation for women's superior verbal skills in contrast to men's stronger visual-spatial ones.[26]

One year later, Simon LeVay's controversial book *The Sexual Brain* (1993) cited brain research from the early 1990s to argue that homosexuality was a neurological condition rooted in the hypothalamus, the portion of the brain that regulates appetite, body temperature, and sexual behavior. LeVay compared the hypothalami of men who had died of AIDS with those of men and women who were (presumed to be) heterosexual. Problematically reading the presence of AIDS as indicative of cadavers' homosexuality, LeVay found the gay men's organ to be smaller than heterosexual men's but nearly the same size as heterosexual women's.[27] Likewise, in 1992, scientists from the UCLA School of Medicine reported, based on autopsy studies, that a brain structure called the "anterior commissure" was 34 percent larger in homosexual men than in heterosexual men.[28] It was even reported in the early to mid-1990s that gay men had more ridges than usual in their fingerprints and that a greater percentage of gay men were left-handed, which, scientists and journalists argued, "bolstered" the theory that sexual orientation was determined in utero.[29] Size did matter, apparently, at least when it came to hypothalami or fingertip ridges.

In making an argument about the congenital nature of homosexuality, LeVay mobilized a medical model of disability to liberate homosexuality from the moral model of choice and from the psychiatric model of deviance. In doing so, LeVay and others hoped that if homosexuality were to be "viewed as something innate, rather than, say, a perverted reaction to a bad upbringing," then homosexuals might gain greater societal acceptance.[30] However, although the findings endeavored to depoliticize and depathologize homosexuality, they ended up scientifically reaffirming heterosexual desire as a prediscursive, brain-based given. For example, the findings equated male homosexuality with a "feminine" desire for men, a finding that biologized as natural the complementary male/female sexual binary, which, as Judith Butler famously argued, constructs heterosexuality as prediscursively natural.

Others were less optimistic than LeVay about the ramifications of such discoveries. Ingeborg L. Ward, a Villanova University professor of psychology, recalled gay and lesbian activism in the 1970s that had resulted in the 1973 removal of homosexuality from the *Diagnostic and Statistical Manual of Mental Disorders* (DSM), and she worried that after the gay community had "worked very hard and long to persuade psychiatrists that [being gay] shouldn't fall into the category of mental illness," new neuroscience research might reaffirm rather than contest the homosexuality-as-mental-illness thesis.[31] As I will discuss in the second part of this chapter, this thrust to biologize gender, sexuality, race, and age by rooting it in the brain was a cultural refraction of postfeminism, gay and lesbian liberation, disability rights, and the long civil rights movement.

Among other controversial brain discoveries, stories about teens' unfinished brains and their bad decisions had reached fever pitch and played out the "nature versus nurture" debate. By the late 1980s, citing an increase in teen accidents and violence, various private foundations, medical professionals, and the federal government took action by undertaking a joint program of research "on why teen-agers take so many foolish risks."[32] A "notoriously reckless group" defined by "acrobatics on skateboards" and "sex without contraceptives," adolescents, the New York Times article reported in 1987, were the only age group with an increasing mortality rate, with reportedly three-quarters of teen deaths caused by accidents, homicide, and suicide, all of which indicated "a lethal propensity for risk-taking."[33] In the words of one developmental psychologist, "young people are essentially . . . dying of their own reckless behavior."[34]

In an attempt to save teens from themselves, psychologists and psychiatrists at the NIMH devised ways "to identify teen-agers most likely to take dangerous risks" along with the risks they were most likely to take.[35] One study, undertaken by a health psychologist at the University of California at San Francisco, profiled likely risk takers, whom she named "bad girls" and "macho boys." Based on a study undertaken on girls aged eleven to fourteen in "inner-city" schools of San Francisco (a designation that hinted at a nonwhite population without officially declaring it), this research defined "bad girls" as being characterized by "drinking, fighting, hitchhiking, arguing with strangers, seeking entertainment in high-crime areas and carrying a knife." However, the "hallmark of the most reckless girls" was their desire to become sexually active within the next year—a desire, reported the study, less common among girls engaging in fewer risky behaviors.[36] Tellingly, no such definitive sexual marker emerged for "macho boys," who often drank, smoked cigarettes and marijuana, rode motorcycles, and got knocked unconscious. Getting knocked up or knocked out seemed the most present threat for bad girls and macho boys, respectively—discoveries that reaffirmed traditional gender roles by assigning gender-differentiated notions of "deviant" behavior.

While the "bad girls" and "macho boys" theory described the psychological underpinnings of and the contributions of environmental stimuli to teen deviance, the article featured another perspective: that biology was a bigger piece of the puzzle. In the same article, another psychologist reported that "sensation-seeking," his neologism for a personality trait that "include[d] the desire for thrills and adventure, the enjoyment of physically risky activities and the need for sensory and social stimulation such as loud music or parties," peaked during the late teen years but declined gradually throughout life.[37] Teenaged thrill seekers possessed a lethal combination of higher testosterone levels and lower levels of monoamine oxidase (MAO), an enzyme that regulates levels of serotonin and other brain chemicals. People with lower MAO levels, psychologists argued, tended to seek out addictive substances and were more likely to have a criminal record.[38]

Essentially, while this article differentiated teenagers from children as a necessary site of intervention, it generally rehashed timeworn "nature versus nurture" debates about childhood development. In doing so, it also linked sexual activity among adolescent girls with delinquency (without making a similar claim about sexually active teen boys), a persistent gendered double standard haunted by eugenic-era associations of "feeblemindedness" with young female promiscuity.[39] However, in 1991, a mere four years later, the first-ever long-term and largest pediatric neuroimaging project in the world would alter forever the terms of this debate. Through the 1990s, Dr. Jay Giedd and his research team at the National Institute of Mental Health (NIMH)'s Child Psychiatry Branch acquired over three thousand MRI scans in the largest pediatric neuroimaging project in the world.[40] Chosen carefully to represent "the racial and socioeconomic mix of America," healthy subjects (defined as those without diagnosed mental illnesses, learning disabilities, or behavioral problems and not wearing braces) between the ages of five and twenty-five volunteered to complete behavior questionnaires and undergo an MRI scan and cognitive testing ("computer games"), after which they could be invited back for follow-up visits at two-year intervals. The NIMH paid families for their participation and even offered souvenir photographs of their children's brains. Maintaining a strict division between normal and abnormal bodies and brains, Giedd asserted that amassing images of normal brains promised cures for diseased or disabled brains, because such a large pool of neurotypical subjects formed a much-needed control group: "We need to study normal teenagers, and we need to look at those same normal teenage brains over and over. How can we ever help kids with problems if we don't know what normal is?"[41]

Previously, theories of neuroplasticity maintained that the period between birth and age five was a "critical period" in development, because once the first five years of life had elapsed, the neurotypical human brain was fully grown and no longer malleable. Since the average adolescent brain is the same size as an average adult's, scientists thought that a teen's hormone-besieged body was the only thing undergoing change during puberty.[42] Jean Piaget, the founder of developmental psychology, had dubbed the final stage of development, from eleven to sixteen years, "formal operational thinking," or when a child learns abstract thinking. Following

Piaget's thinking, developmental psychologists had assumed that neuro-typical children basically had complete, fully functional adult brains "that simply needed more experience to become fully mature."[43] When developmental psychologists discussed biological factors of adolescence (and usually in relation to teen deviance), they assumed that raging hormones only exacerbated the main problem of teens' lack of life experience and identity crises. Physiological factors still remained subordinate to psychological or sociological ones in such analyses.

Giedd's neuroimaging project inexorably shattered cultural and scientific assumptions about teen completeness. "Far from being an innocent bystander to hormonal hijinks," reported Barbara Strauch, the teen brain underwent another period of massive transformation comparable to that which occurred in early brain development of children.[44] If teen brains were previously thought to be completed, inflexible, and recalcitrant objects, by the 1990s they were described by scientists and science journalists as "raw, vulnerable," "work[s] in progress," and "giant construction project[s]."[45] As the teen brain gained new flexibility, it quickly became a new object of intervention. Between 2000 and 2005, *Time*, *U.S. News & World Report*, and *Scientific American Mind* each ran cover stories on the teen brain that linked brain underdevelopment to the emotional turmoil and irresponsible behavior that was imagined to be characteristic of adolescence.

While neuroscientists broke down the adolescent brain into discrete areas that experienced change, science writers/journalists translated their findings into explanations for teenage behavior and advice for more enlightened parenting. By the end of the decade, multiple parenting and education books synthesized new discoveries in adolescent neuroscience for flummoxed parents, teachers of unruly teens, and even teens themselves boasting sensational titles such as *The Primal Teen: What the New Discoveries about the Teenage Brain Tell Us about Our Kids* (2003); *Yes, Your Teen Is Crazy! Loving Your Kid without Losing Your Mind* (2003); *Why Are They So Weird! What's Really Going on in a Teenager's Brain* (2004); *Why Do They Act That Way? A Survival Guide to the Adolescent Brain for You and Your Teen* (2005); and *Parenting the Teenage Brain: Understanding a Work in Progress* (2007).

Books specifically marketed to teens rather than their parents also incorporated neuroparenting insights. For example, the best-selling *Deal with It! A Whole New Approach to Your Body, Brain, and Life as a gURL* (1999) devoted an entire section to the brain, with one subsection called "Surviving the Insanity."[46] Also targeting a teen audience, the cover of Dale Carlson and Nancy Teasdale's *Teen Brain Book: Who and What Are You* (2004) pitched itself to teens with the following promise: "Understand your brain, how it works, how you got the way you are, how to rewire yourself, your personality, what makes you suffer."[47] The multicultural cover art of the book shows cartoon images of teenagers with particular emotions underneath their animated faces. Four white teenagers appear on the cover with the attributes "happy," "sad," "wired," and "lonely." Two dark-skinned girls also appear on the cover with the attributes "angry" and "scared" above their heads. A giant brain, which reaches out to each face with a thin squiggle, appears in the middle to emphasize one shared volatile brain. However, while the cover illustration gestures toward a shared raceless humanism—a universal and multicultural teen experience of "suffering" at the hands of underdeveloped neurology—it is notable that the faces subtly reaffirm racist stereotypes like the "angry black woman."

Teen bodies, always-already crazy, irrational, and explosive, materialized as simultaneously neurologically "proven" and as a preexisting condition into which neuroscience intervened. New neuroscientific discoveries about the teen brain emphasized the importance of the prefrontal cortex (PFC); the "limbic brain," a system that includes sections such as the amygdala, hippocampus, and hypothalamus; and finally, the cerebellum. For example, neuroscientists discovered that when teens were asked to interpret facial expressions, brain scans showed that they used the amygdala rather than the PFC, which led them to (mis)identify a fearful or surprised face as an angry one. However, to make the stakes of these findings legible to a nonscientific audience, neuroparenting book authors relied on strategies of translation that emphasized the correlation between the organs themselves and undesirable teen behaviors. For instance, Strauch's *Primal Teen* describes the amygdala as an almond-shaped "seat of fear and anger" that is responsible for instinctual actions such as "fight-or-flight, anger, or 'I hate you, Mom,'" in contrast to the PFC, which she describes as the "most human" part of the brain.[48] If teens responded to social cues with the amygdala, the brain's "primal emotional center," rather than its rational center, neuroscience helped explicate "why teenagers . . . often seem[ed] to overreact, emotionally erupt for no apparent reason."[49] Now the "myelination" (the development of insulating "sheaths" around neurons that increase the speed and efficiency of neural impulses) occurring in the PFC during adolescence "account[ed] for the lightning-quick flashes of anger" that often accompanied a parental request to an adolescent child to "get off the computer" so other family members could use it.[50] Meanwhile, David Walsh's *Why Do They Act That Way?* describes the PFC as the brain's "CEO" (an interesting economic metaphor in an age of neoliberal upward redistribution), the seat of rationality and adulthood, "the part that helps us cast a wary eye, link cause to effect, decide 'maybe not'—the part, in fact, that acts grown-up."[51] Thus, while neuroscience offered explanations for teens' impulse-driven decision-making processes, neuroparenting experts assigned developmental designations to parts of the brain: the stable PFC henceforth became equated with adulthood, while the more primal and impulsive amygdala became configured as inherently teenaged. Development was then represented as a process of "progressive inhibition," in which the frontal lobes became more adept at inhibiting inappropriate actions, evaluating risks, and making "good decisions."[52] In contrast to stable adults and their stable PFCs, teenagers, in this framework, emerged as irrational, erratic, and perhaps even pre-human, by design.

Linking the new undeveloped teenaged brain to some of the same national problems cited in Bush's proclamation, journalists and neuroparenting experts covered Giedd's discoveries with fervor, making the teen brain culturally legible by explaining the biological roots of good judgment, responsible behavior, and deviance. Since teens' brains weren't fully developed until age twenty-five, one journalist remarked, "it [wa]s no big surprise" that teens were more likely to be victims of car accidents or crime than any other age group; that "the vast majority" of smokers and alcoholics got their start as teens; or that "a quarter of all people with HIV contract[ed] it before age 21."[53] However, rather than problematizing social issues adversely affecting teens, like archaic sex education curricula, inaccessible contraceptives, or racial profiling, "limbic fireworks" became the privileged culprit behind "[a] lot of teen impulsiveness and anger" and deviant behavior.[54] The guilty amygdala incited teen anger, while an underactive ventral striatum caused teen laziness.[55] An underdeveloped PFC explained poor decision making: "most young people don't have all the brain power needed for good judgment."[56]

Other findings often played up and reaffirmed traditional gender binaries between teen girls and boys by emphasizing differences in their affective responses to their underdeveloped neurology. Walsh described boys as "emotional powder kegs" of "anger, aggression, sexual interest, dominance, and territoriality" because of testosterone's "powerful effect on the amygdala."[57] He added that an understanding of "brain chemistry" could "help girls," configured as always-already inherently emotive subjects, "deal with emotional fluctuations" and chemical surges that "amplifi[ed] . . . a wide range of emotions," causing "their moods [to] go haywire."[58] Gender distinctions in neurology were even to blame for gender differences in performance on the SAT. Citing a report from the Society of Neuroscience, a *Washington Post* article titled "Neurobiology: Seasonal Advantage on the SAT?" fretted that "[m]illions" of adolescent "American males may be damaging their academic futures by taking the [SAT] . . . while in the grip of raging hormonal imbalances."[59] Although women performed the same on the SAT in the fall and the spring, men scored nearly 25 percent higher on tests involving spatial reasoning in the spring—"when their testosterone levels were [naturally] the lowest" in their annual cycle. In the age of feminist critiques of sexism in the classroom, like Mary Pipher's best-selling *Reviving Ophelia*, neuroscientific knowledge seemed to bolster claims that perhaps feminists had gone too far in emphasizing girls' scholastic achievement and gendered inequities in education and had placed boys at an unfair disadvantage.

Although science and news media portrayed teens at the mercy of their brains, experts invited parents to train their teens' brains to encourage the development of the proper circuitry essential for successful adulthood by abandoning parenting training that was now "obsolete" in the face of neuro-discoveries.[60] Parenting books explained that "we had no idea why adolescents sometimes act the way they do" until neuroscience granted the tools to "explain adolescence better than ever before."[61] Demystifying adolescent monstrosities, parenting books promised that "[s]eemingly unrelated behaviors, like sleeping late, acting territorial, bursting into tears for no reason, and taking risks" would "make much more sense when you know what's happening inside the adolescent's brain."[62] Neuroparenting proponents asserted that when parents battled with teens, the parent should no longer fault the teen for "being difficult or having a bad attitude." Rather, armed with enlightened neuroparenting skills, the parent should realize "it's his brain's fault" and that he "may really be interpreting the outside world, especially emotional messages, differently" than normal—in other words, differently from adults.[63]

The most common depiction of adolescence offered in neuroparenting discourses was an image of teenagers as temporarily insane or disabled. "What used to be a sad, quiet joke between Mom and Dad," argued Bradley, was now a proven "neurological fact": "*Your kid is crazy . . . Adolescents are temporarily brain-damaged.*"[64] Bradley playfully teases about teens being mentally ill and provides a humorous list of "common adolescent disorders," such as "*Aphasia Whenus Iwannus,*" a "disability" resulting in "sudden loss of speech . . . [and] hearing . . . most pronounced with sounds that mimic parental voices asking questions about chores or homework."[65] Other writers like Strauch labeled teens "crazy by design," while Bradley described teens alternately as "not . . . bad pe[ople], just brain-challenged," "temporarily disabled," "brain-damaged . . . in a value-damaged world," "neurologically handicapped," and exhibiting "insane behaviors" because of a "misfiring brain."[66]

In marshaling metaphors of disability to characterize nondisabled adolescence as a disability, proponents of neuroparenting engaged in two contradictory impulses. First, even when neuroparenting experts recognized the
ableist insensitivity of their claims, they used the language of mental illness
casually and unapologetically to universally characterize adolescence. Bradley is the boldest in this regard, writing that he fully intended to be "flippant
and insensitive" by using the language of mental illness: "Calling teenagers
'crazy' may alarm or offend some of you who have dealt firsthand with true
mental illness, especially in your own families (as I have)," he writes, but he
argues for the validity of this approach, because this language of mental illness derives from "27 years" worth of frustrated parents.[67]

At the same time, neuroparenting texts also tried to draw careful distinctions between "real disability" (i.e., diagnosed mental illness) and "discursive disability" (i.e., normal adolescence). Many publications, bearing
chapter titles such as "Adolescent Insanity: What's Normal, What's Not,"
sought to help parents distinguish between "serious mental illness" and
"normal teenage insanity," whose resemblance to true mental illness "can
get confusing and frightening" for parents and teens.[68] Texts like Bradley's
simultaneously worked to collapse the distinction between "true mental illness" and adolescence, often while paradoxically warning readers against
unjustifiably "tattoo[ing] . . . kids who act out" with "words like 'antisocial,'
'psychopathic,' and sociopathic.'"[69] However, whether or not their teenagers
were "normally brain-disordered from adolescence or more seriously ill,"
Bradley enjoined parents to "*separate the disease from the child bearing it*"
(italics in original) and to bear in mind that their neurotypical teen was
"not insane, just crazy."[70]

A baby boomer model of intensive and nonjudgmental parenting found
a new language, predicated on understanding the inherent qualities and
differences of teen gray matter. The adolescence-as-mental-illness model,
combined with the notion that teen brains were not complete (and thus still
changeable), as previously believed, meant that parents need not worry that
teen behaviors were immutable "character flaws or signs of an evil nature."[71]
For example, encouraging teens to "think before they speak or act," one parenting book maintained, would ensure that the good neural "connections"
associated with emotional restraint would survive the pruning process at the
end of adolescence.[72] This advice rested on the "use-it-or-lose-it" neuroscientific principle that, after the adolescent-stage overproduction of neurons, the
pruning back of underused neurons occurs so that those not "used" are lost.
Even though it was certainly "not the teen's fault that his brain [was]sn't under
his control," the new neuroscience-inflected parenting advice encouraged

parents to provide "guidance and structure" that teens would "eventually internalize" physiologically in their fully developed PFC.[73] Encouraging teens to undertake community service was indispensable "while major brain circuits related to social relationships" were "blossoming and pruning."[74] Conflicts between parents and children were now "just the result of mixed-up wiring" that would fix itself in time if patient parents "calmly but firmly t[aught] brain-challenged children to become functional adults."[75] By linking formerly unexplainable adolescent behavior to underdeveloped parts of the brain, scientists indelibly altered the cultural figure of the teenager and ushered in a new, more compassionate, scientifically enlightened, and increasingly medicalized image of teens as temporarily disabled.

Indeed, neuroparenting's configuration of teenagers as blameless, both for the imperfections of their developing brains and for the bad decisions caused by these imperfections, was indebted to the new post-ADA cultural model of disability, which distinguished "impairment," a natural variation from the norm, from "disability," a condition created by an inaccessible environment or social stigma. Neuroparenting destigmatized adolescence by considering it an "impairment" that was exacerbated by unenlightened parents, teachers, and policy makers. However, even while it traded on newer compassionate rehabilitative logics of effacement and inclusion that had begun to take hold in the wake of the passage of the ADA as well as activism for "neurodiversity," neuroparenting relied on and reinforced a problematic notion of disability as deficiency or insufficiency to be overcome (in the case of teens, through "growing up"). It associated disability with immaturity, bolstering and bolstered by infantilizing images of disabled adults. Since teen brains became understood as "plastic," and thus still susceptible to good as well as bad influences, compassionate parental and governmental disciplinary intervention into teens' proper development into good citizens became not only socially but neurologically imperative. If parents intervened in this "neurological window of opportunity" that previous generations of scientists and parents "never knew existed," they could "*rewire that head*" for healthy citizenship.[76]

"Armed, Alienated, and Adolescent": Race, Masculinity, and Violence

Amid the windfall of new neurological explanations for the condition and symptoms of adolescence, observers debated which types of risk-taking behaviors could be characterized as normal and central to psychological growth and which types indicated something more pathological churning beneath the surface.[77] Moreover, while neuroparenting discourses promoted more compassionate forms of child-centered parenting, the "temporarily insane" teen brain likewise became a financially lucrative cultural norm in the dawning antidepressant age. As direct-to-consumer advertising permeated popular culture, anti-psychiatry and psychiatric survivor movements, galvanized by the passage of the ADA, critiqued the increasing medicalization and pharmaceutical treatment of adolescence. The *New York Times* neatly encapsulated this cultural transition toward the pharmaceutical management of youth in its pithy observation that slacker "Generation X" had become "Generation Rx."[78]

While news media and parenting guides represented adolescent brain discoveries as a way of making adolescence intelligible and manageable, the underdeveloped teen brain also became construed as dangerous, especially when this brain image was juxtaposed with a perceived rise in youth violence.[79] A rash of teenaged violence—both in terms of "school shooting" and "superpredator" epidemics—in the 1990s worked to focus governmental and parental interventions on white teen boys and their mental health. Media coverage of the shootings constructed images of "normal" teen rebelliousness as always-already potentially pathological and produced an image of the teen brain as always-already maladjusted and threatening if not constantly surveilled and disciplined. The potential for teen violence raised the stakes of neurological findings, and did so in racially specific ways. As I will show, the fearsome specter of the superpredator—the unrehabilitatable, nonwhite criminal—provided a necessary foil to the imperiled white, heterosexual, suburban, middle-class boys who were the victims and perpetrators of a school shooting epidemic.

Amid reportage of numerous American school shootings, the need to manage crisis-ridden teenagers had never seemed so dire. In 1993, Pearl Jam, an American grunge rock band, received four MTV Video Music Awards, including Video of the Year, for their song "Jeremy." *Entertainment Weekly*'s Michele Romero described the video as "an *Afterschool Special* from hell."[80] Inspired by a 1991 newspaper account of fifteen-year-old Jeremy Wade Delle, who committed suicide in a Texas classroom filled with his schoolmates, the acclaimed video depicts a young boy who brings a gun to school after being taunted by his peers and ignored by his parents. It opens with collages of newspapers, overlaid with prominent text reading, "62 degrees and cloudy" and "an affluent suburb." The climax of the video occurs when a shirtless Jeremy enters the classroom, tosses an apple to the teacher, and stands before his classmates. Although Pearl Jam's original video featured Jeremy inserting a gun into his mouth over the song's moaning refrain, "Jeremy spoke in class today," MTV's rules about violent imagery restricted the video from showing its footage as originally shot. Shot in black and white, the final sequence features a close-up of Jeremy's face and then pans across the classroom to reveal Jeremy's classmates, frozen in horror and with crimson blood staining their stark white shirts and faces. With the removal of the footage of the gun, many viewers misinterpreted the ending, believing that Jeremy had shot his classmates rather than himself.[81]

Pearl Jam's video was at once timely and prophetic with its ambiguous suicide/homicide ending. According to Jessie Klein, there have been 137 fatal school shootings that have killed 297 victims since 1980, and each decade has witnessed more shooting deaths than the previous.[82] As numerous highly publicized school shootings erupted into the news in the mid- to late 1990s, the most famous of which was the 1999 Columbine massacre, by Dylan Klebold and Eric Harris, Americans feared that school violence was accelerating to reach epidemic proportions.[83] In 1996, Barry Loukaitis, a fourteen-year-old honors student at Frontier Junior High School in Moses Lake, Washington, gunned down two classmates and his teacher and quoted a passage from Stephen King's *Rage* (1977), a story about school violence, to characterize his actions: "This sure beats algebra, doesn't it?"[84] In what became known as the "Pearl Jam defense," lawyers argued that Loukaitis had drawn inspiration from the "Jeremy" music video. Jurors screened the video in the courtroom during Loukaitis's trial.[85] One year later, Evan Ramsey, fifteen, who was often bullied with disability epithets like "retard" and "spaz," killed the principal and one student with a pump action shotgun.[86] A mere two months later, in Springfield, Oregon, fifteen-year-old Kip Kinkel killed his parents, and the next morning, Kinkel opened fire in his cafeteria, killing two students and wounding twenty-two others at Thurston High School, in spite of being arrested and released the day before the shooting for bringing a gun to school. Then, on April 20, 1999, in Littleton, Colorado, the infamous Columbine tragedy occurred: Dylan Klebold, eighteen, and Eric Harris, seventeen, wounded twenty-three students and killed twelve students and a teacher before turning their guns on themselves.[87] Investigations revealed that Harris and Klebold had plotted for at least a year to kill at least five hundred people and blow up their school, and just as in Loukatis's trial, Harris's and Klebold's steady diet of "unhealthy media" (e.g., music by Marilyn Manson and violent videogames like *Quake* and *Doom*) also formed a dominant framing device for understanding their violent impulses, breathing new life (now that experience could become biology) into a longer conversation about youth media consumption and violent behavior extending forward from the Cold War. Until the tragic Virginia Tech school shooting of 2007, in which Cho Seung-Hui killed thirty-two people and wounded twenty-five others, the Columbine massacre was the deadliest school shooting in American history.

Racial and class politics of the shootings were an unacknowledged center strand of the media stories. Without acknowledging the classist and racist assumptions underpinning the shock about school shootings in white middle-class suburbs, some journalists had named the 1996 school shooting incident by Barry Loukaitis a focusing event in which an "urban trend" of schoolyard violence took a "rural turn."[88] The same reporter asked with incredulity "why this is happening now in white, rural areas" when before, it had been contained to "gang-related . . . stabbing . . . involv[ing] money or a fight over a girlfriend." In the wake of the Columbine massacre, journalists noted that it was "ironic that levels of violence among urban youth and gangs" was "down," while violence involving "teens in the suburbs has not received the same amount of attention."[89] Narratives of Columbine cultivated an image of school violence as *naturally* occurring in urban schools and nonwhite populations, by spotlighting its unnaturalness in a white suburban school. As Todd Ramlow argues, journalists actively ignored the suffering of "[u]nderclass and inner-city teens [who] ha[d] faced quotidian school violence for decades" when they accentuated the "surprising" horrors of white suburban school violence.[90] Thus, "school shooters" denoted the *shocking* violence perpetrated by white, middle- to upper-class, suburban adolescent males, prompting one reporter's ominous remark that teen boys were "armed, alienated, and adolescent."[91]

Neurological ideas about the teen brain and its relationship to violent behavior circulated with greater urgency as they quickly entered the conversation about teen school shooters. In the wake of the Charles "Andy" Williams school shooting in 2001, Daniel R. Weinberger, director of the Clinical Brain Disorders Laboratory at the National Institutes of Health (NIH), wrote an op-ed piece for the *New York Times* that made similar assertions.[92] In his op-ed, Weinberger stated that "[t]o understand what goes wrong in teenagers who fire guns, you have to understand something about the biology of the teenage brain"; nonetheless, he reminded readers, his neurobiological perspective was "not meant to absolve criminal behavior."[93] Since teens' PFCs were immature and incomplete, their brains did not possess "the biological machinery to inhibit impulses in the service of long-range planning."[94] Readers, including doctors and psychologists, lined up to respond to Weinberger in subsequent issues under the physiology-inflected title "The Anatomy of a Teenage Shooting." These responses refocused the topic from gun control to teens' biological predispositions toward bad decision making (e.g., "no amount of gun-safety education will serve to endow a child with that which God ha[d] not yet seen fit to grant"); historicizing evidence of responsible adolescence ("Until recent times, children who reached biological maturity . . . were treated as adults[;] Benjamin Franklin was an apprentice printer at age 12, and his brain was evidently well enough developed to plan for the future"); and argued that choice can always win out, even over underdeveloped biology (Andy Williams's classmates "presumably had equally immature brains, and likely none of them came close to losing control in such a manner").[95]

As new neuroimaging technologies emerged, debates about their potential use in criminal trials raged. Neuroimaging had already sparked a nationwide debate on the insanity defense by the mid-1980s, with the introduction of a CT scan of John Hinckley Jr.'s brain as evidence to substantiate a biological explanation for Hinckley's attempt to assassinate President Ronald Reagan.[96] Despite the protestations of many neurologists, brain scans increasingly became regarded as admissible and authoritative courtroom evidence. In a veritable Hinckley trial redux, debates again raged about whether or not brain scans depicting "physical defects" should be admissible as material evidence that Kip Kinkel was schizophrenic and "b[ore] diminished responsibility" for the shootings.[97] Despite prosecutorial protest, two doctors testified in defense of Kinkel, finding similarities in his brain scan to those of thirty-one murderers and substantiating a diagnosis of schizophrenia.[98] Kinkel pled guilty, abandoning his initial insanity plea, and received a sentence of 111 years in prison.[99]

The gender politics of the 1990s also informed cultural perceptions of white school shooters. Massive ongoing societal changes challenged the patriarchal order in the late twentieth century. These included the destabilization of patriarchal power by feminist and gay liberation movements, the elimination of blue-collar jobs in a transitioning economy, and the rise of multiculturalism and affirmative action, all of which represented threats to heteronormative white masculinity, and by extension, white teen boy masculinity. By the mid-1990s, "the angry white male" (AWM) had become a highly visible cultural figure in the press and on-screen, immortalized in vigilante vengeance films such as *Falling Down* (1993) and *White Man's Burden* (1995), and used to characterize the Oklahoma City bomber, Timothy McVeigh, in 1995.[100] The emergence of the AWM was a complex reaction to multiculturalism, feminism, globalization, and neoliberal capitalism. Experienced mainly by working- and lower-middle-class white men, feelings of white male economic disenfranchisement, due to the disappearance of manufacturing jobs (as a result of globalization) and the increasing impossibility of single-income families with a male breadwinner, became crystallized in the figure of the AWM.[101] Masculinity crisis literature emerged, including Robert Bly's *Iron John: A Book about Men* (1990), John Stoltenberg's *End of Manhood: Parables on Sex and Selfhood* (1993), and Susan Faludi's *Stiffed: The Betrayal of the American Man* (1999).[102] Meanwhile, male groups, such as the African American Million Man March and the international male Christian organization the Promise Keepers, organized all-male gatherings on the National Mall in Washington, DC, in 1995 and 1997, respectively. However, rather than focusing its critique on neoliberal capitalism's philosophy of upward redistribution and its role in producing a widening wealth gap, growing poverty, and precarious employment, representations of the AWM blamed minorities, gays, immigrants, and women as well as the legacies of "multicultural" social movements that fought for their equality and recognition for the diminishing quality of white middle-class lives, particularly those of men.

Child development experts also understood school shooters through the framework of masculinity in crisis. Books about boyhood in crisis emerged, including William S. Pollack's *Real Boys: Rescuing Our Sons from the Myths of Boyhood* (1998), which argued that boys were subject to an "emotional straitjacket" of athleticism and aggression that actually concealed a desire for gentler, softer interiority. Pollack often appeared on talk shows as an expert on Columbine and argued that a "national crisis of boyhood" would continue to drive boys to commit Columbine-esque acts of violence "not just because they're copycats, but because they're in pain."[103] Michael Gurian's book *The Good Son: Shaping the Moral Development of Our Boys and Young Men* (2000) took a more brain-based approach than Pollack, arguing that boys' brains, which were "primed for high risk behavior . . . [and] physical aggression," made them more "morally fragile" and less able to control their impulses than girls—a weakness exacerbated by a culture industry that sent boys violent rather than calming messages.[104]

However, Susan Faludi argued in *Newsweek* that "Ritalin-addicted white bad boys in the suburbs" did not suffer from emotional repression; rather, male school shooters were marshaled in service to a broader cultural attack on masculinity.[105] Critics of Pollack argued that his true premise was that teen boys "want . . . to be more like girls": "Pollack advises us to tell our boys, 'If you want to become a beautician, don't let the gender straitjacket get in the way,' or, 'I'm sorry if it's hard for you to get the tears out right now—it's not your fault, it's just the way society has taught you to mask your feelings.'"[106] Fears of male effeminacy, of boy beauticians or teary-eyed sons, revealed thinly veiled homophobic and antifeminist sentiments about generations of queer boys being produced in a "postfeminist" world that prized emotionality over virile, aggressive (read: heterosexual) masculinity. This view was perhaps nowhere more pervasively articulated than in Christina Hoff Sommers's polemic, *The War against Boys: How Misguided Feminism Is Harming Our Young Men* (2000), which argued that boys were in crisis because they were "under siege" by "sensitizing" "anti-boy" "celebrity academic feminists" like Pollack, whose pathologization of boyhood would make boys "tomorrow's second sex."[107] Sommers argued that boys would be served best by all-male classes that would foster "manly character and competition."[108] In a neoliberal era characterized by unrelenting economic crisis imperiling all workers and a fractured fantasy of male breadwinners, Sommers's book implicitly suggested, by invoking capitalist values of "manly competition," that boys made weak by feminism would further exacerbate American economic decline.

The school shooting epidemic dramatized a cultural contestation over shifting heteronormative gender roles in a "postfeminist" world—a world in which notions of proper adolescent development had been inexorably altered by neuroscientific discoveries. The same emerging neuroscience discoveries were used by science journalists to biologize not only a symptomology of adolescence but also other "differences," including sexuality, gender, race, and a propensity for violence. Debates over teen masculinity in crisis were as much about *able-bodied* (which is to say virile, heterosexual, and assertive) masculinity as they were about disenfranchised whiteness. Inherent in the shift to a neurologically compromised teen was an anxiety about "poor development" into proper men, and this new anxiety about the production of an effeminate (and thus queer) masculinity in plastic-teen-boys became increasingly criticized by feminists.[109] While books about boys in crisis, like Pollack's, argued that such instability was a golden opportunity for boys to get in touch with their emotional sides, others felt that boys were imperiled by the "current of opinion that masculinity itself [wa]s a social evil."[110] The question of whether or not boys were "disabled" either by the antiquated notion of masculine competitiveness inherited from previous generations' men or by a new, "softer," masculinity (a masculinity that threatened to turn boys into girls) remained open, crucial, and contested. While all teens were at the mercy of their underdeveloped PFCs and overactive amygdalas, white teen girls were repeatedly described as having more impulse control than their male counterparts of all races. Having benefitted from second-wave feminism's focus on girls' classroom performance and self-image, 1990s girls allegedly became less threatened by their own brains than white teen boys, who were physiologically prone to angry outbursts and imperiled by feminism's gains.

However, while neuroscientific discoveries circulated in neuroparenting and in relation to the culpability of (and even, at times, sympathy for)
white school shooters, the image of the teen brain functioned very differently in relation to African American or Latino teenagers. While coverage
of the school shootings focused on the "surprising" violence of suburban
white teens and their "impaired teen brains," studies of the neurological
origins of violence were already circulating within the emergence of (white)
neuroparenting and exposing cracks in the foundation of 1990s multiculturalism. Scientists had already begun studying links between biology and
violence in the 1970s by focusing on African American and Latino communities. In 1973, the formation of the Center for the Study and Reduction of
Violence was proposed at the University of California–Los Angeles, in part
to study the biological origins of violence by targeting minority groups.
Alondra Nelson's *Body and Soul* details the ways the Black Panther Party,
along with a coalition of organizations that included the National Organization for Women (NOW), resisted and ultimately defeated the center's
formation, by arguing against medicalization and biological determinism.
Among the center's research proposals was a plan to study adults and children with XXY chromosome syndrome; a study of the endocrine system
that would explore the relationship of the menstrual cycle to female violence; and the use of invasive psychiatric surgery on patients (including
incarcerated men and women).[111] However, as Nelson writes, the defeat of
the center was a "Pyrrhic victory" for the Panthers, in that scientists could
(and did) find other means of financing research projects into the biologi-
zation of violence.[112]

One such project, proposed nearly two decades later, was the Violence Initiative. Research at the intersection of race, violence, youth, and
the brain was fueled by events of the era. The 1989 "Central Park jogger"
rape case, in which Trisha Meili, a white woman, was brutally beaten and
raped in Manhattan's Central Park, had set the foundation for a massive
crackdown on juvenile crime that predominantly targeted youths of color.[113]
Although New York City witnessed 2,200 homicides and 5,200 rapes in that
year alone, the media aggressively reported this particular case of a white
woman attacked by teens of color, while Mayor Ed Koch and others called
for the death penalty for "wilding" (a neologism that emerged in reportage
of the case to describe random adolescent group attacks on strangers) and
for the "Central Park Five," the African American and Latino teen boys
between the ages of fourteen and sixteen who were arrested and charged
within hours of the crime.[114]

In February 1992, three years after the Central Park jogger case and one year after the start of Giedd's NIMH pediatric neuroimaging project, Dr. Frederick K. Goodwin, director of the NIMH, began publicizing the "Violence Initiative" as the federal government's "top priority" for psychiatric research.[115] Presented as a public health project, the Violence Initiative promised to identify at-risk children who "might be more likely to go on to becoming labeled eventually as delinquent or criminal" and to design psychiatric or medical interventions that would prevent them from becoming violent or criminal. Goodwin planned to screen over 100,000 "urban" children, as young as five, for biological and genetic markers that signified a predisposition toward violence.[116] When legal scholars from the University of Maryland attempted to organize a meeting to discuss the relationship between genetics and criminal behavior, African American activists, along with some psychiatrists, mobilized such ferocious protest that the NIH abruptly withdrew its $78,000 grant for the meeting, which resulted in its eventual cancellation.[117] In 1994, the infamous "bell curve debate" raged following the publication of *The Bell Curve*, by Richard Herrnstein and Charles Murray, which analyzed and racialized the relationship of IQ to crime, unemployment, premarital pregnancy, and poverty. The book sparked fiery debates among scientists, journalists, activists, academics, and the general public, because it suggested that racial variations in IQ were mainly determined by genetics rather than structural inequities. One year after *The Bell Curve*'s publication, the meeting reconvened, again amid furious controversy, although the organizers assured skeptics that the meeting would address "the possibility that research on the genetics of criminal behavior" was "far more likely to be used against minority groups" than other demographics.[118]

The next heir to the discourse of the congenitally violent, black, inner-city brain figured in the Violence Initiative was the "juvenile superpredator." In a 1995 issue of the newly launched conservative journal the *Weekly Standard*, John Diulio Jr. published his controversial "superpredator" treatise, which described a new generation of "radically impulsive, brutally remorseless youngsters, including ever more preteenage boys, who murder, assault, rape, rob, burglarize, deal deadly drugs, join gun-toting gangs and create serious communal disorders."[119] Mainstream news also covered the story beneath chilling headlines such as *Time* magazine's "Now for the Bad News: A Teenage Timebomb" and *Newsweek*'s "Superpredators Arrive" in 1996.[120] The emergence of the term was often linked to the violent death of a five-year-old African American boy named Eric Morse, who was thrown from a fourteenth-floor window by two laughing African American boys (aged ten and eleven) in the Ida B. Wells housing development (South Side, Chicago), because Morse had refused to steal candy for them.[121]

Although "superpredator" was supposed to function as a catchall designation for particularly heinous juvenile criminals of all races, Diulio commented, in articles such as "My Black Crime Problem, and Ours," that superpredators were overwhelmingly black—a "Crime Bomb" of "fatherless, Godless, and jobless" juvenile criminals.[122] Ignoring structural racism, racial profiling, and the systematic expansion of the prison-industrial complex, Diulio also remarked that if "blacks" were "overrepresented in the ranks of the imprisoned," it was because they were "overrepresented in the criminal ranks—and the violent criminal ranks, at that."[123] Echoing the "public health" sentiments of the Violence Initiative, Diulio once remarked that Medicaid should be thought "not as a health-care program but as 'an anti-crime policy,'" a statement that equated poverty, illness, or both with criminality.[124] At the state level, the superpredator myth buttressed a decision by forty-seven states to amend their laws for tougher sentencing of juvenile criminals that made it easier to funnel juvenile offenders into the criminal justice system.

Significantly, the term "superpredator" was never used to describe white school shooters; rather, it was reserved for African American (and sometimes Latino) youth, constructed as natural-born killers whose exposure to the "moral poverty" of their environment exacerbated their condition. White and nonwhite teenagers were both crippled by neuroscience, but in ways that differed dramatically. Mainstream media never spotlighted the brain of the superpredator as it did with the school shooter. Rather, proponents of the superpredator myth correlated low IQ with a propensity toward violent behavior. The brain was mobilized in discourses of school shootings to explain that white teens who perpetrated violence may not have the wiring necessary to commit premeditated crimes or to conceptualize consequences. However, an extension of the *Bell Curve* debate and the Violence Initiative, the superpredator treatise argued that superpredators (and implicitly, all teen boys of color), rather than possessing the vulnerable, developing teen brains of their white peers, had been wired for violence from the very beginning. Thus, a compassionate neuroparenting model relied upon the identification of white teens as rehabilitatable, medicalized subjects in opposition to teens of color, who materialized as congenitally criminal and unrehabilitatable.

This conception of biologized deviance, which played out on the bodies of adults as well as teens of the era, was a palimpsest of earlier eugenic and sexological discourses that pathologized difference to maintain racial, sexual, and bodily hierarchies.[125] Lisa Duggan argues that, as the nine-teenth-century white patriarchal home became "threatened" by women's and African Americans' increasing involvement in public social life, all women were construed as having the potential to act in ways that would contribute to the home's further dissolution, even while certain spectacular pathologized figures (e.g., mannish lesbians) emerged as embodied figures who personified the most imminent threat.[126] Similarly, discourses of teen "craziness" worked to collapse the distinction between competing symp-tomologies of "normal adolescence" and "true mental illness," so that the "most troubling figure" in neuroparenting discourse in the era of school shootings was the "normal" white teen boy, whose normative neurologi-cal development into a nonviolent, heterosexual, economically viable, able-bodied man was far from assured.

By the end of the Decade of the Brain, the pathologized "typical ado-lescent" was now in need of psychological (and often pharmaceutical) intervention. In an article about the Columbine tragedy, Kenneth How-ard, a psychologist, warned parents that, although all teens faced emo-tional turmoil, "[I]f your kid is behaving like a 'typical adolescent'—sullen, depressed, getting poor grades, having trouble with friends—that kid needs help, and it's not a phase."[127] After all, Harris and Klebold, the article noted, had "seemed . . . like normal children from normal families, rattling along the bumpy emotional road" that was accepted as "the normal course of the teen-age years."[128] Against the backdrop of a school shooting epidemic, Katie Couric warned viewers of the evening news, "The 90s has seen how dangerous misdirected teen-age rage can be."[129] The line between "crazy by design" and psychopathic became increasingly blurred for teen boys of the 1990s, now that "normal" teen outbursts might mask something more sinis-ter. Brain imagery of school shooters was used, at first, to make the shooter into an exception, a pathologically distinct and abnormal teen. However, by the end of the Decade of the Brain, the specter of the pathological teenager, without the necessary "wiring" to control impulses, haunted representations of all teens, especially testosterone-drenched teen boys. Although "their behavior always had been annoying and sometimes even troublesome," the *Boston Globe* identified American teenage boys of the 1990s as "Public Enemy Number One."[130]

However, in spite of fears of school violence and teen rage, many remained critical about the new pathologization of rebellious teenagers as ill, because it fueled corporate pharmaceutical power and profit. In 1989 a *Washington Times* article, "Brain Sitters for Teens," posed the sardonic question, "Sick of the breakdown in communication with a young rebel? Too tired to deal?

Help is at hand."[131] Rather than dealing with "the differences that fall painfully into the generation gap," the article noted the increasingly "popular remedy" for exasperated parents: the psychiatric hospital. Noting the transition from a law-based delinquency model to the medical model of adolescence this book has traced, the report noted that "troublesome teens," who might previously have been enrolled in military school, labeled "juvenile delinquents," or "described . . . as rebels without a cause . . . in less enlightened times," were now being institutionalized with "disturbing trendiness" for new diagnoses such as "adolescent adjustment reaction."

Fueled both by school shootings themselves and by reports that many of the school shooters were on various antidepressants or other prescription "psychotropic drugs," debates about teen mental illness and the acceptability of adolescent antidepressant use raged in the media. Myriad accounts of Columbine and of school shootings in general mention that Eric Harris had been taking Luvox, an antidepressant often prescribed for obsessive-compulsive behavior, which had led to his rejection from enlistment in the Marines; accounts of Kip Kinkel often mention that he was undergoing psychiatric treatment and taking Prozac when he committed murder.[132] Thus, the shootings sparked controversy about the increasing frequency with which young people were prescribed new psychotropic drugs like Ritalin, Prozac, and Zoloft, especially when such drugs were imagined to have contributed to the deluge of school shootings rather than stemming their flow. The federal government intervened by spotlighting teen mental health as a national health issue. In response to the Columbine tragedy, President Clinton hosted the first-ever White House Conference on Mental Health in July 1999 and the one-day "White House Conference on Teenagers: Raising Responsible and Resourceful Youth" in May 2000, which gathered parents, teenagers, educators, youth workers, foundation leaders, researchers, and policy makers.[133]

From the 1970s onward, adult and youth activists in burgeoning "anti-psychiatry" and "psychiatric survivor" movements formed a significant and vocal resistance to the medicalization of adolescence, which had become profitable for pharmaceutical industries and psychiatric institutions alike. The psychiatric survivor movement united former psychiatric patients in a critique of psychiatry. Anti-psychiatry publications, including Maia Szalavits's *Help at Any Cost: How the Troubled-Teen Industry Cons Parents and Hurts Kids* (2006), emerged to critique the institutionalization and psychiatric treatment of teens.[134] Another similarly motivated organization, Mind-Freedom International (MFI), established in 1986, began holding counter-conferences protesting the annual meeting of the American Psychiatric

Association in New York City.[135] MindFreedom, whose interests are globally positioned, became accredited by the United Nations as a nongovernmental organization with consultative roster status, enabling its leaders to join in international negotiations regarding the human rights of people with disabilities.[136] MFI directly encourages youth activism, as evidenced by the MindFreedom Youth Campaign, a sector dedicated specifically to youth issues relating to psychiatric treatment and drugs. In addition, MFI initiated MadPride, a movement "that celebrates the human rights and spectacular culture of people considered very different by our society."[137] Part of this celebration of difference involves the gathering and online publishing of oral histories of psychiatric "survivors," many of whom were medicated or institutionalized as teenagers.[138]

Youth activists have developed websites to talk back to the ongoing medicalization of adolescence and its construction as a lucrative market opportunity for pharmaceuticals. One such website is Fritz Flohr's Againstpsychiatry.com, which features a scan of the brain with sardonic reference to the famous 1980s anti-drug commercial slogan, "This is your brain on drugs"; beneath the images of "well" and "schizophrenic" brains, the caption reads, "Look! Kids! This is your brain on psych meds!"[139] Flohr's article "Don't Listen to Him, He's Crazy" describes his experiences at the True Spirit Conference, arranged by an organization seeking to empower progressive activists with mental health diagnoses. Flohr not only describes the persistent diagnosing of queer and transgendered youth with psychiatric disorders but also critiques the way liberal progressives and radicals accept standard mental health treatment all too easily while offering "feel good claims about how 'special' and 'gifted' . . . bipolar folks are."[140] Thus, resistance against the medicalization of adolescence and against the mental health industry by adults and youths with disabilities and mental illness was ongoing during the period. It existed within and alongside debates about the potential negative effects of psychiatric drugs on teenagers, which were fueled by the school shooting epidemic, and represented yet another way disability, as a politicized identity, circulated in a post-ADA world.

Teenscreen, Neoliberalism, and Surveillance

Amid an ongoing school shooting epidemic, the U.S. government implemented neuroscientifically and psychologically produced preventative measures to protect teenagers from themselves and from each other. One year prior to the Columbine massacre, President Clinton appeared at Kip Kinkel's grieving high school to announce that his administration was producing a guidebook of "early warning signs for potential school violence" that would be given to every school in the nation.[141] The guide, "Early Warning, Early Response," was the first of many lists of warning signs for dangerous youth.[142] Meanwhile, the Secret Service established a National Threat Assessment Center with a specialized team of investigators focused on researching adult and youth "American assassins," and the Federal Bureau of Investigation released its own report, "The School Shooter: A Threat Assessment Perspective" (2000). However suggestive its title was, the document was not meant to profile students to identify potential school shooters, according to the FBI's public statements.[143] Typical warning signs from various lists included "chronic feelings of isolation or rejection, frequent angry outbursts, social withdrawal or depression, fascination with or possession of weapons, alcohol or drug dependency, history of bullying behavior (or of being bullied), and lack of interest in school or poor school performance," while other lists included such subjective judgments as "dresses sloppily," is "a geek or nerd," or "characteristically resorts to name calling, cursing, or abusive language."[144] Harking back to developments in neuroinformatics that emerged during the Decade of the Brain, a partnership between the Alcohol, Tobacco, and Firearms Bureau (ATF) and a private security corporation, Gavin de Becker Incorporated, adapted Mosaic 2000 (a counterterrorist software program originally used by government agencies to profile "potentially dangerous individuals") for use in schools.[145]

Invoking the ADA, President George W. Bush's administration also established the New Freedom Commission on Mental Health in 2002 to improve the nation's mental health service delivery system for adults and children with mental illness. In a 2003 report, the commission emphasized the centrality of voluntary mental health screening in the early detection of and intervention into mental illness and applauded Columbia University's TeenScreen Program as "a model screening program for youth."[146] Offered through schools, clinics, doctors' offices, juvenile justice facilities, and other youth-oriented organizations and settings, TeenScreen was a "national mental health and suicide risk screening program" that offered voluntary health screenings (with parental consent) to teens and their families. To participate, teens filled out a questionnaire and, when necessary, secured a one-on-one appointment with a mental health professional to determine whether s/he was at risk of depression, suicide, or other mental health issues. At the conclusion of the assessment, the parents of potentially at-risk teens were notified.[147] As of 2012, TeenScreen had claimed more than 2,800 active sites in forty-seven U.S. states as well as in ten other nations, including fifty sites in the United Kingdom, three each in

India and Canada, and one each in Colombia, Scotland, the United Arab Emirates, New Zealand, Australia, Malaysia, Germany, and Brazil. Critics of the program note that TeenScreen used passive consent forms rather than requiring written parental approval and lured children to participate with free gifts like candy, prizes, movie tickets, or gift certificates. Perhaps most disturbing is that the financial backers and creators of the program had strong connections to major pharmaceutical companies. The program's creator, Dr. David Shaffer, was a consultant for Hoffman LaRoche, Wyeth, and GlaxoSmithKline, manufacturers of antidepressants that stand to profit handsomely from inroads into a teen mental health market. TeenScreen announced in November 2012 that it would be ceasing its program by the close of the year. The center did not give a reason for its closure. Invoking a "commitment to eliminate inequality for Americans with disabilities," the New Freedom Commission on Mental Health is one outgrowth of a post-ADA United States to ensure, in Bush's words, that people with mental illnesses can "live, work, learn and participate fully in their communities."[148] However, its association with TeenScreen underscores the extent to which disability civil rights discourse has been mobilized in an ongoing neoliberal project to privatize and profit from health services, individualize pathology, and implement new forms of surveillance—all of which have been facilitated by the commodification of disabling adolescence across myriad industries.

As the meaning of rehabilitation became increasingly social for some, it has become increasingly juridical for others. California undertook an unprecedented prison construction project between 1982 and 2000, during which time the state's prison population, disproportionately made up of Latinos and African Americans, grew by 500 percent.[149] As adolescence became a site of rehabilitation, harsher state laws for juvenile offenders have been enacted, placing ever more youth offenders in adult prisons, which have been run increasingly by profit-driven private corporations. Human Rights Watch cited the theory of the superpredator for moves by states to put more teenagers, especially teens of color, into the adult criminal justice system. By its estimate, in 1988, approximately 1,600 juvenile offenders were incarcerated in adult jails. By 1997, this number had skyrocketed to approximately 9,000, disproportionately composed of youths of color and formative of what some critics have named a "school-to-prison pipeline."[150] Increasingly, new and financially lucrative forms of surveillance (counterterrorist, psychological, and internalized), incarceration, and pharmaceutical markets have been legitimated and depoliticized through rehabilitative discourses of disability inclusion.

In one sense, the story of the 1990s teen brain is the story of how the logics of rehabilitation have progressed to ensure, in Henri Jacques Stiker's brutally prescient words, that the designation "*disabled* will increasingly be synonymous with *maladjusted*."[151] Popular neuroscience discourses in the Decade of the Brain worked simultaneously to normalize and pathologize adolescence as "brain damage" or "temporary insanity" that was inextricably rooted in the brain and tied to national health. In the case of teenagers, this version of compassionate neurologization ushered in a new approach to parenting, animated a lively debate about the place of prescription drugs in regulating teen moods and behaviors, and legitimated increased surveillance of teen behavior on a variety of fronts. Adolescence became a temporary disability to be overcome, while the teenager became a species defined by its incomplete and malleable brain.

Neuroparenting discourses conjured a universalizing image of adolescence as a shared state of disability to be overcome as the brain wires itself for adulthood. This was an image that traded in shared humanity—a universal experience of adolescent development that promised to transcend other identity categories like race, class, gender, or sexuality. Rehabilitative citizenship's pathologization of the individual accompanied an effacement of structural injustice. A philosophy of endless self-makeover, rehabilitative citizenship strongly resonated with ascendant neoliberal politics of the 1990s that emphasized personal responsibility ("overcoming" through individual will) and multicultural inclusion ("Aren't we all disabled or different in some way?"). However, this intense focus on the individual elided the political reality and overlapping persistence of structural ableism and racism like racial profiling and an expanding prison-industrial complex, which, according to Loïc Wacquant, became a preferred American neoliberal containment strategy for the endemic poverty and social unrest created by increasingly unstable labor and the privatization (or total dismantling) of public services.[152] As I discussed in the third chapter, this form of multiculturalism fueled and was fueled by a post–civil rights "Ellis Island whiteness" and the rise of color-blind racism as a reaction against downward redistribution and affirmative action. In the post–civil rights and post-ADA era, the raceless teen brain, disabled by adolescence, offered one such unifying affirmation of universal human struggle that, at best, elided ongoing gendered, racial, ableist, and sexual inequities, and at worst, bolstered them.

Thus, although a commonsense alignment of disability and adolescence may have begun as a storytelling convention, this metaphoric alignment had dramatic ramifications in criminal, neurological, and pharmaceutical debates about teen depression and violence. Most broadly, the same discourses of neuroplasticity and rehabilitation of disability at work on the teen body during the Decade of the Brain were inextricably linked to neoliberal discourses of inclusion and rehabilitation of conditions like racism, homophobia, and sexism. These entangled discourses of inclusion were emblematized profoundly in one neurologist's claim that, through "directed neuroplasticity," scientists might one day "untangle our circuits to relieve depression, cure learning disabilities, rehabilitate stroke victims, postpone the worst of Alzheimer's disease," and "even undo the brain wiring that supports racism."[153] Like adolescence and disability, racism and other bodily and social ills might be neurobiologically inevitable and hardwired, but, perhaps, capable of being rehabilitated, reprogrammed, or overcome into tolerance.

Conclusion

Susceptible Citizens in the Age of Wiihabilitation

An epidemic worse than flu is terrifying our quacks
As GPs over Britain suffer Internet Attacks.
"Doctor have a look at this. It's only twenty pages.
I would have printed out the rest but fear I'm in the stages
Of something fairly terminal. I've made a diagnosis.
I found it on the Internet. I think it's psittacosis.
Or mononucleosis. Or arteriosclerosis.
I also know which drug to use and in what strength of doses."
"The Internet." A doctor writes:
The symptoms are a cue of people in my waiting room
With sod all else to do
But ask me what I think they've got then tell me my mistakes
While reeling off prescriptions which the cyber-doctor makes.
Regrettably the only cure for this disease today,
or Chronic Cyberchondria, as doctors like to say.
Apart from application to your neck of a tourniquet
is log off from the website, get a life, and go away.
—Martin Newell, 1999

In this era, self-diagnosis is inevitable. We, as physicians, need to approach this as teachers.
—Dr. Kit C. Lee, 2012

In 1999 Martin Newell, a British rock musician and poet, penned the above poem for the *Independent*'s "Weekly Muse" that poked fun at a new disorder and the problems it posed for doctors. He jokes that exhaustive self-diagnosis not only leads to unnecessarily overfull waiting rooms but also unproductively challenges doctors' authority over diagnosis and treatment. The neologism "cyberchondria" began circulating in the late 1990s to describe a new variation of hypochondria for the information age: an anxiety concerning one's wellness that is triggered by the obsessive visiting of health and medical websites. As the poem illustrates, cyberchondria is an ill-defined terminology with vague diagnostic criteria. Those invoking it—journalists, computer scientists, and doctors, among others—often draw little distinction between the self-education efforts of diligent health information seekers and the frenzied searches of so-called hypochondriacs who overreact to banal symptoms.[1] A diagnosis of dysfunction by degree, cyberchondria lurks along the fine and ever-shifting line between health consciousness and health obsession.

Often described as an outgrowth of Internet addiction, cyberchondria has spawned a windfall of studies, ranging from the anecdotal and confessional to the longitudinal and technological, undertaken by journalists, technology researchers, psychiatrists, and bloggers trying to understand the cultural changes wrought as ever more people seek health information online.[2] More than a decade after the disorder's emergence, two Microsoft researchers, Ryen W. White and Eric Horvitz, undertook the first-ever scientific study of cyberchondria, which they defined as "the unfounded escalation of concerns about common symptomology based on review of search results and literature online."[3] As part of an effort to add more personalized features to Microsoft's search service, White and Horvitz studied the behavior of health information seekers and concluded that "the intrinsic problems with the implicit use of Web search as a diagnostic engine"—where queries describing symptoms are input as search terms and the rank and information of results are interpreted as diagnostic conclusions—can lead users to believe that common symptoms are likely the result of serious illnesses.

In many ways, cyberchondria is just a new diagnosis for an ongoing cultural problem. Studies of cyberchondria, whether serious or sardonic, tell us less about actual minds and bodies (or actual illness) and more about broader historical changes and cultural values at the nexus of the body, technology, medical knowledge, and citizenship in the age of neoliberal capitalism—the same convergences that *Chronic Youth* has traced in relation to adolescence. The transition toward neoliberalism has been a multifaceted economic, cultural, and technological project occurring across a wide swath of global cultural locations and with a variety of implications that are still very much in formation. This brief conclusion cannot possibly endeavor to map them all. Instead, I would have us begin by imagining cyberchondria as an orientation toward history, technology, medical knowledge, and embodiment in an "era" in which, following from Dr. Kit Lee's resigned words in this chapter's second epigraph, "self-diagnosis is inevitable."[4] By positioning cyberchondria in relation to the cultural history of media, citizenship, and embodiment that I have traced from the 1970s into the twenty-first century, I am suggesting that cyberchondria, an endless cycle of desire for self-diagnosis enacted through popular media, has, in a way, *always* been rehabilitative citizenship's preferred subjectivity. That said, as this book has historicized how rehabilitative citizenship has naturalized a culture of endless individual readjustment, I also want to consider what new forms of interdependence might emerge as collective readjustments undertaken by susceptible citizens in unstable times.

Of course, the era of self-diagnosis and rehabilitative self-discipline significantly predates the Internet age. To resist the technological determinism implicit in the term itself, we must position cyberchondria alongside and within longer crises over media use as well as its role in the democratization and commodification of medical knowledge. As *Chronic Youth* has shown, these sutured processes of education and entertainment have been and remain profitable for a number of industries. This book has described how rehabilitative edutainment—problem-driven, pedagogical commercial media—ascended as a predominant mode of address for teen citizens, who were imagined as always-already in crisis and in need of the type of intervention that healthy media were best suited to provide. Rehabilitative edutainment, such as "disease-of-the-week" made-for-TV movies, ABC's *After School Specials*, teen sick-lit, and later, neuroscience-inflected parenting books, operated pedagogically to rehabilitate denigrated popular media by endeavoring to rehabilitate teenagers into healthy citizens. Specifically, this book has argued that adolescence and disability increasingly became conjoined categories as rehabilitative narratives of "overcoming disability" aligned with "coming of age." In teen television and literature as well as in conversations about their value, this discursive alignment has served a crucial citizenship training function, as rehabilitative edutainment cultivated disciplined teen citizens who aspired to "stable" able-bodied, heterosexual adulthood through an endless ritual of self-surveillance, emotional management, and makeover. Amid an exploding 1970s self-help industry and culture, this was an extraordinarily profitable formula that centralized ideas about debility, capacity, and endless improvement potential (or, in rehabilitative citizenship terms, "growth" and "overcoming").

Rehabilitative edutainment also addressed teenagers as sexual proto-citizens rather than as innocent children, as sexual identity formation became imagined as a crucial step in healthy adolescent development in a United States inexorably altered by various sexual revolutions. In this way, rehabilitative edutainment negotiated a broader cultural conversation about sexuality and sexual pleasure in a post–sexual liberation world characterized by desire for greater openness about sex. Rehabilitative edutainment offered a disciplined version of sexual liberation, one that fostered and contained the volatility of teen sexual expression within the intertwined normative regimes of compulsory able-bodiedness and heterosexuality. However, the teenager, as an anxious site of potentiality and development, revealed the instability of heterosexuality and able-bodiedness since, much like the unstable teenager him/herself, these normative regimes required constant maintenance. Thus, by disciplining the rebel into the patient, rehabilitative edutainment naturalized self-surveillance, an endless ritual of self-diagnosis and rehabilitative management, as healthy and essential to good citizenship. As a tool of governmentality, rehabilitative edutainment formed one cultural location in which health itself became "seen as a side effect of successful normativity."[5]

Rehabilitative citizenship marshaled rehabilitation's polytemporal desire—an ambivalent, nostalgic vision of a more coherent, more innocent past and the possibility that rehabilitating the present might restore that former stability. In this way, rehabilitative citizenship was responding to a perceived loss of innocence in the post-Vietnam, post-Watergate era—an era in which, cultural producers believed, young adults needed to be better prepared to confront deep social problems because childhood, too, might be lost forever. Instead of eliminating corrupting influences like sex or violence (or even the mass media themselves) to remedy the loss, liberal pedagogues dealt with this cultural trauma through the rehabilitation of mass entertainment like television or popular literature into healthy edutainment that promised to rehabilitate teens into stable, socially responsible adults. However, its images of coming of age and overcoming disability still predominantly spotlighted white middle-class protagonists, offering up their struggles as universal. Moreover, its vision of health, of the stability promised by normativity and adulthood, was already quickly becoming illusory in an age of post-Fordism in which "Stayin' Alive" and making a good living were becoming increasingly difficult.[6]

Just as teen identity crisis was becoming normalized, so was the "crisis ordinary" of post-Fordism and later, neoliberalism.[7] Broad shifts in the American economy and government in favor of privatization relied upon and fueled rehabilitation's privatization of citizenship: good citizenship was refashioned as endless self-surveillance, makeover, and enhancement amid increasing economic and social instability. The precarious economic circumstances of post-Fordist deindustrialization—declining wages, the global export of blue-collar jobs, increasingly unstable employment, and the systematic retraction of "Great Society" social welfare programs—challenged the validity of the American "bootstraps" mentality and the self-made man, as the chasm between the rich and the poor widened dramatically along racial, gendered, sexual, class, and dis/ability lines. By the 1990s, unflagging neoliberal faith in the free market had ascended as an economic policy and as a set of cultural values embraced by liberals and conservatives alike. This philosophy enshrined economic deregulation and privatization, or, in other words, the belief that corporations are the most agile, innovative, and effective in responding to social problems. By contrast, government-administered social safety nets like welfare or universal health care are cast as sluggish, unprofitable, and "dependency-breeding" (often through overlapping racist and ableist language that describes not only the programs themselves but also the perceived populations who need them). This neoliberal cultural/ economic faith in the free market has naturalized phenomena such as the upward redistribution of wealth, the dismantling of social services through the moralizing language of entrepreneurialism ("personal responsibility"), or the idea that economic and personal security and success are achieved largely through individual willpower ("hard work") rather than severely circumscribed by ongoing structural inequalities.

Perhaps self-diagnosis has become inescapable in the Internet age of cyberchondria. However, *Chronic Youth* has shown that the cultural shift that has undergirded the naturalness or healthiness of self-surveillance or personal responsibility has been neither "inevitable" nor solely individual. Rather, it has required cultural work, undertaken within and across diverse sites, including cultural representation, government policy, media regulation, medical knowledge and industries, and even individual embodiment. By tracing how the rebel became the patient, this book has shown that this transition toward self-surveilling citizenship has been, in every instance, political, affective, and deeply historical. Through the depoliticizing narratives of coming of age and overcoming disability, rehabilitative edutainment had the crucial effect of naturalizing certain neoliberal cultural values, such as endless flexibility and individual adjustment to increasingly precarious living conditions, as apolitical and universal matters of "growing up" or "getting well" rather than historically contingent matters of economics and politics. Namely, rehabilitative edutainment's problem-driven cultural narratives about disabling and crisis-ridden adolescence—the individual overcoming of which was figured as natural, universal, and above all, responsible—did not just endeavor to create good citizens. Rather, these texts, and the coalition of government, parents, and cultural producers who endorsed them, endeavored to create citizens who could meet post-Fordism's new affective and economic demands. The story of how the rebel became the patient, then, is itself a story of the privatization of citizenship, as post–World War II sociological understandings of externally induced teen deviance gave way to medicalizing, psychological explanations of teen identity crisis, wherein teens' very bodies became the source of and solution to all of the problems they experienced in the social world. Thus, by tracing the entanglement of rehabilitation and self-surveilling citizenship through cultural representations of adolescence and disability, *Chronic Youth* has offered a new cultural history of neoliberalism.

Rehabilitative citizenship shows few signs of abatement, especially in an era of neoliberal privatization that parallels and fuels media's transition away from collectivizing "mass" media and toward miniaturization and personalization.[8] Thus, in the so-called era of cyberchondria, rehabilitative edutainment's torch has been passed to diverse new media offerings that we might call "diagnostic media," which serve a variety of age and demographic groups. Diagnostic media encompass a tidal wave of health-focused, consumer-oriented media, from interactive health information sites like WebMD, to full-body "exergaming" on the Wii or X-Box Kinect, to reality TV health makeover shows, or to health-oriented iPhone applications. As the *After School Specials* did for television, exergaming has rehabilitated the image of videogaming, a formerly denigrated medium and practice, as play has become productive and economically lucrative. The Wii has not only appeared increasingly in school physical fitness programs, configured as a timely antidote to American cultural panics about childhood obesity, but it has also become a rehabilitative tool in nursing homes.[9] Health professionals have endorsed the Wii's entertainment value as well as its therapeutic potential to increase mobility and fine motor skills in aging residents and sedentary students alike—an exercise regimen that has been called "Wii-habilitation."[10]

Diagnostic media, like the teen sick-lit that preceded them, offer a wealth of accessible medical information and detailed symptomologies that also encourage users to engage in various forms of self-diagnosis. Armed with information, patients certainly can use WebMD to maintain their health, ask more informed questions of doctors about treatment options, and advocate for themselves or others during appointments with doctors, many of whom encourage their patients to be more proactive in their medical care. However, WebMD also offers an endless interface of self-diagnosis, most powerfully epitomized by its Symptom Checker's clickable avatar. One click to the abdomen produces an exhaustive list of checkable symptoms indexed to their causes, ranging from common to serious. Profile creation enables users to amass their symptom histories, print out a "doctor's report," or access health information tailored to their symptoms and potential conditions. And of course, for self-diagnosis-on-the-go, users can now access individually tailored health information through a WebMD iPhone application. Diagnostic media net further profits from increased personalization, as users yield personal health information that becomes valuable as consumer data and then sold back as empowering consumer-citizenship.

While self-diagnosis might very well fuel cyberchondria, both also, and more importantly, fuel revenue drawn by health information sites from pharmaceutical and other advertising investments. This codependency was nowhere more obvious than in WebMD's controversial depression test, which was funded by the pharmaceutical company Eli Lilly. Advertisements for Lilly's antidepressant Cymbalta not only flanked the test, but a journalist also found that the test's default position was to find depression in everyone who took it. Even if users answered no to all ten of the questions (which were framed so that a "yes" answer indicated depressed behavior), they received a result of "Lower risk: You may be at risk for major depression."[11] As Nikolas Rose has argued, in the coming decade depression will become the most prevalent disability in the United States and the United Kingdom— not only through a broad increase in (and normalization of) depression but also through a gradating approach in its assessment.[12] Namely, as the above test illustrates, the operative diagnostic question will no longer be "Are you depressed?" but rather "How depressed are you?"—questions that bear a haunting resemblance to the one posed in 1978 by the *Journal of Adolescence*, "Adolescent Depression: Illness or Developmental Task?"

While "ordinary" sadness certainly differs substantially from depression, the naturalized image of trauma-filled moody adolescence has often glossed over the differences. As *Chronic Youth* has shown, sadness gained use value in the 1970s, as coming of age became recast, emotionally and later neuro-logically, as a gradual and progressive process of emotional inhibition that would culminate in the stability of adulthood. Rehabilitative edutainment, as an affective tool of governmentality, offered lessons in emotional manage-ment for impressionable and volatile teenagers. Yet teen sadness and its cul-tural and economic value not only remain important and unacknowledged sites in an ongoing genealogy of depression and cyberchondria (especially as teens have become a lucrative site of pharmaceutical investment), but also constitute a significant and unexamined cultural aspect of the 1970s shift toward affective labor.

Just as rehabilitative edutainment offered empowering messages of per-sonal responsibility to teen audiences, diagnostic media trade in a philos-ophy of individual health empowerment through the democratization of health information for self-diagnosis. Yet this movement toward "democ-ratizing" health empowerment is still a privatizing one that neglects (or, at worst, impedes) a collective imperative to address the structural barri-ers to democratically available health care. A vision of community health empowerment, redistributive justice, and health care as a human right rather than a capitalist commodity—in other words, the progressive vision offered in different but interrelated ways by patient activist, feminist, black nationalist, and disability rights movements from the 1970s onward—remains unfulfilled in a country that recorded roughly 49 million Americans without health insurance and another 46.2 million living in poverty in 2012.[13] Diagnostic media, with their emphasis on individual health empowerment, have transformed this activist call for the downward redistribution of health knowledge/power into corporate profits—soothing and profiting from an anxiety felt by many in an age of increasingly precarious relationships to economic security and access to health insurance and care. WebMD, along with other diagnostic media, emerges as yet another inadequate neoliberal corporate solution to a social problem—consumer-oriented, profit-driven industries offering the democratization of health knowledge in a culture in which actual government-sponsored universal health care remains demonized as antithetical to democracy.

Within a *longue durée* of cultural panics about unhealthy media (content or use) and their potential to produce unstable citizens, cyberchondria emerges as a seemingly new crisis of mediation and self-control. However, cyberchondria *actually* names an ongoing cultural anxiety about the increasing centrality of self-surveillance in our neoliberal cultural moment—a self-surveillance that *seems* natural but has been made necessary as an adjustment to unyielding bodily and economic precarity. Part of this story has been economic and cultural, as the transition from 1970s deindustrialization to 1990s neoliberal privatization has produced the rise of an economic and political precarity that cuts across class, geographical location, and other categories of social difference. Part of this cultural story has related to increasingly personalized media that facilitate ever more intimate forms of self-diagnosis, media forms that emphasize the precarity of health as a source of knowledge production and consumption, entertainment, play, and profit.

However, perhaps the most intimate part of this cultural story has been a bodily one: the cultural shift in the very categorical meanings of disability and able-bodiedness in the post-genomic age of biomedicine. Now, on an ever more microscopic scale, genetic and prenatal testing offer us assessments of "risk factors" for future abnormalities. As "predisposition" becomes a form of pre-debility, *all bodies*, disabled and nondisabled alike, become characterized by a state of asymptomatic pre-illness or "susceptibility" as a neoliberal culture of rehabilitation meets the post-genomic age.[14] As Jasbir K. Puar observes, all of these histories of precarity—bodily, economic, and cultural—are interrelated, as neoliberal and post-genomic

bodies are now "debilitated in relation to [their] ever-expanding potentiality," whether in a quest to meet neoliberal labor demands for endless
capacity or configured as investment opportunities for biomedical projects.[15] Disability activists as well as disability studies scholars often have
argued that disability is more permeable than other "traditional" identity
categories, because whether through accidental injury or the aging process, life itself, in this view, is nothing more than a progressive process of
debilitation.[16] However, as *Chronic Youth* has argued, this understanding
of disability remains perilously close to the falsely inclusive rehabilitative
language of personal responsibility, which maintains that, if we're all disabled in some way, then individual determination to overcome renders the
amelioration of structural injustice an irrelevant project, or to put this idea
into age-related terms, if we're all growing old, then *surely* we can all "just
grow up" and accept responsibility for our circumstances.

In a culture of rehabilitation, debility and capacity become equally profitable sites of investment. In mapping the various sites of self-surveilling
citizenship, from the rehabilitative edutainment of the 1970s to the cyberchondria of our contemporary moment, we might find new ways of using
the master's tools to dismantle the master's house.[17] At the very least, historicizing how rehabilitative citizenship has been naturalized and maintained
exposes the instability rather than the inevitability of governmentality itself.
Perhaps precarity, as a political and affective recognition of our shared vulnerability, might just incite the right kind of identity crisis—one that does
not simply compel the endlessly insular rehabilitative readjustment of individual overcoming, but rather incites a collective reckoning about citizenship and well-being. As neoliberal citizenship is conceived in ever more contractual terms, the expanding precariat reveals it to be a Faustian bargain,
because its terms are always subject to renegotiation rather than guaranteed
in advance as a human right. Part of this collective identity crisis of shared
vulnerability must involve thinking about precarity in historical and affective
terms that pay close attention to how individuals' proximities to vulnerability expand and contract, based on other cultural differences like race, class,
gender, sexuality, dis/ability, global location, or age. Perhaps we might begin
by reimagining growing as an economic and cultural commitment to interdependency rather than an individual proposition, one that extends sideways, backwards, and downward rather than only indefatigably forward or
upward.[18] By abandoning the forever-deferred promise of stability, we might
embrace the ongoing work of collective human care rather than the insular
paternalism of individual improvement that perpetuates the chronic youth
of neoliberal capitalism.

NOTES

NOTES TO THE INTRODUCTION

1. Shales, "Life and Love in a Bubble."
2. This phrase is drawn from Hall, *Policing the Crisis*.
3. Acland, *Youth, Murder, Spectacle*, 12.
4. Ibid., 24.
5. Observers have often historicized teenagers as little more than an invention of U.S. capitalism, either by emphasizing their emergence as a post–World War II market segment or by spotlighting their consumption patterns as inherently resistive. Grace Palladino's foundational *Teenagers: An American History* maintains the linkage between the etymology of "teenager" and the rise of the teen market (especially the emergence of *Seventeen* magazine), linking the emergence of high school youth subcultures to the social power and leverage gained by teens as they increasingly became targeted as consumers. Likewise, Jon Savage argues that the "invention of the teenager" occurred when advertisers and manufacturers devised it as a marketing term "that reflected the newly visible spending power of adolescents" (*Teenage: The Creation of Youth Culture*, xv). See also Cohen, *Consumer's Republic*, 318–19. On commodification and youth, see Banet-Weiser, *Authentic™*; Frank, *Conquest of Cool*; Cook, *Commodification of Childhood*; Quart, *Branded*; Kearney, *Girls Make Media* and *Mediated Girlhoods*; Milner, *Freaks, Geeks, and Cool Kids*; Nash, *American Sweethearts*; and Doherty, *Teenagers and Teenpics*. See also Clover, *Men, Women, and Chainsaws*. For an account of the emergence of the medical category of adolescence, see Prescott, *Doctor of Their Own*.
6. See Hall and Jefferson, *Resistance through Rituals*; and Hebdige, *Subculture*. See also Palladino, *Teenagers*; Hine, *Rise and Fall*; and Schrum, *Some Wore Bobby Sox*.
7. Post–World War II "mental hygiene" films were a media precursor to rehabilitative edutainment. These were ten-minute instructional films, bearing titles such as "Are You Popular?," "Dating Dos and Don'ts," or "Narcotics: Pit of Despair" and shown in American classrooms to mold the values and attitudes of students. Like mental hygiene films, rehabilitative edutainment also hoped to reshape the attitudes and behaviors of impressionable young citizens, but edutainment was meant to be profitable rather than solely educational, developing out of established *commercial* television networks and literary publishers rather than educational industries. For more information on mental hygiene films, see Schaefer, *"Bold! Daring! Shocking! True"*; and Smith, *Mental Hygiene*.
8. Norden devises ten visual and narrative tropes within which disability continues to be represented in film: "Civilian Superstar," "Comic Misadventurer,"

"Elderly Dupe," "Noble Warrior," "Obsessive Avenger," "Saintly Sage," "Sweet Innocent," "Tragic Victim," "High Tech Guru," and "Techno Marvel." See Norden, *Cinema of Isolation*. See also Garland-Thomson, *Extraordinary Bodies*; Mitchell and Snyder, *Narrative Prosthesis*; Haller, *Representing Disability*; and Chivers and Markotic, *The Problem Body*.

9. In her foundational text *Claiming Disability*, Simi Linton analyzes the ableism implicit in language and common idiomatic expressions like "blind justice," "falling on deaf ears," or "crippling debt."

10. Mitchell and Snyder, *Narrative Prosthesis*, 63.

11. Garland-Thomson, *Extraordinary Bodies*, 6. Likewise, Mitchell and Snyder argue that to examine the sociopolitical and discursive logics of disability is not to "deny the reality of physical incapacity or cognitive difference" but rather to analyze the cultural reception and disqualification of "those labeled deviant on ideological as well as on physical planes" (*Narrative Prosthesis*, 7).

12. Clare, *Exile and Pride*, 8.

13. See Berlant, *Queen of America*; and Edelman, *No Future*.

14. Arguably, the anxious category "tween" emerged in many ways in the late 1990s, not only as another niche market segment but also as a way of marking the physical changes of puberty while maintaining the sexual innocence of childhood—"too old for toys, too young for boys."

15. See Berlant, *Queen of America*; and Stockton, *The Queer Child*.

16. Levine, *Wallowing in Sex*.

17. Coining the term "intimate public sphere," Berlant reframes the study of "the nation" from one of political belonging to one of emotional attachment, as she studies the legacies of Reagan-era conservatism's emphasis on personal morality and the family as the bedrock of political discourse. See Berlant, *Queen of America*. See also Berlant, *The Female Complaint*.

18. See Kafer, "Compulsory Bodies"; and McRuer, *Crip Theory*. See also Clare, *Exile and Pride*; and Snyder and Mitchell, *Cultural Locations of Disability*. Crip theory builds on Adrienne Rich's influential essay "Compulsory Heterosexuality and Lesbian Existence."

19. McRuer, *Crip Theory*, 2.

20. Here, I invoke Ramlow's notion of "disabling adolescence." See Ramlow, "Bad Boys."

21. Bush argues that the story of twentieth-century juvenile justice is the story of how poor and nonwhite youth have been excluded from modern categories of childhood and adolescence. See Bush, *Who Gets a Childhood?*

22. The term "metaphoric abstraction" is Todd Ramlow's. See Ramlow, "Bad Boys."

23. Bederman, *Manliness and Civilization*, 43. Similarly, Kidd argues that a tension between two persistent and seemingly conflictive narratives has inexorably shaped the education, supervision, and cultural representation of American boys: "boyology," comprising professional writing about the biological and social development of boys, and the "feral tale," a literary and folkloric narrative

of cross-cultural encounter that "dramatizes but also manages the 'wildness' of boys." This tension persists in "boyhood crisis" literature of the late twentieth century, which is partly the subject of his fourth chapter. See Kidd, *Making American Boys*, 1.

24. See Chinn, *Inventing Modern Adolescence*.
25. Snyder and Mitchell, *Cultural Locations of Disability*, 72.
26. See Rembis, *Defining Deviance*.
27. See Baynton, "Disability and the Justification of Inequality."
28. See Ordover, *American Eugenics*; Black, *War against the Weak*; and Stern, *Eugenic Nation*.
29. Acland, *Youth, Murder, Spectacle*, 24.
30. See Gilbert, *A Cycle of Outrage*. See also Boddy, *Fifties Television*.
31. See especially Medovoi, *Rebels*, 1–52. Toby Miller also argues that cultural capitalism produces a form of bifurcated subjectivity and mode of citizenship when he contends that the "ideal citizen" is formed by two seemingly opposed subjectivities: one a selfless, community-minded individual and the other a self-ish, ravenous consumer. These opposing impulses are "tempered" by civility as a prized virtue that produces "well-tempered," self-surveilling citizen-selves, but both are necessary to the maintenance of democracy and consumer capitalism as mutually reinforcing. Likewise, the tension between rebelliousness and self-lessness I am tracing in representations of teenagers is constitutive of American notions of democracy. See Miller, *Well-Tempered Self*.
32. Medovoi, *Rebels*, 6.
33. Merriam-Webster.com, http://www.merriam-webster.com/dictionary/ rehabili-tate (accessed March 25, 2013).
34. See Halberstam, *In a Queer Time*; Muñoz, *Cruising Utopia*; Stockton, *Queer Child*; and Freeman, *Time Binds*.
35. Stiker, *History of Disability*, 144.
36. Ibid., 124. See also the first chapter of Serlin, *Replaceable You*.
37. Stiker, *History of Disability*, 124.
38. Erikson, *Identity*, 17.
39. Ibid., 68. A prototype, in cognitive psychological terms, is a model of a concept used by people to typify members or objects of a particular category. For instance, "chair" is often the prototype associated with the more general term "furniture."
40. Erikson, *Identity*, 68.
41. Ibid.
42. Erikson also likens "confused rebels" to autistic children, in terms of their shared inability to articulate "a coherent 'I.'" Ibid., 217.
43. Here, I am indebted to Margaret Somers's invaluable analysis of the contractu-alization of citizenship. Somers's central thesis is that market fundamentalism, or the ideological regime that understands free market logic as the best way to organize all realms of social life and the public sphere, creates the conditions

whereby wealth can replace social citizenship rights. By determining moral worth and equality in terms of economic productivity, marketization enables the "contractualization of citizenship," whereby all civil rights become conditional on quid pro quo exchange rather than guaranteed a priori. As full employment becomes less and less guaranteed, expendable "internal stateless" populations are created and disavowed rather than protected by the state. See Somers, *Genealogies of Citizenship*.

44. Reiff, *Triumph of the Therapeutic*.
45. For a history of self-help, see McGee, *Self Help Inc*. See also Illouz, *Saving the Modern Soul*.
46. On consumerism and citizenship, see Chasin, *Selling Out*; McRuer, *Crip Theory*; Sender, *Business, Not Politics*; and Miller, *Cultural Citizenship*.
47. Categories of adolescence and disability also figured prominently in critiques of the rehabilitation culture of the 1970s. Progressives worried that the "inward turn" of rehabilitative citizenship meant nothing less than the devolution of "real" political dissent (the leftist political idealism of the 1960s) into atomized self-fulfillment through commodity fetishism or pop psychology rather than the collective empowerment of social movements. For conservatives, the "therapeutic sensibility" of the 1970s threatened the cohesiveness of the nation in a variety of interrelated ways. They argued that the sexual "openness" of post–sexual liberation culture was sexually excessive, unproductive, and immature. Others, like Christopher Lasch, who penned *A Culture of Narcissism* (1979), used the language of disability and adolescence to argue that the inward turn toward the therapeutic led to "weak" complaining and self-absorption rather than proactivity, as "connecting with oneself" replaced the (able-bodied) "rugged individualism" and entrepreneurial spirit that had made America great. Finally, a conservative attack on the philosophy of downward redistribution espoused by leftist social movements (the "culture wars") recast these social justice movements as "special interest groups" whose self-serving agendas only fractured the cohesiveness of the United States. Notoriously named the "Me Decade" by Tom Wolfe, the 1970s were castigated by conservatives and progressives, in different but interrelated ways, as the collective adolescence of the nation itself—besieged by the "identity crises" of social movements and struggling to overcome the selfishness of an inward focus. This idea of the 1970s as the nation's collective adolescence pervaded discourses about AIDS as a penalty for the immature sexual excesses that occurred in the wake of sexual liberation. See Crimp, *Melancholia and Moralism*, 4–5; and Treichler, *How to Have Theory in an Epidemic*. As late as 1992, Marilyn Quayle reiterated this sentiment of the 1970s as the nation's adolescence in her Republican National Convention speech, when she lambasted political rival Bill Clinton's immaturity and irresponsibility, refuting his claim to a new generation of leadership by arguing that "[n]ot everyone demonstrated, dropped out, took drugs, joined in the sexual revolution or dodged the draft" in the late sixties and seventies. See Purdum, "What They're Really Fighting About."

48. Stiker, *History of Disability*, 134.
49. Ibid., 150.
50. Duggan, "The New Homonormativity." On homonormativity, see also Warner, *Trouble with Normal*; and McRuer, "As Good as It Gets."
51. Stiker, *History of Disability*, 135.
52. Todd Ramlow observes that disabled people and youth "have been perceived to threaten the reproduction of labor and economic systems of value, as well as the political and ideological norms of bodily and national life with which these systems are aligned." I quote him here at length:

    The crisis of labor and value posed by people with disabilities is that their "special needs" interrupt the Fordist rhythms of capitalist America. People with disabilities are often perceived as nonproductive members of society or, worse, as unnecessary burdens on industry, which must accommodate their needs. At times, of course, capitalism is directly responsible for the production of disability (whether through work-related accidents, unsafe working conditions, repetitive-motion or stress-related injuries, or environmental toxins that affect reproduction). . . . The threat that youth apparently poses to capitalist systems of labor is that, because youth is a time of instruction and indoctrination between childhood and adulthood, it might come to reject or fail to learn or conform to traditional patterns of labor or of socioeconomic and political value. This economic crisis created by youth was most clearly elaborated in the late 1980s and early 1990s in the cultural panics and debates over "Gen-Xers" and "slacker" youth, who were perceived as listless and, most important, unproductive. (Ramlow, "Bad Boys," 115–16)

53. This book does not discuss youth and popular music, but much critical and productive work has been done on the subject. See Hebdige, *Subculture*; Ross and Rose, *Microphone Fiends*; Grossberg, *We Gotta Get Out*; Rose, *Black Noise*; and Neal, *Soul Babies*. This book also does not discuss comic books, though there is also excellent work on comic books and youth. See Wright, *Comic Book Nation*; and Fawaz, *New Mutants*. For an account of the cultural work of adolescence on the teenage-ing of the Internet, see Schulte, *Cached*.
54. Robert McRuer categorizes this type of activism as "depathologizing movements." See McRuer, *Crip Theory*, 12. On the disability rights movement, see Shapiro, *No Pity*; Fleischer and Zames, *Disability Rights Movement*; and Nielsen, *Disability History*. For an overview of LGBT activism that led to the removal of homosexuality from the American Psychiatric Association's list of mental disorders, see Bayer, *Homosexuality and American Psychiatry*.
55. Following Berlant and Halberstam, *Chronic Youth* analyzes a "silly" archive, comprising affective objects that form the "waste materials of everyday communication" that are nonetheless "pivotal documents in the construction, experience, and rhetoric of quotidian citizenship in the United States." Berlant, *Queen of America*, 12. See also Halberstam, *Queer Art*.

56. Levine, *Wallowing in Sex*; McCarthy, *Citizen Machine*; Ouellette, *Better Living*; Weber, *Makeover TV*; Banet-Weiser, *Kids Rule!*; and Miller, *Makeover Nation*.

57. On the cultural work of affect, see Sedgwick, *Touching Feeling*; Cvetkovich, *Archive of Feelings*; Ahmed, *Cultural Politics*; Clough and Halley, *Affective Turn*; Illouz, *Cold Intimacies*; Love, *Feeling Backward*; Berlant, *Female Complaint* and *Cruel Optimism*; and Gould, *Moving Politics*.

58. For analyses of the interplay of cultural constructions of gender roles, sexuality, and medical and scientific discourse and technology, see Fausto-Sterling, *Sexing the Body*; Haraway, *Simians, Cyborgs, and Women*; Brumberg, *Body Project*; Martin, *Woman in the Body*; Treichler, Cartwright, and Penley, *Visible Woman*; and Wilkerson, *Diagnosis: Difference*. For discussions of the relationship of medical knowledge and the construction of race, see Washington, *Medical Apartheid*; Somerville, *Queering the Color Line*; and Metzl, *Protest Psychosis*. For analyses of the connections between medical knowledge and representations of medicine in the realm of film and television, see Cartwright, *Screening the Body*; Treichler, *How to Have Theory*; and Reagan, Tomes, and Treichler, *Medicine's Moving Pictures*.

59. Palladino's analysis valuably suggests that adolescence is historically contingent rather than an essential category, but it also establishes generational conflict between adults and teens as a transhistorical trend when, for example, she likens the bobby soxers of the 1940s to the Beatlemaniacs of the 1960s as rebellious consumers (*Teenagers*). See also Douglas, *Where the Girls Are*. Some examples of analyses that identify the resistive or liberatory qualities of the teen market or the agency that teens express as consumers include Davis and Dickinson, *Teen TV*; LeBlanc, *Pretty in Punk*; Driver, *Queer Girls*; and Harris, *All about the Girl*.

60. See Green, *Fault in Our Stars* for a parodic interpretation of teen sick-lit's conventions. See also Comedy Central's *Strangers with Candy* (1999–2000), which lampooned ABC's *After School Specials*.

NOTES TO CHAPTER 1

1. Simon, *Graceland*.

2. See "The Bubble Boy," *Seinfeld*. See also Disney's *Bubble Boy*.

3. The ethical dilemmas posed by David's isolation are more characteristic of contemporary accounts of the story than of public accounts of David written during his lifetime. For a discussion of the ethical issues presented by David Vetter's confinement to the bubble, see *American Experience: The Boy in the Bubble*. See also the website supporting the documentary, http://www.pbs.org/wgbh/amex/bubble/, especially the section called "Bioethics Opinions," http://www.pbs.org/wgbh/amex/bubble/sfeature/sf_ethics.html (accessed June 11, 2008). The historian James H. Jones, author of *Bad Blood: The Tuskegee Syphilis Experiment* (1993), is also currently working on a book that will scrutinize the roles of doctors and family members involved in the decision to put David Vetter into the bubble.

4. Garland-Thomson, *Extraordinary Bodies*, 3.

5. For her performance, Hyland garnered a posthumous Emmy for outstanding performance by a supporting actress in a comedy or drama special.

6. "Germ-Free 'Home.'" See also Auerbach, "Boy Spending Life in Plastic Bubble."

7. A laminar airflow room was created to house and protect leukemia patients whose immune systems had been compromised by chemotherapy. The 13-East section was constructed in 1969. Larger than the earlier "Life Island," a bed entirely encased in a plastic bubble, the laminar airflow room surrounded by plastic sheeting containing a door-sized space through which things and occasionally doctors could pass in and out.

8. See Cohn, "Boy with Fatal Disease Kept Alive."

9. Ibid.

10. David's parents asked that their last name be omitted from news stories about their son.

11. DeVita-Raeburn, *Empty Room*, 4.

12. Ibid., 3.

13. See Bogdan, *Freak Show*; and Snyder and Mitchell, *Cultural Locations*.

14. According to Oshinsky, the March of Dimes campaign, through its use of celebrity images, poster children, and other advertising media, revolutionized fundraising activities undertaken by charities, in that prior to the Depression, fund raising typically consisted of large donations from a few very affluent donors rather than small donations from the masses. See Oshinsky, *Polio*. See also Longmore, "Conspicuous Contribution."

15. "Infantile citizenship" is Berlant's term. See *Queen of America*.

16. Auerbach, "Boy Spending Life."

17. Selected examples include Auerbach, "Boy Spending Life"; Auerbach, "Three-Year-Old Boy's Life"; "Boy, 12, Out of 'Bubble'"; "Boy Leaves His 'Bubble'"; King, "Signs Hopeful for Boy Out of Bubble"; Taylor, "Emergence"; "Headliners"; and King, "Houston 'Bubble Boy' Dead."

18. "Boy with Immune Deficiency Challenges Theories."

19. Mansfield, "8 Years in Germ-Free Chamber."

20. Cohn, "Boy with Fatal Disease."

21. Mansfield, "8 Years in Germ-Free Chamber."

22. Bruce Jennings, interview in *American Experience: The Boy in the Bubble*.

23. *Life*, September 14, 1962. Between 1960 and 1980, *Life* magazine featured over twenty cover stories on medical triumphs and insights into the human body, including a multi-issue series on the brain and the first-ever portraits of a fetus in the late 1960s and early 1970s. There were also at least four issues devoted to open-heart transplants in this period.

24. DeVita-Raeburn, *Empty Room*, 205–6.

25. Ibid.

26. United Press International, "Quest for Normal Life."

27. Whether or not David liked the suit is a subject of debate. David's psychiatrist, Mary Murphy, described David's terror and refusal to enter the suit. While

David wasn't coerced to use the suit, she said that he was pressured in spite
of his obvious fear. David's mother says that although he was "nervous" the
first time he entered the suit, "for every entry into that suit, David thoroughly
enjoyed it and was thrilled to be in the suit." See McVicker, "Bursting the
Bubble." See also *American Experience: The Boy in the Bubble.*

28. Spigel, "From Domestic Space to Outer Space," 214.
29. Penley, *NASA/Trek,* 14–15.
30. NASA tried to attract women and minorities into the astronaut corps by hiring
    the actress Nichelle Nichols (Lieutenant Uhura) to assist in recruitment efforts.
    Mae Jemison, the first black female astronaut, also began each of her radio com-
    munications with Uhura's signature line, "Hailing frequencies open." See Penley,
    NASA/Trek, 19–20.
31. Penley, *NASA/Trek,* 9–10.
32. The impetus to create TA began as an outgrowth of environmental activism. See
    National Library of Medicine, "HTA 101."
33. Auerbach, "Boy Spending Life."
34. Mansfield, "8 Years in Germ-Free Chamber."
35. McVicker, "Bursting the Bubble."
36. DeVita-Raeburn, *Empty Room,* 91–92.
37. Ibid., 92.
38. "Germ-Free 'Home.'"
39. According to Elizabeth DeVita-Raeburn, Ted's girlfriend was the niece of a
    patient undergoing treatment for cancer in 13-East, the same ward as Ted.
40. Edelman, *No Future,* 4.
41. Jameson, *Political Unconscious,* 104.
42. Shales, "Life and Love in a Bubble."
43. For more information about the rise of the made-for-TV movie, see Levine,
    Wallowing in Sex; and Gomery, "Television, Hollywood, and the Development
    of Movies Made-for-Television." For a comprehensive listing of all made-for-TV
    movies, see the multivolume set Marill, *Movies Made for Television.*
44. Levine, *Wallowing in Sex,* 25.
45. On "disease-of-the-week" television narratives, see Longmore, "Conspicuous
    Contribution," 134–58. On disease-of-the-week shows that focus on sexu-
    ally transmitted diseases, see Patton, *Fatal Advice;* and Treichler, *How to Have
    Theory.*
46. Shales, "Life and Love in a Bubble."
47. Treichler, *How to Have Theory,* 182.
48. O'Connor, "TV Weekend."
49. Shales, "Life and Love in a Bubble."
50. Auerbach, "Three-Year-Old Boy's Life."
51. McPherson, "David's Choice."
52. McRuer, *Crip Theory,* 92.
53. Gerber, *Disabled Veterans,* 3–4. See also Scarry, *Body in Pain.*

54. Roy and Tod's casual conversation about "dirty" unprotected sex is striking from a contemporary vantage point. Less than a decade later, this conversation would likely have a much different tone and message, as the pervasiveness of HIV/AIDS prompted the question of "how to have sex in an epidemic," the title of a 1983 sex-positive safe-sex pamphlet by Richard Berkowitz and Michael Callen.

55. White, "Sex Education; or How the Blind Became Heterosexual," 133–47.

56. McRuer, *Crip Theory*, 8–9.

57. Rich, "Compulsory Heterosexuality and Lesbian Existence."

58. See Chapter 10 of Gitlin, *Inside Prime Time*.

NOTES TO CHAPTER 2

1. Lemanczyk, "After School Specials."

2. ABC's *After School Specials* dealt with homosexuality implicitly, in episodes about AIDS and in one episode about ballet dancing ("A Special Gift."). On racism, see "Color of Friendship," "Class Act: A Teacher's Story," "Taking a Stand," "Girlfriend," and "Shades of a Single Protein." On teen pregnancy, see "Schoolboy Father," "Jacqui's Dilemma," and "Too Soon for Jeff." On child molestation, see "Don't Touch." On child abuse, see "Please Don't Hit Me, Mom" and "Terrible Things My Mother Told Me." On physically abusive teen relationships, see "Love Hurts." On divorce, see "What Are Friends For?" and "Divorced Kids' Blues." On sexual harassment, see "Boys Will Be Boys." On rape, see "Did You Hear What Happened to Andrea?" and "Date Rape." On teen suicide, see "Amy and the Angel" and "Face at the Edge of the World" (a.k.a. "A Desperate Exit"). On illegal drugs, see "Stoned," "Tattle: When to Tell on a Friend," and "Desperate Lives."

3. I treat psychological ideas about adolescence and their codification of universal "normal" developmental stages as one historical context for the *Specials*. As I am invested in disability studies' critique and deconstruction of medical knowledge/power, I would argue that the establishment of universalizing psychological norms of development are invested in what the disability studies scholar Lennard Davis has named the historical and cultural process of "enforcing normalcy." "Normal" stages of development rely on juxtaposition with deviations from normal development and are thus invested in the creation of able-bodiedness as a norm. See Davis, "Constructing Normalcy." For a disability studies critique of theories of childhood development and their use in education, see Ferri and Bacon, "Beyond Inclusion." Psychiatric survivor and anti-psychiatry activist movements have also critiqued psychological and psychiatric authority.

4. See Spigel, *Make Room for TV*.

5. The *After School Specials* had many clones, including CBS *Schoolbreak Special* (1984–1995); CBS's *Afternoon Playhouse* (1981–1983); NBC's *Special Treat* (1975–1986); and USA's *Lifestories: Families in Crisis* (1992–1996).

6. Establishing the total number of ABC's *After School Specials* is nearly impossible, since there is no complete archive of the series. Individual episodes were

produced by small production companies and then sold to ABC. The Internet Movie Database (IMDB) records a total of 154 episodes. Individual episodes of the *Specials* are scattered throughout the country in different libraries and museums, and some have been released on DVD. New York's Paley Center for Media boasts the largest (unindexed) collection.

7. Lemancyk, "After School Specials."

8. Ibid.

9. Ibid.

10. Martin Tahse, telephone interview by author, February 22, 2007. Unless otherwise cited, all quotes from Martin Tahse are from this telephone interview.

11. Psychological theories of the role of separation from the family of origin and its essential relationship to individuation, identity formation, and teen coming of age were being formed by the end of the 1960s through the early 1980s, most notably by the psychoanalyst Margaret Mahler. See Mahler, Pine, and Bergman, *Psychological Birth*. See also Blos, "The Second Individuation Process of Adolescence."

12. There is a growing body of work in queer rural studies that is critical of "metronormativity," a term that describes how sexual liberation has been linked to a compulsory migration from rural to urban spaces, which configures rural spaces as "backwards" and sexually repressive. See Herring, *Another Country*; Gray, *Out in the Country*; Halberstam, *In a Queer Time*; and Tongson, *Relocations*. On metronormativity and disability, see Clare, *Exile and Pride*.

13. Garisto, "Why 'Afterschool Specials' Are Special."

14. Tahse noted that he focused on parental alcoholism often because his father was an alcoholic. See the episodes "Francesca, Baby," "She Drinks a Little" (a.k.a. "First Step"), "Can a Guy Say No?," and "Just Tipsy, Honey."

15. Discourses of developmental psychology in the late 1960s and early 1970s were one of many locations in which the configuration of adolescence as crisis was codified and reproduced. The psychologist Lawrence Kohlberg's theories of moral development share many similarities with the problem novel formula. For a historical analysis of identity politics and youth in reference to Erik Erikson's work on identity crisis, see Medovoi, *Rebels*.

16. No ABC *After School Specials* about cognitive disability feature disabled girls, and very few episodes about physical disability feature a female protagonist, except "Blind Sunday" and "Run, Don't Walk."

17. Tahse's notion of girls liking a "boy show" (but not boys' liking a "girl show") was of a piece with dominant developmental psychological ideas about adolescence, which were presented as gender-neutral and universal but generally based on white, able-bodied, all-male subjects. One famous critique of this tendency was offered by Carol Gilligan, who argued, based on her study of girls and women, that females make moral decisions through the relationship-driven principle of "care" as opposed to the abstract principle–driven "justice." Gilligan's work became influential in shifting attention to the specificities of

adolescent female development by the late 1980s. See Gilligan, "In a Different Voice."

18. See "A Very Delicate Matter" and "Private Affairs." This author did not see any shows dedicated to herpes, HPV, or chlamydia, although all were also prevalent at the time. During the AIDS epidemic, the series devoted at least three episodes to HIV/AIDS: "Just a Regular Kid: An AIDS Story" (1987); "In the Shadow of Love: A Teen AIDS Story" (1991); and "Positive: A Journey into AIDS" (1995). "In the Shadow of Love" featured the following disclaimer, which was uncharacteristic of *After School Specials*: "Today's *Afterschool Special* deals with the subject of AIDS infection and contains frank discussions of teenage sexuality. Parents are encouraged to watch and discuss with their children." "Don't Touch," an episode about child molestation, seems to be the only other *Special* that featured a parental warning about the episode's disturbing content, which suggests that narrative renderings of certain issues, such as sexuality, HIV/AIDS, and child molestation, were deemed more controversial than other episodes that dealt with nonsexual child abuse or other STDs (that were not so closely associated with homosexuality, as HIV/AIDS was).

19. O'Connor, "Those Adaptations."

20. Although Brad Silverman, an actor with Down syndrome, appeared at the end of "The Kid Who Wouldn't Quit" to address the audience, different able-bodied actors played Silverman at various stages of life. An able-bodied actor also played Hewitt in "Hewitt's Just Different."

21. In "Hewitt's Just Different," Hewitt's younger friend, Willy, finds a sexy poster of a scantily clad blonde woman and ridicules Hewitt, "Wow! Hewitt! Gonna hang it in a special place? . . . Got a crush on her?" Hewitt angrily yanks the poster away from Willy, who apologizes. Meanwhile, "The Kid Who Wouldn't Quit" establishes Brad Silverman's coming of age through his bar mitzvah and through his energetic flirting with able-bodied high school girls. He flirts openly with a cheerleader without realizing that she is making fun of him to a group of girls. An African American basketball player, Kevin Washington (Eric D. Wallace), rescues Brad, encouraging him to "be cool" rather than coming on so strongly to the girls.

22. Mitchell and Snyder, *Narrative Prosthesis*, 48–49. Mitchell and Snyder importantly note that disability's centrality to representation poses a problematic conundrum: the ubiquity of disability as a "symbolic figure" in representation is rarely accompanied by its depiction as "an experience of social and political dimensions."

23. Ibid.

24. Clowse, *Brainpower*, 162–67.

25. U.S. Senate, Hearings Before the Committee on Interstate and Foreign Commerce, cited in Perlman, "Reforming the Wasteland," 25.

26. The phrase "vast wasteland" originated in FCC Chairman Newton Minow's 1961 address to the National Association of Broadcasters (NAB). One report, *The Impact of Educational Television* (1960), described commercial television

as "encourage[ing] chiefly passivity and minimum effort rather than activity, a minimum of social interaction, a concern with fantasy rather than real life, and living in the present rather than concerning oneself either with self-improvement or the problems of tomorrow." See Schramm, *The Impact of Educational Television*, 26, cited in Perlman, "Reforming the Wasteland," 36.

27. See Perlman, "Reforming the Wasteland."

28. "Does Video Violence Make Johnny Hit Back?"; "Ending Mayhem." See also U.S. Surgeon General, *Television and Growing Up*; Wertham, "How Movie and TV Violence Affects Children"; Cline, "TV Violence"; and Kiester, "TV Violence."

29. Levine, *Wallowing in Sex*, 82.

30. Schramm, cited in Perlman, "Reforming the Wasteland," 36.

31. O'Connor, "Saturday Is No Picnic."

32. O'Connor, "ABC's 'No Greater Gift.'"

33. Michel Foucault argues that one effect of modernity was the production of a discourse of children's asexuality. See Foucault, *History of Sexuality*. Television scholars have chronicled the history of accusations of the adverse effects of television content and viewing practices. See Spigel, *Make Room for TV*; and Boddy, "Senator Dodd Goes to Hollywood."

34. See "The Second Sexual Revolution." This was the cover story.

35. Nash, "Hysterical Scream or Rebel Yell?," 144.

36. Ibid.

37. For secondary literature on the history of sex education controversies, see Luker, *When Sex Goes to School*; Irvine, *Talk about Sex*; and Moran, *Teaching Sex*. In the late sixties, many publications debated whether or not sex education should occur in schools or in the home. See Furlong, "It's a Long Way"; Iseman, "Sex Education"; "Sex in the Classroom"; Goodman, "Controversy over Sex Education"; "Sex-Education Controversy"; Bell, "Why the Revolt"; Bettelheim, "Right and Wrong Way"; Rabinovitz, "How to Talk to Your Parents"; "Let's Learn to Make Love"; Reuben, "Everything You Always Wanted"; Butts, "Sex Education"; Faier, "Sex-Education Controversy"; Gordon, "Let's Put Sex Education Back"; Keefauver, "Dick and Jane"; and Tenver, "Talk to Your Teen-Agers."

38. See Goodheart, "Sex in the Schools"; Rowan et al., "Sex Education"; Kobler, "Sex Invades the Schoolhouse"; and Stanton, "Bring Back the Stork!"

39. White, "How the Blind Became Heterosexual," 136.

40. See Gitlin, *Inside Prime Time*, 203–20.

41. Shales, "The Initiation of James." For a historical account of the *James at 15* controversy, see Levine, *Wallowing in Sex*, 42–43.

42. Levine, *Wallowing in Sex*, 96–99.

43. Stiker argues that the obliteration of differences among disabilities is the modus operandi of rehabilitation when he says that "Two discourses arise [in rehabilitation]. The one proposes to make careful distinctions among the kinds and classes of disability, the other to make the boundaries so fuzzy that there is

scarcely more than a single class of the disabled." See Stiker, *History of Disability*, 156.

44. "TV Highlights."
45. Fisher, "Icy Tale with a Happy Ending."
46. Ibid.
47. IMDB describes the story as one of "overcoming shyness"; http://www.imdb.com/title/tt0295614/ (accessed June 11, 2008). The DVD sleeve from Netflix features this description: "A gawky lad learns to skate."
48. For an analysis of the representation of rural space, see Johnson, *Heartland TV*.
49. While I chose not to include it in this article, this theme of a rural boy's participation in a feminized sport (ballet) is taken up again in "A Special Gift" (1979), which won a prestigious Peabody Award. Like "The Ice Skating Rink's" Tucker Faraday, the farmer Peter Harris and his "sissy" ballet dancing are often crosscut with traditionally masculine images like playing basketball or bailing hay in the barn with his father.
50. Fisher, "Icy Tale with a Happy Ending."
51. See Savran, *Taking It*. My use of the term "flexible" derives from Emily Martin's work. See Martin, *Flexible Bodies*.
52. Savran, *Taking It*, 125.
53. "'Heartbreak' Tale."
54. Mitchell and Snyder, *Narrative Prosthesis*, 48–49.
55. Network affiliates were actually part of the show's success and its demise. Tahse noted that "once critics started reviewing the shows, the affiliates really joined in and made it all possible" because "every city started showing them, and then the advertisers jumped in." However, the *Specials* were always economically precarious, because they were "really at the whim of affiliates," which had to voluntarily "give up" hour timeslots for the *Specials* rather than filling them with more profitable commercial programming. He says the show's cancellation "is a mystery because it happened after Disney bought ABC, because you'd think that Disney would be interested in keeping these shows on the air. But they were stealing the time from the affiliates, it wasn't network time that was being used. . . . the affiliate had to take something they'd have programmed out, in which they got all the money, and put in the *After School Special*, in which they'd have to share with the network." From Tahse, KPCC interview and Tahse, telephone interview.
56. I thank Laura Cook Kenna for illuminating this significant distinction.
57. Brown, *Regulating Aversion*, 11.
58. McRuer, *Crip Theory*, 2.
59. Brown, *Regulating Aversion*, 5.
60. Fisher, "Icy Tale with a Happy Ending."

NOTES TO CHAPTER 3

1. Whitfield, "Missions of Mercy."
2. Drew, *100 Most Popular*, 274.

3. Kamen has used the term "sick-lit" to describe a third-wave feminist form of self-actualization by disclosing "invisible illnesses." She uses "sick-lit" to describe a form of what some scholars have called "autopathography," an autobiographical account of oneself that focuses on a disease, disorder, or disability that affects the artist. See Kamen, "A 'Sick-Lit' Manifesto." This chapter will not focus on autopathographies. For more information about autopathography, see Brody, *Stories of Sickness*; Frank, *The Wounded Storyteller*; and Couser, *Recovering Bodies*.

4. There is YA literature about HIV/AIDS from this period that would certainly fall into the category of teen sick-lit, though I chose not to include it here, for reasons both of length and representativeness of authors' work. While Jean Ferris has never published a novel about AIDS, Lurlene McDaniel has published only two books out of over fifty that focus on people with AIDS: *Sixteen and Dying* (1992) and *Baby Alicia Is Dying* (1993). *Sixteen*'s protagonist, Anne Wingate, contracted HIV from a blood transfusion, and an anonymous benefactor's donation grants her "one last wish" to travel to a ranch out west, where she meets Morgan, her love interest. *Baby Alicia* is the story of white teenaged Desi, a volunteer at a home for HIV-positive babies, and her attachment to Alicia, an African American baby whose mother abandoned her at birth. HIV and AIDS are underrepresented in comparison with other diseases in McDaniel's oeuvre. This omission is consistent with its cultural moment, in which HIV/AIDS were considered diseases that mainly affected gay men, drug users, and "innocent victims," such as hemophiliacs or medical professionals who contracted the disease unknowingly. For an analysis of how AIDS was presented as a disease not affecting "normal" heterosexuals, see Patton, *Fatal Advice*. While the problem novel was an outgrowth of 1970s liberalism, teen sick-lit often reaffirmed conservative political and sexual values, and the way the novels deal with HIV/AIDS (and certainly, the way they dealt with this disease substantially less than other diseases) is certainly part of this reaffirmation.

5. Although it is outside the historical period in this study, Green's novel *A Fault in Our Stars* (2012) deviates significantly from the teen sick-lit formula described in this chapter. It is told in first-person narration and often mocks the melodramatic conventions of "teen sick-lit." Hazel falls in love and has sex with a disabled cancer survivor, Augustus, rather than pursuing a "normal" boy. The book also does not configure their romance as a rehabilitative treatment for cancer in the way that other books discussed in this chapter do.

6. On classic narratives about illness, see Herndl, *Invalid Women*; and Keith, *Take Up Thy Bed*. For literary criticism on mental illness, femininity, and literature, see Showalter, *Female Malady*; and Gilbert, *Madwoman in the Attic*. See also Klages, *Woeful Afflictions*; Holmes, *Fictions of Affliction*; and Garland-Thomson, *Extraordinary Bodies*.

7. McDaniel received a RITA Award from the Romance Writers of America in 1992; three of her novels were selected as International Reading Association

(IRA) and Children's Book (IRA/CBC) Children's Choices in 1989 and 1990, and her novels have appeared on several best-seller lists. *Invincible Summer* was an ALA Best Book for Young Adults, a Booklist Young Adult Editors' Choice, and a School Library Journal Best Book of the Year. McDaniel and Ferris's publications would have enjoyed increased visibility from such recognition. Although Lowry was best known for her Newberry Award–winning novel *The Giver* (1994), her first novel, *A Summer to Die* (1977), was teen sick-lit. Benning's books were all teen sick-lit similar to McDaniel's.

8. The final book in the series, *To Live Again* (2001), takes place nearly eight years after *No Time to Cry* and details Dawn's struggle with "another medical crisis" that causes partial paralysis. Since it was published well after the emergence of teen sick-lit, I do not discuss it here.

9. See Smith-Rosenberg, "Female World of Love and Ritual."

10. In considering the interconnected disciplinary power of gender and sexual and bodily normativity in teen sick-lit, my analysis responds to Kenneth Kidd's recent call for a greater queer theoretical engagement with youth literature. See Kidd, "Queer Theory's Child."

11. Mitchell and Snyder, *Narrative Prosthesis*, 48–49. See also Sontag, *Illness as Metaphor*.

12. On the cultural work of affect, see Ahmed, *Cultural Politics of Emotion*; Clough and Halley, *Affective Turn*; Love, *Feeling Backward*; Gould, *Moving Politics*; and Berlant, *Female Complaint* and *Cruel Optimism*. On the relationship between reading and sadness, see Warhol, *Having a Good Cry*.

13. Gould, *Moving Politics*, 27.

14. Rose addresses this issue in *The Case of Peter Pan*, 12–42.

15. See Williams, *Marxism and Literature*.

16. "From Pooh to Salinger."

17. Fitzgerald, "The Influence of Anxiety." See also Aronson, *Exploding the Myths*, 53.

18. "The Paperback Revolution."

19. For more information about problem novels, see Egoff, "The Problem Novel." See also Egoff, *Thursday's Child*; Murray, *American Children's Literature*, 175–212; and MacLeod, *American Childhood*, 198–210.

20. Rose, *Peter Pan*, 10.

21. Ibid., 2.

22. Ibid., 141. Rose is "referring to . . . the very constitution of the adult as a subject, a process which the adult then *repeats* through the book which he or she gives to the child" (141).

23. See Trites, *Disturbing the Universe*, x.

24. McDaniel won the RITA Award for *Now I Lay Me Down to Sleep*. *Goodbye Doesn't Mean Forever* (1989), *Too Young to Die* (1989), and *Somewhere between Life and Death* (1990) were selected as IRA/CBC Children's Choices.

25. Whitfield, "Missions of Mercy."

26. Kumbier, "Chronic Popularity."
27. Spelman, *Fruits of Sorrow*, 1.
28. Whitfield, "Missions of Mercy."
29. Two notable exceptions to this suppression of the voice and perspective of characters with disease or disability are Cynthia Voight's *Izzy Willy Nilly* (1986) and Judy Blume's *Deenie* (1991).
30. Egoff in Feinberg, *Welcome to Lizard Motel*, 40. For a further discussion of the YA illness narrative's obsessive recounting of symptoms, see Kumbier, "Chronic Popularity," 72–77.
31. McDaniel, *Six Months*, 27. From this point onward, this chapter will use in-text parenthetical citations when quoting from novels by McDaniel and Ferris.
32. By contrast, John Green's author's note in *A Fault in Our Stars* (2012), *Time*'s number one fiction book of 2012, reminds readers, "This book is a work of fiction. I made it up. Neither novels nor their readers benefit from attempts to divine whether any facts hide inside a story. Such efforts attack the very idea that made-up stories can matter."
33. McDaniel webpage.
34. McDaniel also thanks "all the dedicated health personnel who are warring with childhood cancer" in *Six Months to Live*, while *She Died Too Young* (1994) expresses "gratitude to Tennessee Donor Services, whose valuable input helped in the creation of th[e] manuscript." Meanwhile *Baby Alicia Is Dying* (1993) thanks the staff of Childkind, an organization that began in 1989 as a group home for children born with HIV/AIDS, and *If I Should Die before I Wake* ends with information on how to become a hospital program volunteer. *A Time to Die* (1992) is dedicated to Karen Leigh Fleming (October 6, 1967–February 20, 1991), "a victim of cystic fibrosis."
35. Imaging was a popular alternative treatment for cancer in the 1980s in which cancer patients mobilize their imagination to conjure war imagery of their body battling enemy cancer cells. Dawn often imagined cancer cells as blobs battling her teddy bear army.
36. Teen sick-lit could very well be one form of cultural response to a perceived childhood/adolescent cancer epidemic, since it experienced its surge in popularity in the 1980s, a decade that also witnessed a surge in childhood cancer cases. The National Cancer Institute reports that childhood leukemias and brain tumors seemed to escalate in the early 1980s, while rates in succeeding years have not demonstrated consistent upward or downward movement. See National Cancer Institute, "Childhood Cancers"; and Kaiser, "No Meeting of the Minds." Newspaper articles about childhood cancer also steadily increased throughout the 1980s into the 1990s, especially reportage about the dangers of prolonged exposure to power lines and the benefits of breastfeeding in preventing childhood cancer. The historian Gretchen Krueger argues that unlike most adult cancers, leukemia and other common childhood tumors were responsive to drug therapies in observable ways, making them ideal poster children for publicists, journalists, investigators,

and politicians who wanted to highlight advancement in cancer research and treatment while eliding "the negative realities such as the limited gains made in certain pediatric cancers, the high costs of treatment, and the high prevalence of mental and physical disabilities caused by experimental chemotherapy protocols." See Krueger, "'For Jimmy, and the Boys and Girls of America.'"

37. Lipsyte, "For Teen-Agers, Mediocrity?"

38. See Mickenberg, *Learning from the Left.*

39. Murray, *American Children's Literature*, 185. For more information about young adult genres, see the library resource Herald, *Teen Genreflecting.*

40. MacLeod in Feinberg, *Welcome to Lizard Motel*, 40.

41. There was also a resurgence of series fiction, which competed with the problem novel formula, serving in many ways as its antithesis. A wildly popular format of YA literature for teen girl readers from the 1950s, the famed girl sleuth Nancy Drew reinvented herself in the mid-1980s with a spinoff, *The Nancy Drew Files* (1986–1991). However, new girls' series, such as Ann M. Martin's *Babysitters Club* series (1986–1991) and Francine Pascal's *Sweet Valley High* (1983–1991), also burst on the YA lit scene. Both series featured affluent suburban girls partaking in normative teen girl staples, such as cheerleading, babysitting, and boyfriends. However, girls' series fiction usually cultivated a world that, while brimming with adventure, was eminently, "reassuringly knowable," according to Sherrie Inness. Unlike the precarious protagonists of teen sick-lit, "Nancy Drew is not going to get seriously injured in a car accident; Cherry Ames is not going to discover that she has cancer." See Inness, *Nancy Drew and Company*, 3.

42. Feinberg, *Welcome to Lizard Motel*, 34. Likewise, Marc Aronson argues that "physical ailments" and "grave diseases" were central to the problem novel. See Aronson, *Exploding the Myths*, 55.

43. Feinberg, *Welcome to Lizard Motel*, 37.

44. Feinberg in "Up Front: Barbara Feinberg," *New York Times*, May 7, 2009, http://www.nytimes.com/2009/ 05/10/books/review/ Upfront-t.html.

45. Lipsitz, *Possessive Investment.*

46. "Ellis Island whiteness" is Matthew Frye Jacobsen's term. See Jacobsen, *Roots Too.* I thank Nikhil Pal Singh for pushing me to more fully consider the racial politics of teen sick-lit.

47. Davis, *Bending Over*, 5.

48. Bell, "Introducing White Disability Studies," 275.

49. Audre Lorde describes a similar experience with a nurse who encourages her to wear a prosthesis to conceal the loss of her breast after her radical mastectomy, in spite of its causing her physical and emotional discomfort. See Lorde, *Cancer Journals*, 49–50.

50. I thank the anonymous reader from the *Journal of Literary and Cultural Disability Studies* for making this observation. See Sontag, *Illness as Metaphor*; Lorde, *Cancer Journals*; Hooper, "Beauty Tips for the Dead"; and Ehrenreich, "Welcome to Cancerland."

51. Grossman, "Dying Teenagers in Love."

52. Ibid.

53. It is worth noting that Jean Ferris's characters are slightly older than McDaniel's. Robin and Rick's ages aren't specified, but we know that Rick is in college while Robin is still in high school. Dawn Rochelle's saga begins at thirteen, but by the end of the books, she is roughly as old as Robin.

54. Stiker, *History of Disability*, 136.

55. "Piss on Pity" is a famous disability rights slogan from the twentieth century.

56. Library of Congress, "Promoting Literacy." Established in 1977, the Library of Congress's Center for the Book celebrates American literary heritage, promotes an appreciation for books, and fosters reading. Later, the center focused on literacy programs in cooperation with other reading advocacy organizations at state and local levels. Fostering a relationship between the government and the private sector, the center subsists primarily on tax-deductible donations from corporations and individuals. Moreover, since 1984, many affiliated, state-based centers for the book have been established throughout the fifty states and the District of Columbia, promoting their own individual state literary heritage via themes, projects, and events in partnership with the Library of Congress.

57. Maeoff, "Dismay over Those Who Shun Reading"; Ringle, "Technology Isn't Enemy of Books"; Kidder, "How Illiteracy, and Aliteracy, Waste the Wisdom of the Ages"; McDowell, "New U.S. Law"; "A Nation of Lookers-Into"; Stephens, "Pen and Paper"; Cohen, "If the Written Word Is Really Dying"; Collins, "Aliteracy . . . You Wouldn't Read about It"; Will, "Tempting Readers"; and Donahue, "Books Pushed to the Back."

58. Maeoff, "Dismay over Those Who Shun Reading."

59. McDowell, "New U.S. Law."

60. Library of Congress, *Television, the Book, and the Classroom*, 7–8.

61. Ibid., 11–12.

62. The program was developed out of an experiment in Philadelphia when an advance copy of the script for a two-part TV dramatization of the Roosevelt family was printed as an insertion for the *Philadelphia Inquirer* with additional copies printed and sent for all of the city's junior and senior high school students. Students worked with the script on various assignments, and the show drew excellent ratings as a result of the participatory nature of the program.

63. In keeping with larger national concerns about reading practices in the face of the distractions posed by new technologies like television and videogames, quite a few *After School Specials* in this period also focused on illiteracy—illiterate parents or children who conceal their inability to read from their loved ones and schoolteachers. See the following ABC *After School Specials*: "Backwards: The Riddle of Dyslexia" (1984), "The Hero Who Couldn't Read" (1984), and "Daddy Can't Read" (1988). "Backwards" and "Daddy Can't Read" featured a white illiterate child and factory worker, respectively, while "Hero" featured an African American illiterate basketball player.

64. Teachers registered their class with the BOOK-IT! Program and received educational materials to use in class, such as reading charts to track students' individual and class progress. By the late 1980s, Pizza Hut came into schools to throw a free pizza party for an entire class if all students met their individual and collective reading goals.
65. Cohen, "If the Written Word Is Really Dying."
66. The metastasizing magazine market was also blamed for reading's decline. The *Economist* reported that according to a magazine audit firm, Mediamark Research Inc., "look-into-ship" was becoming an alternative to reading, in that most people (94 percent of American adults) were "look[ing] into" at least one magazine per month. See "A Nation of Lookers-Into."
67. Cohen, "The Lost Book Generation."
68. Ibid. See also Henderson, "Literacy Campaign
69. Maeoff, "Dismay over Those Who Shun Reading."
70. Gardner, "Case of the Vanishing Reader." See also Donahue, "Books Pushed to the Back Shelf," which reported that "60% of American households did not purchase a single book in a given year . . . not even *How to Satisfy a Woman Every Time*. Or *French for Cats*."
71. Lipsyte, "For Teen-Agers, Mediocrity?"
72. Gardner, "Case of the Vanishing Reader"; and Donahue, "Books Pushed to the Back Shelf."
73. Maeoff, "Dismay over Those Who Shun Reading."
74. Ibid.
75. For an examination of the intertwined processes of welfare reduction and prison expansion, see Wacquant, *Punishing the Poor*.
76. Kidder, "How Illiteracy, and Aliteracy, Waste the Wisdom of the Ages."
77. McDaniel, webpage.
78. Grossman, "Dying Teenagers in Love."
79. Feinberg, *Welcome to Lizard Motel*, 35. Likewise, the YA literature scholar Marc Aronson cites debates on the American Library Association listserv about YA lit's penchant for "bleakness." See Aronson, *Exploding the Myths*, 70.
80. Aronson, *Exploding the Myths*, 55.
81. Egoff in Feinberg, *Welcome to Lizard Motel*, 40.
82. Baker, "Adolescent Depression."
83. McDaniel, webpage.
84. Lurlene McDaniel, "Question from Ph.D. Student writing about you," February 17, 2008, personal email.
85. *Six Months to Live* revolves around Ecclesiastes 3, "To everything there is a season." *Saving Jessica* (1996) features the following epigraph: "This is how we know what love is: Jesus Christ laid down his life for us. And we ought to lay down our lives for our brothers. . . . Dear children, let us not love with words or tongue but with actions and in truth (1 John 3:16 and 18)." *Till Death Do Us Part* (1997) quotes from 1 Corinthians 13:4–8 with "Love is patient, love is kind."

86. Cvetkovich, *Archive of Feelings*, 10.
87. Ibid., 7.
88. See Reissman, "Women and Medicalization."
89. Hochschild, *Managed Heart*, 2.
90. Ibid., 6.
91. Ibid., 108.
92. Hardt and Negri, *Empire*, 292–93.
93. The first use of the term "emotional intelligence" is usually attributed to Wayne Payne's doctoral thesis, "A Study of Emotion: Developing Emotional Intelligence" (1985).
94. Gould, *Moving Politics*, 40.
95. See Lauren Berlant's discussion of precarity and the precariat in *Cruel Optimism*, 194–96.

NOTES TO CHAPTER 4

1. Bradley, *Yes, Your Teen Is Crazy!*, 5.
2. See also Thornton, *Brain Culture*; Wexler, *Brain and Culture*; Johnson, *Mind Wide Open*; and Restak, *Naked Brain*.
3. See Rajan, *Biocapital*; Rose, *Politics of Life*; and Wailoo, Nelson, and Lee, *Genetics and the Unsettled Past*. See also Haraway, *Modest_Witness*.
4. See Duster, *Backdoor to Eugenics*; Roberts, *Killing the Black Body*; Kevles, *In the Name of Eugenics*; and Gould, *Mismeasure of Man*.
5. See Hubbard, "Abortion and Disability"; Saxton, "Disability Rights and Selective Abortion"; Rapp, *Testing Women*; Sandel, *Case against Perfection*; and Glover, *Choosing Children*.
6. Dr. Peter D. Kramer used this famous phrase to describe the antidepressant drug Prozac in his book *Listening to Prozac*.
7. Friend, "Scientists Trek to Inner Space."
8. Yemma, "Imaging Moves Scientists Closer."
9. Begley, "Mapping the Brain." See also Allen, "Mapping the Brain."
10. Bush, "Presidential Proclamation 6158."
11. Judd, "Statement Concerning Fiscal Year 1995."
12. Ibid.
13. Ibid.
14. Ibid.
15. Ibid.
16. U.S. Equal Employment Opportunity Commission, "Remarks of President Bush."
17. Ibid.
18. Ibid.
19. Begley, "Mapping the Brain."
20. McKernan, "Global Map of the Mind."
21. Ibid.

22. See Dumit, *Picturing Personhood*, 6–8. See also Hixson, "New Seeing-Eye Machines."

23. Begley, "Mapping the Brain." Note that the *Newsweek* article draws a careful distinction between a "retarded patient" and a "normal volunteer," a distinction that enables the disabled person to appear as a medical subject while the "normal" person appears autonomous. See also Dumit, *Picturing Personhood*, 160.

24. Begley, *Mind and the Brain*, 24.

25. For a discussion of these articles, see Fausto-Sterling, *Sexing the Body*, 115–45.

26. Ibid., 115.

27. Schwartz, "Genes, Hormones, and Sexuality."

28. "Sexual Preference Linked to Brain Region, Study Says"; Price, "Scientist Links Brain Anomaly." See also LeVay, "Difference in Hypothalamic Structure."

29. There are hundreds of articles on the genetic and neurological arguments for a biologized notion of sexual orientation. Selected primary source articles include the following: "Study Links Genetics, Male Homosexuality Research"; "The Gay Brain: Corpus Callosum"; Knox, "Gene May Help Explain"; Katz, "US Scientists Find Sex on the Brain"; Price, "Scientists Link Brain Anomaly, Homosexuality"; Connor, "Homosexuality Linked to Genes"; Angier, "Zone of Brain"; Suplee, "Brain May Determine Sexuality"; Kong, "Researcher Finds Clue"; Hurst, "New Study"; "'Gays' Wary of Problem with Brain"; Gelman et al., "Born or Bred"; Begley and Hager, "Does DNA Make Some Men Gay?"

30. Angier, "Zone of Brain."

31. Ward in Angier, "Zone of Brain." McRuer also notes the parallel histories of medicalization shared by homosexuality and disability in *Crip Theory*.

32. Coleman, "Teen-Age Risk-Taking."

33. Ibid.

34. Ibid.

35. Ibid.

36. Ibid.

37. Ibid.

38. Ibid.

39. See Rembis, *Defining Deviance*.

40. National Institute of Mental Health Child Psychiatry Branch, http://intramural.nimh.nih.gov/chp/ brainimaging/index.html.

41. Strauch, *Primal Teen*, 12.

42. Walsh, *Why Do They Act*, 16.

43. Ibid.

44. Strauch, *Primal Teen*, 7–8 and 63.

45. Ibid., 8.

46. Drill, McDonald, and Odes, *Deal With It!*

47. Carlson and Teasdale, *Teen Brain Book*.

48. Strauch, *Primal Teen*, 204.

49. Ibid., 67–68.

50. Ibid., 37.

51. Walsh, *Why Do They Act*, 78.
52. Strauch, *Primal Teen*, 32.
53. Crenson, "Parents Just Don't Understand."
54. Walsh, *Why Do They Act*, 29.
55. Ibid., 30.
56. Ibid.
57. Ibid., 65.
58. Ibid.
59. The article also reported that women performed better on spatial problems when their testosterone levels were at their peak. See Suplee, "Neurobiology." See also Begley, "Thinking Looks Like This."
60. Bradley, *Yes, Your Teen Is Crazy!*, xvi.
61. Walsh, *Why Do They Act*, 12.
62. Ibid.
63. Ibid., 79.
64. Bradley, *Yes, Your Teen Is Crazy!*, xv. Italics in original.
65. Ibid., 10.
66. Ibid., 8.
67. Ibid., xviii.
68. Ibid., 61.
69. Ibid., 64–69.
70. Ibid., xvii. Italics in original.
71. Ibid., 8.
72. Walsh, *Why Do They Act*, 33.
73. Ibid., 46.
74. Ibid., 37.
75. Ibid., 8.
76. Ibid., xvi.
77. Coleman, "Teen-Age Risk-Taking." See also Siegfried, "Adolescents' Risky Rebellion."
78. Bloom, "The Way We Live Now."
79. Especially in superpredator stories, many newspapers reported a rise in juvenile violence more generally. See Diulio, "Stop Crime Where It Starts"; Atkinson, "Superpredators"; Leonard, "Are 90s Teens This Terrible"; Zoglin, "Now for the Bad News." See also Becker, "Superpredators."
80. Romero, "Music Review."
81. Weisbard et al., "Ten Past Ten."
82. Seventeen of the shootings occurred in elementary schools, the most famous of which, as of this writing, has been the 2012 Sandy Hook Elementary School shooting, the third deadliest school shooting in American history. See Kirk, "Since 1980, 297 People Have Been Killed."
83. Although cultural representations and journalistic reportage on school shooters (and the demographics of school shooters themselves) have been overwhelmingly

focused on teen boys, the first modern school shooting is often cited as that of Brenda Spencer, seventeen, who used her birthday rifle to shoot at an elementary school playground across the street from her home in January 1979.

84. Egan, "Where Rampages Begin."

85. Ryan, "Accused Teen Killer."

86. Todd Ramlow analyzes the cultural use of such epithets and their place in cultures of bullying surrounding the school shooters Andy Williams, Eric Harris, and Dylan Klebold. See Ramlow, "Bad Boys," 107–8 and 118.

87. For an account of media coverage, see Cullen, *Columbine*.

88. Egan, "Where Rampages Begin."

89. Kass, "They Called Themselves the 'Trenchcoat Mafia.'"

90. Ramlow, "Bad Boys," 117.

91. Bowles, "Armed, Alienated, and Adolescent."

92. Giedd and two colleagues, Dr. Daniel R. Weinberger and Dr. Brita Elvevåg, coauthored a paper for the National Campaign to Prevent Teenage Pregnancy called "The Adolescent Brain: A Work in Progress" (2005). In her introduction to the paper, Sarah S. Brown, the campaign's director and treasurer, argued that although her organization and others had developed lists of "background and contextual" contributing factors to teen pregnancy, "What is striking about this list—in addition to its sheer length—is that it is almost entirely confined to psychological and social factors. . . . Aside from the age of puberty, physiological factors are virtually absent." Thus, discoveries about the teen brain also animated interventions into teen sexuality and pregnancy prevention as a new form of adolescent sexual containment.

93. Weinberger, "A Brain Too Young."

94. Ibid. In 2004, *Roper v. Simmons*, a Missouri case that questions whether or not the Eighth Amendment ban on "cruel and unusual" punishment prohibits the execution of juvenile murderers, was heard by the Supreme Court in an attempt to overturn *Stanford v. Kentucky* (1989). A 5–4 majority ruled that "cruel and unusual" did not apply because an "American consensus against the use of capital punishment" did not exist. Justices were encouraged to consider new adolescent neuroscience discoveries ("biological reasons why teens younger than 18 tend not to be as adept as adults in controlling their impulses"). An amicus brief filed by numerous health care organizations, including the American Medical Association and the American Academy of Child and Adolescent Psychiatry, argued that "to hold [teens] accountable . . . for the immaturity of their neural anatomy and psychological development" was unjust. See Jacoby, "Op-Ed: Some Juvenile Killers."

95. Various letters to the editor appear in the March 13, 2001, edition of the *New York Times* under the title "Anatomy of a Teenaged Shooting," including letters by Simon Turkel, Thomas Szasz, M.D., and Laurens D. Young.

96. Many scholars, including the historians Joseph Dumit and Sander Gilman, have argued that, legally and socially, there is no definitive correlation between an

abnormal brain and an insane person. Dumit argues that neuroimaging is so persuasive because it enables onlookers to actually see an abnormal brain rather than relying on the seemingly more subjective diagnosis of an abnormal mind. Visual knowledge bolsters a comforting cultural fantasy that "the brain of an insane person should somehow be different from a sane person's" (118–19). See Dumit, *Picturing Personhood*, 109–33. See also Ader, "Investigational Treatments." For more information about the controversial nature of these scans as diagnostic tools or in/as expert testimony, see Kulynych, "Psychiatric Neuroimaging Evidence"; Mayberg, "Functional Brain Scans"; Rojas-Burke, "PET Scans Advance"; and Dumit, *Picturing Personhood*, 107–38.

97. "Defense Doesn't Want State to Look for Physical Defects."

98. O'Connor, "Medical Expert."

99. Most recently, in the 2012 mass school shooting at Sandy Hook Elementary School, the shooter Adam Lanza's brain was autopsied to search for abnormalities (none were found), and as of this writing, geneticists at the University of Connecticut are studying Lanza's DNA to search for abnormalities or mutations that might be associated with aggressive behavior—the first study of its kind. See Walsh, "DNA of Newtown Shooter."

100. Edsall, "Understanding Oklahoma."

101. Ibid.

102. Portions of *Stiffed* also appeared in article form earlier than the book's publication from 1994 to 1996 in the *New Yorker*, *Double Take*, and *Esquire*. See Faludi, "Betrayal of the American Man." See also Levant, "Masculinity Crisis," 221.

103. *Dateline NBC with Katie Couric*, "The Fury." See also Hall, "The Troubled Life of Boys."

104. Peterson, "Raising Sons in the Age of Columbine." Another thoughtful op-ed piece argued that the "murderous attack in Littleton" was not "a manifestation of individual pathologies," and not something that reveals a crisis in youth culture, but rather a crisis fueled by a celebrated cultural norm of "violent masculinity" in spite of how much cultural critics attempt to speak about "violent teens" in "gender-neutral" terms. See Katz and Jhally, "Crisis in Masculinity."

105. Faludi, "Betrayal of the American Man," 48.

106. Lemann, "Battle over Boys." See also Doten, "Without Guidance."

107. Lemann, "Battle over Boys."

108. Ibid.

109. Ruth Feldstein discusses the problems of male development in an earlier period. See Feldstein, *Motherhood*.

110. Bernstein, "Books of the Times."

111. Nelson, *Body and Soul*, 161. See also Washington, *Medical Apartheid*.

112. Nelson, *Body and Soul*, 155.

113. Ibid.

114. As teenagers, the boys were held and interviewed by the police for more than twenty-four hours before they confessed, and all recanted almost immediately

and have maintained their innocence ever since. In two separate trials, all five were convicted based largely on their confessions rather than other physical evidence. After spending years in prison, all were exonerated when Matias Reyes, a convicted rapist and murderer serving a life sentence for other crimes, admitted that he committed the crime alone. His involvement in the rape was confirmed by DNA evidence.

115. See Angier, "Disputed Meeting."
116. Breggin, "U.S. Hasn't Given Up." Breggin was an outspoken critic of the Violence Initiative, and one of the best-known critics of the mainstream psychiatric treatment of youth. See Breggin and Breggin, *The War against Children*. On criticism of the Violence Initiative from a radical perspective, see Progressive Labor Party, "Position Paper"; and Cohen, "Beware the Violence Initiative Project."
117. Angier, "Disputed Meeting."
118. Ibid.
119. See Bennett, Diulio, and Walters, *Body Count*.
120. Zoglin, "Now for the Bad News"; and Annin, "Superpredators Arrive." See also Dusseau, "Superpredators Prowl"; "New Age Killer Kids"; Gray, "Invasion of the Superpredators"; and Montgomery, "Young Lawbreakers."
121. See Annin, "Superpredators Arrive"; and Atkinson, "Superpredators."
122. Butterfield, "Crime Continues to Decline." See also Diulio, "My Black Crime Problem."
123. Diulio, "My Black Crime Problem."
124. Zoglin, "Now for the Bad News."
125. Duggan asserts the emblematic similarity of two fearsome figures that emerged in cultural narratives of the late nineteenth century: the "black beast rapist" and the "homicidal lesbian," as they are both "threats to white masculinity and to the stability of the white home as fulcrum of political and economic hierarchies." Duggan, *Sapphic Slashers*, 3.
126. Ibid., 29. Here, I invoke Duggan's argument that in the discourse of the pathological lesbian, "the most troubling figure" of all was "the 'normal' woman . . . [who] became a figure of potential instability and betrayal located in the position of any (white) woman" and positioned "alongside the foregrounded image of the fixed, identifiable, deviant lesbian."
127. Goode, "Terror in Littleton."
128. Ibid.
129. *Dateline NBC with Katie Couric*, "The Fury."
130. Leonard, "Are 90s Teens This Terrible?"
131. Fields, "Brain Sitters for Teens."
132. Kaufman, "Are Psychiatric Drugs Safe"; McKenzie and Mora, "Kids' Antidepressants"; Reed, "Does a Drug Lead Boys to Kill?"; Cohen, "Just Say No"; Lore, "Teen Use of Drugs"; Goff, "Medicines for the Mind"; Price, "School Shooter"; Hoeller, "Dubious Drug Therapy."
133. White House, press release.

134. The Bay Area Radical Mental Health Collective specializes in addressing the "emotional and mental crises in the radical left" in order to create sustainable, emotionally supported activism instead of paternalistic intervention. Its website features a large selection of zines, which have been a mainstay of the youth anti-psychiatry movement and provide a valuable record of its concerns, activities, and individual activist stories. The website features a fairly strong feminist critique of traditional heteronormative gender roles, including a critique of conventional, aggressive masculinity and its role in violence against women. See Bay Area Radical Mental Health Collective, http://www. radicalmentalhealth.net.
135. MFI's website does not include archival information, but includes many up-to-the-minute press releases regarding its current projects, activities, and events. MindFreedom International, "Frequently Asked Questions," http://www.mindfreedom.org/mfi-faq/intro-FAQs/.
136. MindFreedom International, "Global Campaign," http://www.mindfreedom.org/campaign/global.
137. MindFreedom International, "Youth Campaign," http://www.mindfreedom.org/campaign/usa.
138. MindFreedom International, "Personal Stories," http://www.mindfreedom.org/personal-stories.
139. AgainstPsychiatry.com, http://www.againstpsychiatry.com. Flohr's site includes news stories regarding psychiatric drugs and their effects and YouTube videos of personal testimonies of psychiatric survivors. There are also writings by homeless youth and foster children regarding their experiences with the psychiatric system.
140. Flohr, "Don't Listen to Him, He's Crazy."
141. PBS, "Profiling School Shooters."
142. Ibid. In 1998, the American Psychological Association issued a pamphlet entitled "22 Warning Signs" that might signal a "serious possibility" or "potential" for violence, while the National School Safety Center, a California-based nonprofit group, produced a twenty-point "Checklist of Characteristics of Youth Who Have Caused School-Associated Violent Deaths." The National Center for the Prevention of Crime also developed a list of warning signs for troubled kids who might require "action."
143. See FBI, "The School Shooter." See also "FBI: School Threat Report"; and PBS, "Profiling School Shooters."
144. PBS, "Profiling School Shooters."
145. The Mosaic 2000 program used a questionnaire for children that rated their answers from 1 (low potential for violence) to 10 (high potential for violence). The program was meant to help school officials better assess school threats. See PBS, "Profiling School Shooters." See also Thomas, "Mosaic 2000."
146. PBS, "Profiling School Shooters."
147. See TeenScreenTruth, http://www.teenscreentruth.com.

148. See President's New Freedom Commission on Mental Health, http://www.mentalhealthcommission.gov. See also Columbia University TeenScreen Program, http://www.teenscreen. org/.
149. See Gilmore, *Golden Gulag.* See also Davis, *Are Prisons Obsolete?*
150. Moriearty and Carson, "Cognitive Warfare and Young Black Males." See also Hing, "Shocking Details."
151. Stiker, *History of Disability,* 160.
152. Wacquant, *Punishing the Poor.*
153. Begley, "Rewiring Your Gray Matter."

NOTES TO THE CONCLUSION

1. In spite of how dismissive of actual and legitimate health anxiety the term "cyberchondria" is, some researchers have found a strong correlation between people researching "depression" online and people who eventually receive a diagnosis of depression. Of course, this analysis neglects myriad economic, cultural, professional, and interpersonal complexities involved in the depression diagnostic procedures. See Leykin, Muñoz, and Contreras, "Are Consumers of Health Information 'Cyberchondriacs'?"
2. Pew surveys tracking health information seeking found in 2011 that 80 percent of Internet users gather health information online. Over a third of U.S. adults reported in 2012 that they went online to diagnose a medical condition, either their own or someone else's, to supplement (or, in some cases, to avoid) a visit to the doctor's office. See Fox, "Health Report." See also Fox and Duggan, "Health Online 2013."
3. White and Horvitz, "Cyberchondria."
4. Moyer, "Cyberchondria."
5. Berlant, "Slow Death," 765.
6. "Stayin' Alive" was a disco song by the Bee Gees that became a hit as part of the soundtrack for *Saturday Night Fever* in 1977.
7. "Crisis ordinary" is Lauren Berlant's characterization of neoliberalism. See "Affect, Noise, Silence, Protest." See also Duggan, *Twilight of Equality.*
8. Diagnostic media's emergence is, in part, related to the shifting technological landscape of the late twentieth century, which, as cultural historians of the Internet have argued, has increasingly transitioned away from collectivizing "mass" media and toward miniaturization and individualization. See Dean, *Democracy;* Chun, *Programmed Visions;* and Schulte, "Occupying a Node of Our Own."
9. The establishment of a WiiFit user profile begins with a weigh-in, which could prompt a startled "Oh!" from the game if it perceives the user to be too heavy as he/she steps on the Wii balance board. The gaming system often gives comically contradictory health advice. The WiiFit scolds users for not playing enough to meet weight loss goals, while Wii gaming sessions are punctuated by gentle Wiiminders to "take a break" or "go outside for a bit."

10. Tanner, "Break a Leg?" Scientists have also studied the Wii's potential application as a training tool for surgeons. See Reilly, "A Wii Warm-Up."

11. Edwards, "WebMD's Depression Test."

12. Rose in Puar, "Cost of Getting Better," 155–56.

13. Galewitz, "Census: Uninsured Numbers Decline."

14. See Rose, *The Politics of Life Itself*.

15. Puar, "Cost of Getting Better," 153. McRuer refers to this as our "haunt[ing]" by "the disability to come" in *Crip Theory*, 207.

16. Disability activists often refer to able-bodied people as "TABs," or "temporarily able-bodied." For examples of scholarship about disability as a meta-identity that is more fluid than others, see Davis, *Bending Over*; and Siebers, *Disability Theory*.

17. Here, I invoke Audre Lorde's famous essay, "The Master's Tools Will Never Dismantle the Master's House." See Lorde, *Sister Outsider*, 110–14.

18. Here, I tease out the crip implications of Katherine Bond Stockton's queer account of "growing sideways" in *Queer Child*.

BIBLIOGRAPHY

ABC *After School Specials*. "Amy and the Angel." September 22, 1982. Paley Center for Media Archives, New York.

———. "Are You My Mother?" March 5, 1986. Paley Center for Media Archives, New York.

———. "Backwards: The Riddle of Dyslexia." March 4, 1984. Paley Center for Media Archives, New York.

———. "Blind Sunday." April 21, 1976.

———. "Boys Will Be Boys." September 15, 1994. Paley Center for Media Archives, New York.

———. "Can a Guy Say No?" February 12, 1986. Paley Center for Media Archives, New York.

———. "Cindy Eller: A Modern Fairy Tale." October 9, 1985. Paley Center for Media Archives, New York.

———. "Class Act: A Teacher's Story." March 18, 1987. Paley Center for Media Archives, New York.

———. "Color of Friendship." November 11, 1981. Paley Center for Media Archives, New York.

———. "Daddy Can't Read." March 16, 1988. Paley Center for Media Archives, New York.

———. "Date Rape." September 15, 1988. Paley Center for Media Archives, New York.

———. "Desperate Lives." March 3, 1982.

———. "Did You Hear What Happened to Andrea?" December 27, 1983. Paley Center for Media Archives, New York.

———. "Divorced Kids' Blues." March 4, 1987. Paley Center for Media Archives, New York.

———. "Don't Touch." November 6, 1985. Paley Center for Media Archives, New York.

———. "Face at the Edge of the World" (a.k.a. "A Desperate Exit"). September 19, 1986. Paley Center for Media Archives, New York.

———. "Francesca, Baby." October 6, 1976. Paley Center for Media Archives, New York.

———. "Girlfriend." April 15, 1993. Paley Center for Media Archives, New York.

———. "Heartbreak Winner" (a.k.a. "The Gold Test"). February 13, 1980. DVD.

———. "The Hero Who Couldn't Read." April 18, 1984. Paley Center for Media Archives, New York.

———. "Hewitt's Just Different." October 12, 1977. Paley Center for Media Archives, New York.

———. "The Ice Skating Rink." February 5, 1975. DVD.

———. "In the Shadow of Love: A Teen AIDS Story." September 18, 1991. Paley Center for Media Archives, New York.

——. "I Want to Go Home." February 13, 1985. Paley Center for Media Archives, New York.

——. "Jacqui's Dilemma." June 2, 1994. Paley Center for Media Archives, New York.

——. "Just a Regular Kid: An AIDS Story." September 9, 1987. Paley Center for Media Archives, New York.

——. "Just Tipsy, Honey." March 16, 1989. Paley Center for Media Archives, New York.

——. "The Kid Who Wouldn't Quit: The Brad Silverman Story." September 23, 1987. Paley Center for Media Archives, New York.

——. "The Late Great Me! Story of a Teenaged Alcoholic." November 14, 1979. Paley Center for Media Archives, New York.

——. "Love Hurts." September 16, 1993. Paley Center for Media Archives, New York.

——. "A Matter of Time." February 11, 1981. DVD.

——. "A Mile from Here to Glory." May 5, 1978. DVD.

——. "Mom and Dad Can't Hear Me." April 5, 1978.

——. "My Dad Can't Be Crazy . . . Can He?" September 14, 1989. Paley Center for Media Archives, New York.

——. "Please Don't Hit Me, Mom." September 19, 1983. Paley Center for Media Archives, New York.

——. "Positive: A Journey into AIDS." December 7, 1995. Paley Center for Media Archives, New York.

——. "Private Affairs." October 26, 1989.

——. "Run, Don't Walk." March 4, 1981.

——. "Schoolboy Father." October 15, 1980. DVD.

——. "Shades of a Single Protein." January 28, 1993. Paley Center for Media Archives, New York.

——. "She Drinks a Little" (a.k.a. "First Step"). September 23, 1981. Paley Center for Media Archives, New York.

——. "A Special Gift." October 24, 1979. Paley Center for Media Archives, New York.

——. "Stoned." November 12, 1980. Library of Congress Moving Image Collections.

——. "Taking a Stand." January 19, 1989. Paley Center for Media Archives, New York.

——. "Tattle: When to Tell on a Friend." October 26, 1988. Paley Center for Media Archives, New York.

——. "Terrible Things My Mother Told Me." January 20, 1988. Paley Center for Media Archives, New York.

——. "Too Soon for Jeff." September 12, 1996. Paley Center for Media Archives, New York.

——. "Torn between Two Fathers." April 20, 1989. Paley Center for Media Archives, New York.

——. "Tough Girl." September 22, 1982; October 28, 1981. Paley Center for Media Archives, New York.

——. "A Very Delicate Matter." November 10, 1982. Paley Center for Media Archives, New York.

———. "What Are Friends For?" March 19, 1980. Paley Center for Media Archives, New York.

Abramson, Barry. "Game Parlors Face Curbs." *New York Times*, August 9, 1981, LI11.

Acland, Charles R. *Youth, Murder, Spectacle: The Cultural Politics of Youth in Crisis*. Boulder: Westview, 1994.

Adams, Rachel, and David Savaran, eds. *The Masculinity Studies Reader*. New York: Blackwell, 2002.

Ader, Mary. "Investigational Treatments: Coverage, Controversy, and Consensus." *Annals of Health Law* 5 (1996): 45–61.

AgainstPsychiatry.com. Website. http://www.againstpsychiatry.com.

Ahmed, Sara. *The Cultural Politics of Emotion*. New York: Routledge, 2004.

Allen, William. "Mapping the Brain." *St. Petersburg Times*, April 12, 1994, 1D.

American Experience. "Bioethics Opinions." http://www.pbs.org/wgbh/amex/bubble/ sfeature/sf_ethics.html.

———. Online forum on *The Boy in the Bubble*. http://www.pbs.org/wgbh/amex/bubble/sfeature/sf_forum.html.

American Experience: The Boy in the Bubble. DVD. Directed by Barak Goodman and John DiMaggio. WGBH Educational Foundation and Ark Media LLC, 2006.

Angier, Natalie. "Disputed Meeting to Ask if Crime Has Genetic Roots." *New York Times*, September 19, 1995, C1.

———. "Elementary, Dr. Watson: The Neurotransmitters Did It." *New York Times*, January 23, 1994, sec. 4, p. 1.

———. "Study Links Brain to Transsexuality." *New York Times*, November 2, 1995, B15.

———. "Zone of Brain Linked to Men's Sexual Orientation." *New York Times*, August 30, 1991, A1.

Annin, Peter. "Superpredators Arrive." *Newsweek*, January 22, 1996.

Aronson, Marc. *Exploding the Myths: The Truth about Teenagers and Reading*. Lanham: Scarecrow Press, 2001.

Atkinson, Peter. "Superpredators." *Sunday Mail* (Queensland), January 21, 1996.

Auerbach, Stuart. "Boy Spending Life in Plastic Bubble." *Washington Post*, October 3, 1974, A1.

———. "A Three-Year-Old Boy's Life in a Sterile Bubble." *Washington Post*, October 6, 1974, A3.

Backe, John D. Introduction to *Television, the Book, and the Classroom: A National Seminar, April 26, 1978*. Washington: Library of Congress, 1978.

Baker, Ronald. "Adolescent Depression: Illness or Developmental Task." *Journal of Adolescence* 1.4 (1978): 297–307.

Banet-Weiser, Sarah. *Authentic™: The Politics of Ambivalence in a Brand Culture*. New York: New York University Press, 2012.

———. *Kids Rule! Nickelodeon and Consumer Citizenship*. Durham: Duke University Press, 2007.

Bay Area Radical Mental Health Collective. Website. http://www.radicalmentalhealth.net.

Bayer, Ronald. *Homosexuality and American Psychiatry: The Politics of Diagnosis.* New York: Basic Books, 1981.

Baynton, Douglas. "Disability and the Justification of Inequality in American History." In *The New Disability History*, edited by Paul Longmore and Lauri Umansky, 33–57. New York: New York University Press, 2001.

Becker, Elizabeth. "Superpredators: An Ex-Theorist on 'Young Superpredators,' Bush Aide, Has Regrets." *New York Times*, February 9, 2001, A2.

Bederman, Gail. *Manliness and Civilization: Cultural History of Gender and Race in the United States, 1880–1917.* Chicago: University of Chicago Press, 1996.

Begley, Sharon. "Gray Matters: New Brain-Scanning Technologies Show Differences between Men and Women." *Newsweek*, March 27, 1995.

———. "Mapping the Brain." *Newsweek*, April 20, 1992.

———. *The Mind and the Brain: Neuroplasticity and the Power of Mental Force.* New York: Harper Collins, 2002.

———. "Rewiring Your Gray Matter." *Newsweek*, January 1, 2000.

———. "Thinking Looks Like This: PET Scans Show the Brain Recalling and Cogitating. (Positron Emission Topography)." *Newsweek*, November 25, 1991.

Begley, Sharon, with Mary Hager. "Does DNA Make Some Men Gay?" *Newsweek*, July 23, 1993.

Bell, Chris. "Introducing White Disability Studies: A Modest Proposal." In *The Disability Studies Reader*, edited by Lennard Davis, 2nd ed., 275–82. New York: Routledge, 2006.

Bell, Joseph N. "Why the Revolt against Sex Education?" *Good Housekeeping*, November 1969.

Bennett, William J., John J. Diulio Jr., and John P. Walters. *Body Count: Moral Poverty . . . And How to Win America's War against Crime.* New York: Simon and Schuster, 1996.

Berlant, Lauren. "Affect, Noise, Silence, Protest: Ambient Citizenship." Social Science Research Council, November 20, 2009. http://publicsphere.ssrc.org/berlant-affect-noise-silence-protest-ambient-citizenship/.

———. ed. *Compassion: The Culture and Politics of an Emotion.* New York: Routledge, 2004.

———. *Cruel Optimism.* Durham: Duke University Press, 2011.

———. *The Female Complaint: The Unfinished Business of Sentimentality in American Culture.* Durham: Duke University Press, 2008.

———. *The Queen of America Goes to Washington City.* Durham: Duke University Press, 1997.

———. "Slow Death (Sovereignty, Obesity, Lateral Agency)." *Critical Inquiry* 33 (2007): 754–80.

Bernstein, Richard. "Books of the Times: Boys, Not Girls, as Society's Victims." *New York Times*, July 31, 2000, E6.

Bettelheim, B. "Right and Wrong Way to Teach Sex." *Ladies' Home Journal*, January 1970.

Black, Edwin. *War against the Weak: Eugenics and America's Campaign to Create a Master Race*. New York: Four Walls Eight Windows, 2003.

Bloom, Amy. "The Way We Live Now: Generation Rx." *New York Times*, March 12, 2000, sec. 6, p. 23.

Blos, P. "The Second Individuation Process of Adolescence." *Psychoanalytic Study of the Child* 22 (1967): 162–86.

Blume, Judy. *Deenie*. New York: Bradbury Press, 1973.

Boddy, William. *Fifties Television: The Industry and Its Critics*. Reprint, Chicago: University of Illinois, 1992.

———. "Senator Dodd Goes to Hollywood: Investigating Video Violence." In *The Revolution Wasn't Televised: Sixties Television and Social Conflict*, edited by Lynn Spigel and Michael Curtin, 161–85. New York: Routledge, 1997.

Bogdan, Robert. *Freak Show: Presenting Human Oddities for Amusement and Profit*. Chicago: University of Chicago Press, 1988.

Bowles, Scott. "Armed, Alienated, and Adolescent." *USA Today*, March 26, 1998, 9A.

"Boy, 12, Out of 'Bubble' for Treatment." *New York Times*, February 8, 1984, A20.

"The Boy in the Bubble." *New York Times*, February 26, 1984, E16.

The Boy in the Plastic Bubble. ABC. November 12, 1976. Dir. Randall Kleiser.

"Boy Leaves His 'Bubble.'" *Washington Post*, February 9, 1984, D10.

"Boy with Immune Deficiency Challenges Theories in 3 Years of His Life in Plastic Bubble." *New York Times*, October 7, 1974, 41.

Bradley, Michael J. *Yes, Your Teen Is Crazy! Loving Your Kid without Losing Your Mind*. Gig Harbor: Harbor Press, 2003.

Breggin, Peter. "U.S. Hasn't Given Up Linking Genes to Crime." Letter to the Editor. *New York Times*, September 18, 1992. http://query.nytimes.com/gst/ fullpage.htm l?res=9E0CE6DC1338F93BA2575AC0A964958260&n=Top/Reference/Times%20 Topics/Subjects/C/Crime%20and%20Criminals.

Breggin, Peter R., and Ginger Ross Breggin. *The War against Children: Psychiatry Targets Inner City Youth*. Monroe: Common Courage Press, 1998.

Brody, Howard. *Stories of Sickness*. 2nd ed. New York: Oxford University Press, 2002.

Brown, Wendy. *Regulating Aversion: Tolerance in the Age of Identity and Empire*. Princeton: Princeton University Press, 2008.

Brumberg, Joan Jacobs. *The Body Project: An Intimate History of American Girls*. New York: Vintage, 1998.

Buckley, Tom. "TV: Afterschool Gluttony." *New York Times*, November 15, 1978, C30.

Bush, President George H. W. "Presidential Proclamation 6158." From Project on the Decade of the Brain. http://www.loc.gov/loc/brain/proclaim.html. Accessed May 29, 2008.

Bush, William. *Who Gets a Childhood? Race and Juvenile Justice in Twentieth-Century Texas*. Athens: University of Georgia Press, 2010.

Butterfield, Fox. "Crime Continues to Decline, but Experts Warn of Coming 'Storm' of Juvenile Violence." *New York Times*, November 19, 1995, A18.

Butts, J. D. "Sex Education: Who Needs It?" *Ebony*, April 1977, 96–98.

Carlson, Dale, and Nancy Teasdale, eds. *The Teen Brain Book: Who and What Are You.* Madison: Bick Publishing, 2004.

Cartwright, Lisa. *Screening the Body: Tracing Medicine's Visual Culture.* Minneapolis: University of Minnesota Press, 1995.

Chasin, Alexandra. *Selling Out: The Gay and Lesbian Movement Goes to Market.* New York: Palgrave Macmillan, 2001.

Chinn, Sarah. *Inventing Modern Adolescence: The Children of Immigrants in Turn-of-the-Century America.* New Brunswick: Rutgers University Press, 2008.

Chivers, Sally, and Nicole Markotic. *The Problem Body: Projecting Disability on Film.* Columbus: Ohio State University Press, 2010.

Cho, David. "Parents Pan 'Bubble Boy' Film: Disney Movie Makes Light of Illness, Say Advocates for Afflicted Children." *Washington Post,* August 17, 2001.

Chun, Wendy Hui Kyong. *Programmed Visions: Software and Memory.* Cambridge: MIT Press, 2011.

Clare, Eli. *Exile and Pride: Disability, Queerness, and Liberation.* Cambridge: South End, 1999.

———. "Stolen Bodies, Reclaimed Bodies: Disability and Queerness." *Public Culture* 13.3 (2001): 359–65.

Cline, V. B. "TV Violence: How It Damages Your Children." *Ladies' Home Journal,* February 1975.

Clough, Patricia, and Jean Halley. *The Affective Turn: Theorizing the Social.* Durham: Duke University Press, 2007.

Clover, Carol. *Men, Women, and Chainsaws: Gender in the Modern Horror Film.* Princeton: Princeton University Press, 1993.

Clowse, Barbara Barksdale. *Brainpower for the Cold War: The Sputnik Crisis and the National Defense Education Act of 1958.* Westport: Greenwood, 1981.

Cohen, David. "Just Say No to Classroom Drugs: Never Have So Many Children—Especially Boys—Been Given Drugs That Affect Mind, Mood and Behavior." *Toronto Globe and Mail,* December 6, 1999, A17.

Cohen, Liz. *A Consumer's Republic: The Politics of Mass Consumption in Postwar America.* New York: Random House, 2003.

Cohen, Mitchel. "Beware the Violence Initiative Project—Coming Soon to an Inner City Near You." *Synthesis/Regeneration* 19, Spring 1999. http://www.greens.org/s-r/19/19-07.html. Accessed July 18, 2008.

Cohen, Roger. "If the Written Word Is Really Dying, Who Is Patronizing the Superstores?" *New York Times,* September 30, 1990, sec. 4, p. 6.

———. "The Lost Book Generation." *New York Times,* January 6, 1991, 4A.

Cohn, Victor. "Boy with Fatal Disease Kept Alive 3½ Years in Germ-Free NIH Room." *Washington Post,* March 27, 1976, B1.

Coleman, Daniel. "Teen-Age Risk-Taking: Rise in Deaths Prompts New Research Effort." *New York Times,* November 24, 1987, C1.

Collins, K. "Aliteracy . . . You Wouldn't Read about It." *Sunday Mail* (Queensland), December 1, 1991.

Columbia University TeenScreen Program. Website. http://www.teenscreen.org/index. php? option=com_content& task=view&id=43&Itemid=124. Accessed June 11, 2008.

Connor, Steve. "Homosexuality Linked to Genes; Ethical Dilemmas Loom as Genetic Study of Gays' Families Suggests Predisposition Is Inherited through Men's Mothers." *Independent* (London), July 16, 1993, 1.

———. "Science: The Last Great Frontier." *Independent* (London), May 21, 1995, 52.

Cook, Daniel Thomas. *The Commodification of Childhood: The Children's Clothing Industry and the Rise of the Child Consumer*. Durham: Duke University Press, 2004.

Couser, G. Thomas. *Recovering Bodies: Illness, Disability, and Life Writing*. Madison: University of Wisconsin Press, 1997.

Crenson, Matt. "Parents Just Don't Understand: Brain Changes, Not Hormones, Explain Many Adolescent Behaviors." Associated Press, December 26, 2000.

Crimp, Douglas. *Melancholia and Moralism: Essays on AIDS and Queer Politics*. Cambridge: MIT Press, 2002.

Cuban, Larry. "Required TV for Students: A Proposal for Home Educational Programming." *Washington Post*, May 21, 1978, B8.

Cullen, Dave. *Columbine*. New York: Twelve, 2009.

Cvetkovich, Ann. *Archive of Feelings: Trauma, Sexuality, and Lesbian Public Culture*. Durham: Duke University Press, 2003.

Danesi, Marcel. *Cool: The Signs and Meanings of Adolescence*. Toronto: University of Toronto Press, 1994.

Dateline NBC with Katie Couric. "The Fury: Why Boys Are Always the Ones to Commit Teen Violence." May 18, 1999.

Davis, Angela Y. *Are Prisons Obsolete?* New York: Seven Stories Press, 2003.

Davis, Glyn, and Kay Dickinson, eds. *Teen TV: Genre, Consumption, and Identity*. London: British Film Institute, 2008.

Davis, Lennard. *Bending Over Backwards: Disability, Dismodernism, and Other Difficult Positions*. New York: New York University Press, 2002.

———. "Constructing Normalcy: The Bell Curve, the Novel, and the Invention of the Disabled Body in the Nineteenth Century." In *The Disability Studies Reader*, edited by Lennard Davis, 2nd ed., 3–17. New York: Routledge, 2006.

———. *Enforcing Normalcy: Disability, Deafness, and the Body*. New York: Verso, 1995.

Dean, Jodi. *Democracy and Other Neoliberal Fantasies: Communicative Capitalism and Left Politics*. Durham: Duke University Press, 2009.

Decade of the Brain. http://www.loc.gov/loc/brain/proclaim.html. Accessed April 15, 2008.

"Defense Doesn't Want State to Look for Physical Defects in Kinkel's Brain." Associated Press, September 9, 1999.

DeVita-Raeburn, Elizabeth. *The Empty Room: Surviving the Loss of a Brother or Sister at Any Age*. New York: Simon and Schuster, 2004.

Diulio, John J. "My Black Crime Problem, and Ours." *City Journal*, Spring 1996. http://www.city-journal.org/html/6_2_my_black.html.

———. "Stop Crime Where It Starts." *New York Times*, July 31, 1996, A15.

"Does Video Violence Make Johnny Hit Back?" *Science Digest*, January 1972.

Doherty, Thomas. *Teenagers and Teenpics: The Juvenilization of American Movies in the 1950s*. Philadelphia: Temple University Press, 2002.

Donahue, Deirdre. "Books Pushed to the Back of the Shelf." *USA Today*, June 24, 1992, 1D.

Doten, Patti. "Without Guidance, Boys Will Be Troubled Boys." *Boston Globe*, July 20, 1998, C7.

Douglas, Susan. *Where the Girls Are: Growing Up Female with the Mass Media*. New York: Three Rivers Press, 1994.

Drew, Bernard. *The 100 Most Popular Young Adult Authors: Biographical Sketches and Bibliographies*. Englewood: Libraries Unlimited, 1997.

Drill, Esther, Heather McDonald, and Rebecca Odes. *Deal With It! A Whole New Approach to Your Body, Brain, and Life as a gURL*. New York: Pocket Books, 1999.

Driver, Susan. *Queer Girls and Popular Culture: Reading, Resisting, and Creating Media*. New York: Peter Lang, 2007.

Duggan, Lisa. "The New Homonormativity: The Sexual Politics of Neoliberalism." In *Materializing Democracy: Toward a Revitalized Cultural Politics*, edited by Russ Castronovo and Dana D. Nelson. Durham: Duke University Press, 2002.

———. *Sapphic Slashers: Sex, Violence, and American Modernity*. Durham: Duke University Press, 2000.

———. *The Twilight of Equality? Neoliberalism, Cultural Politics, and the Attack on Democracy*. New York: Beacon, 2004.

Dumit, Joseph. *Picturing Personhood: Brain Scans and Biomedical Identity*. Princeton: Princeton University Press, 2004.

Dusseau, Brigitte. "Superpredators Prowl Where 'Killing Time' Is Taken Literally." *Daily Telegraph Mirror* (Australia), December 28, 1995.

Duster, Troy. *Backdoor to Eugenics*. New York: Routledge, 2003.

Eccleshare, Julia. "Teenage Fiction: Realism, Romances, Contemporary Problem Novels." In *International Companion Encyclopedia of Children's Literature*, edited by Peter Hunt, 2nd ed., vol. 1. London: Routledge, 2004.

Edelman, Lee. *No Future: Queer Theory and the Death Drive*. Durham: Duke University Press, 2004.

Edsall, Thomas B. "Understanding Oklahoma: Masculinity on the Run; From Workplace to Bedroom—to Timothy McVeigh." *Washington Post*, April 30, 1995, C01.

Edwards, Jim. "WebMD's Depression Test Has Only One (Sponsored) Answer: You're 'At Risk.'" CBSNews.com, February 10, 2012. http://www.cbsnews.com/8301-505123 _162-42844266/ webmds-depression-test-has-only-one-sponsored-answer-youre- at-risk/?tag=bnetdomain.

Egan, Timothy. "Where Rampages Begin: A Special Report: From Adolescent Angst to Shooting Up Schools." *New York Times*, June 14, 1998.

Egoff, Sheila. "The Problem Novel." In *Only Connect: Readings on Children's Literature*, edited by Sheila Egoff, G. T. Stubbs, and L. F. Ashley, 2nd ed. Toronto: Oxford University Press, 1980.

————. *Thursday's Child: Trends and Patterns in Contemporary Children's Literature.* Chicago: American Library Association, 1981.

Ehrenreich, Barbara. "Welcome to Cancerland." *Harper's Magazine*, November 2001, 43–53.

"Ending Mayhem." *Time*, June 7, 1976.

Erikson, Erik H. *Identity: Youth and Crisis.* 1968. Reprint, New York: Norton, 1994.

Faier, J. S. "Sex-Education Controversy." *Harper's Bazaar*, July 1977.

Faludi, Susan. "The Betrayal of the American Man: At Ground Zero of the Masculinity Crisis, the Ornamental Culture, beyond the Politics of Confrontation." *Newsweek*, September 13, 1999.

Fausto-Sterling, Anne. *Sexing the Body: Gender Politics and the Construction of Sexuality.* New York: Basic Books, 2000.

Fawaz, Ramzi. *The New Mutants: Comic Book Superheroes and Popular Fantasy in Postwar America.* New York: New York University Press, forthcoming.

"FBI: School Threat Report Not Meant for Student Profiling." CNN.com, September 6, 2000. http://archives.cnn.com/2000/ US/09/06/fbi.school.violence.02/. Accessed June 11, 2008.

Federal Bureau of Investigation. "The School Shooter: A Threat Assessment Perspective." http://www.fbi.gov/publications/school/school2.pdf. Accessed June 11, 2008.

Feinberg, Barbara. *Welcome to Lizard Motel: Children, Stories, and the Mystery of Making Things Up.* Boston: Beacon, 2004.

Feldstein, Ruth. *Motherhood in Black and White: Race and Sex in American Liberalism, 1930–1965.* Ithaca: Cornell University Press, 2000.

Ferri, Beth A., and Jessica Bacon. "Beyond Inclusion: Disability Studies in Early Childhood Teacher Education." In *Promoting Social Justice for Young Children*, edited by B. S. Fennimore and A. L. Goodwin, 137–46. New York: Springer, 2011.

Ferris, Jean. *Invincible Summer.* New York: Farrar, Straus, and Giroux, 1987.

Fields, Suzanne. "Brain Sitters for Teens: New Psychiatric Pitch." *Washington Times*, August 1, 1989, F1.

Fisher, Emily. "An Icy Tale with a Happy Ending." *Washington Post*, February 5, 1975, B9.

Fishman, K. D. "Sex Becomes a Brand-New Problem." *New York Times Magazine*, March 13, 1966.

Fitzgerald, Frances. "The Influence of Anxiety." *Harper's Magazine*, September 2004, 62–70.

Fleischer, Doris Zames, and Frieda Zames. *The Disability Rights Movement: From Charity to Confrontation.* Philadelphia: Temple University Press, 2001.

Flohr, Fritz. "Don't Listen to Him, He's Crazy." http://www.againstpsychiatry. com/ Dontlisten.html.

Foucault, Michel. *Discipline and Punish: The Birth of the Prison.* New York: Vintage, 1995.

————. *History of Sexuality.* Vol. 1, *An Introduction.* New York: Vintage, 1990.

————. "Nietzsche, Genealogy, History." In *The Foucault Reader*, edited by Paul Rabinow. New York: Pantheon, 1984.

Fox, Susannah. "Health Report." Pew Internet and American Life Project, February 1, 2011. http://www.pewinternet.org/ Reports/2011/HealthTopics.aspx.

Fox, Susannah, and Maeve Duggan. "Health Online 2013." Pew Internet and American Life Project, January 15, 2013. http://pewinternet.org/Reports/ 2013/Health-online. aspx.

Frank, Arthur. *The Wounded Storyteller: Body, Illness, Ethics*. Chicago: University of Chicago Press, 1997.

Frank, Thomas. *The Conquest of Cool: Business Culture, Counterculture, and the Rise of Hip Consumerism*. Chicago: University of Chicago Press, 1998.

Freeman, Elizabeth. *Time Binds: Queer Temporalities, Queer Histories*. Durham: Duke University Press, 2010.

Friend, Tim. "Scientists Trek to Inner Space." *USA Today*, October 26, 1992, 6D.

"From Pooh to Salinger." *Time*, December 13, 1963.

Furlong, W. B. "It's a Long Way from the Birds and the Bees [Sex Education Program]." *New York Times Magazine*, June 11, 1967, 24–25.

Galewitz, Phil. "Census: Uninsured Numbers Decline as More Young Adults Gain Coverage." Kaiser Health News, September 12, 2012. http://www.kaiserhealthnews. org/Stories/ 2012/September/12/census-number-of-uninsured-drops.aspx.

Gamson, Joshua. *Freaks Talk Back: Tabloid Talk Shows and Sexual Nonconformity*. Chicago: University of Chicago Press, 1999.

Gardner, Marilyn. "The Case of the Vanishing Reader." *Christian Science Monitor*, January 28, 1992, 13.

Garisto, Leslie. "Why 'Afterschool Specials' Are Special; 'Afterschool' Fare." *New York Times*, August 5, 1985, H21.

Garland-Thomson, Rosemarie. *Extraordinary Bodies: Figuring Physical Disability in American Culture and Literature*. New York: Columbia University Press, 1997.

———, ed. *Freakery: Cultural Spectacles of the Extraordinary Body*. New York: New York University Press, 1996.

"The Gay Brain: Corpus Callosum." *Gazette* (Montreal), November 18, 1994, A12.

"'Gays' Wary of Problem with Brain." *Courier-Mail* (Queensland), April 1, 1991.

Gelman, David, Donna Foote, Todd Barrett, and Mary Talbot. "Born or Bred." *Newsweek*, February 24, 1992.

Gerber, David A. *Disabled Veterans in History*. Ann Arbor: University of Michigan Press, 2000.

"Germ-Free 'Home' Shields Baby Boy." *New York Times*, September 23, 1972, 62.

Gilbert, James. *A Cycle of Outrage: America's Reaction to the Juvenile Delinquent in the 1950s*. New York: Oxford University Press, 1986.

Gilbert, Sandra M. *The Madwoman in the Attic: The Woman Writer and the Nineteenth-Century Literary Imagination*. 2nd ed. New Haven: Yale University Press, 2000.

Gilligan, Carol. "In a Different Voice: Women's Conceptualizations of Self and Morality." *Harvard Educational Review* 47 (1977): 481–517.

Gilmore, Ruth Wilson. *Golden Gulag: Prisons, Surplus, Crisis and Opposition in Globalizing California*. Berkeley: University of California Press, 2007.

Gitlin, Todd. *Inside Prime Time*. New York: Pantheon, 1983.

Glover, Jonathan. *Choosing Children: Genes, Disability, and Design*. Oxford: Oxford University Press, 2008.

Goff, Karen Goldberg. "Medicines for the Mind." *Washington Times*, May 7, 2000, D1.

Goleman, Daniel. "When Rage Explodes, Brain Damage May Be the Cause." *New York Times*, August 7, 1990, C1.

Gomery, Douglas. "Television, Hollywood, and the Development of Movies Made-for-Television." In *Regarding Television*, edited by E. Ann Kaplan. Frederick: University Publications of America, 1983.

Goode, Erica. "Terror in Littleton: The Psychology; Deeper Truths Sought in Violence by Youths." *New York Times*, May 4, 1999, A28.

Goodheart, B. "Sex in the Schools: Education or Titillation?" *Today's Health*, February 1970.

Goodman, W. "Controversy over Sex Education: What Our Children Stand to Lose." *Redbook*, September 1969.

Gordon, S. "Let's Put Sex Education Back Where It Belongs—in the Home." *Good Housekeeping*, October 1977.

Gould, Deborah. *Moving Politics: Emotion and ACT UP's Fight against AIDS*. Chicago: University of Chicago Press, 2009.

Gould, Stephen Jay. *The Mismeasure of Man*. 2nd ed. New York: Norton, 1996.

Gray, Mary L. *Out in the Country: Youth, Media, and Queer Visibility in Rural America*. New York: New York University Press, 2009.

Gray, Stephen. "Invasion of the Superpredators." *Sunday Times* (London), February 16, 1997.

Green, John. *A Fault in Our Stars*. New York: Dutton, 2012.

Grossberg, Lawrence. *We Gotta Get Out of This Place*. New York: Routledge, 1992.

Grossman, Marni. "Dying Teenagers in Love." *Bust*, July/August 2010. http://www.utne. com /Literature/Sick-Lit-Lurlene-McDaniel.aspx. Accessed March 5, 2013.

Halberstam, Judith. *In a Queer Time and Place: Transgender Bodies, Subcultural Lives*. New York: New York University Press, 2005.

———. *The Queer Art of Failure*. Durham: Duke University Press, 2011.

Hall, Stephen S. "The Troubled Life of Boys: The Bully in the Mirror." *New York Times* online, August 12, 1999. http://query.nytimes.com/gst/fullpage.html?res =9A02E2D91E39F931A 1575BC0A96F958260. Accessed June 6, 2008.

Hall, Stuart. *Policing the Crisis: Mugging, the State, and Law and Order*. New York: Palgrave Macmillan, 1978.

Hall, Stuart, and Tony Jefferson, eds. *Resistance through Rituals: Youth Subcultures in Post-War Britain*. New York: Holmes and Meier, 1976.

Haller, Beth A. *Representing Disability in an Ableist World: Essays on Mass Media*. Louisville: Avocado Press, 2010.

Haraway, Donna. *Modest_Witness@Second_Millenium.FemaleMan_Meets_Onco Mouse: Feminism and Technoscience*. New York: Routledge, 1997.

————. *Simians, Cyborgs, and Women: The Reinvention of Nature*. New York: Routledge, 1991.

Hardt, Michael, and Antonio Negri. *Empire*. Cambridge: Harvard University Press, 2001.

Harris, Anita, ed. *All about the Girl: Culture, Power, and Identity*. New York: Routledge, 2004.

Hawkins, Anne Hunsaker. *Reconstructing Illness: Studies in Pathography*. West Lafayette: Purdue University Press, 1998.

"Headliners." *New York Times*, February 12, 1984, E7.

"'Heartbreak' Tale: All Is Not Olympic Gold That Glitters." *Washington Post*, February 10, 1980, TV43.

Hebdige, Dick. *Subculture: The Meaning of Style*. New York: Routledge, 1981.

Henderson, Keith. "Literacy Campaign Moves to TV." *Christian Science Monitor*, August 8, 1986, 19.

Herald, Diane Tixier. *Teen Genreflecting: A Guide to Reading Interests*. 2nd ed. Englewood: Libraries Unlimited, 1997.

Herndl, Diane Price. *Invalid Women: Figuring Feminine Illness in American Fiction and Culture*. Chapel Hill: University of North Carolina Press, 1993.

Herring, Scott. *Another Country: Queer Anti-Urbanism*. New York: New York University Press, 2010.

Hine, Thomas. *The Rise and Fall of the American Teenager*. New York: Harper Collins, 1999.

Hing, Julianne. "The Shocking Details of a Mississippi School-to-Prison Pipeline." ColorLines, November 26, 2012 http://colorlines.com/archives /2012/11/school_prison_pipeline_meridian.html.

Hixson, Joseph R. "New Seeing-Eye Machines . . . Look inside Your Body, Can Save Your Life." *Vogue*, July 1983.

Hochschild, Arlie Russell. *The Managed Heart: Commercialization of Human Feeling*. Berkeley: University of California Press, 2003.

Hoeller, Keith. "Dubious Drug Therapy." *Washington Times*, March 29, 2005, A15.

Holmes, Martha Stoddard. *Fictions of Affliction: Physical Disability in Victorian Culture*. Ann Arbor: University of Michigan Press, 2004.

Hooper, Judith. "Beauty Tips for the Dead." In *Minding the Body: Women Writers on Body and Soul*, edited by Patricia Foster, 107–38. New York: Anchor/Doubleday, 1994.

Hubbard, Ruth. "Abortion and Disability: Who Should and Should Not Inhabit the World." In *The Disability Studies Reader*, edited by Lennard J. Davis, 2nd ed., 93–104. New York: Routledge, 2006.

Hurst, Lynda. "New Study on What Makes Men Gay Splits Homosexual Community." *Toronto Star*, September 14, 1991, D5.

Illouz, Eva. *Cold Intimacies: The Making of Emotional Capitalism*. Cambridge: Polity, 2007.

———. *Saving the Modern Soul: Therapy, Emotions and the Culture of Self-Help*. Berkeley: University of California Press, 2008.

Inness, Sherrie A., ed. *Delinquents and Debutantes: Twentieth Century American Girls' Cultures*. New York: New York University Press, 1998.

———. *Nancy Drew and Company: Culture, Gender, and Girls' Series*. New York: Popular Press, 1997.

Irvine, Janice M. *Talk about Sex: The Battles over Sex Education in the United States*. Berkeley: University of California Press, 2004.

Iseman, M. F. "Sex Education: What Do Children Actually Learn?" *McCall's*, January 1968.

Jacobsen, Matthew Frye. *Roots Too: White Ethnic Revival in Post–Civil Rights America*. Cambridge: Harvard University Press, 2006.

Jacoby, Jeff. "Op-Ed: Some Juvenile Killers Deserve to Die." *Boston Globe*, October 21, 2004, A19.

Jameson, Frederic. *The Political Unconscious: Narrative as a Socially-Symbolic Act*. Ithaca: Cornell University Press, 1981.

Johnson, Steven. *Mind Wide Open: Your Brain and the Neuroscience of Everyday Life*. New York: Scribner, 2004.

Johnson, Victoria. *Heartland TV: Prime Time Television and the Struggle for U.S. Identity*. New York: New York University Press, 2008.

Judd, Lewis L. "Statement concerning Fiscal Year 1995 Appropriations for the National Institute of Mental Health, National Institute of Neurological Disorders and Stroke, National Institute on Drug Abuse, National Institute on Deafness and Other Communication Disorders, National Eye Institute, National Institute on Aging, National Institute of Child Health and Human Development, National Institute on Alcohol Abuse and Alcoholism." Senate Appropriations Subcommittee on Labor, Health, and Human Services, and Education, and Related Agencies. Federal Document Clearing House Congressional Testimony. March 1, 1994.

Kafer, Alison. "Compulsory Bodies: Reflections on Heterosexuality and Able-Bodiedness." *Journal of Women's History* 15.3 (2003): 77–89.

Kaiser, Jocelyn. "No Meeting of the Minds on Childhood Cancer." *Science*, December 3, 1999, 1832–34.

Kamen, Paula. "A 'Sick-Lit' Manifesto: I Am Woman, Hear Me Kvetch." Cupcakeseries. com, March 3, 2005. http://cupcakeseries.blogspot.com/ 2005/03/editors-note-paula-kamen-will-be-guest.html. Accessed February 27, 2008.

Kass, Jeff. "They Called Themselves the 'Trenchcoat Mafia.'" *Christian Science Monitor*, April 22, 1999.

Katz, Ian. "US Scientists Find Sex on the Brain." *Guardian*, August 30, 1991.

Katz, Jackson, and Sut Jhally. "Crisis in Masculinity." *Boston Globe*, May 2, 1999.

Kaufman, Marc. "Are Psychiatric Drugs Safe for Children?" *Washington Post*, May 4, 1999, Z07.

Kaufman, Marjorie. "Long Island Q&A: David G. Amral, What Makes Memory Tick?" *New York Times*, April 10, 1994, 14LI, p. 2.

Kearney, Mary Celeste. *Girls Make Media*. New York: Routledge, 2006.

———, ed. *Mediated Girlhoods: New Explorations of Girls' Media Culture*. New York: Peter Lang, 2011.

Keefauver, J. "Dick and Jane and a Dread Disease." *National Review*, June 9, 1978, 721.

Keith, Lois. *Take Up Thy Bed and Walk: Death, Disability, and Cure in Classic Fiction for Girls*. New York: Routledge, 2001.

Kevles, Daniel. *In the Name of Eugenics: Genetics and the Uses of Human Heredity*. Cambridge: Harvard University Press, 1998.

Kidd, Kenneth B. *Making American Boys: Boyology and the Feral Tale*. Minneapolis: University of Minnesota Press, 2004.

———. "Queer Theory's Child and Children's Literature Studies." *PMLA* 126.1 (2011): 182–88.

Kidder, Rushworth M. "How Illiteracy, and Aliteracy, Waste the Wisdom of the Ages." *Christian Science Monitor*, July 8, 1985, 21.

Kiester, E. "TV Violence: What Can Parents Do?" *Better Homes and Gardens*, September 1975.

King, Wayne. "Houston 'Bubble Boy' Dead; Could Not Fight Any Disease." *New York Times*, February 13, 1984, A1.

———. "Signs Hopeful for Boy Out of Bubble and One Who Fell in Lake." *New York Times*, February 11, 1984, 12.

Kirk, Chris. "Since 1980, 297 People Have Been Killed in School Shootings." *Slate*, December 19, 2012. http://www.slate.com/articles/news_and_politics/ map_of_ the_week/2012/12/sandy_hook_a_chart_of_all_196_fatal_school_shootings_ since_1980_map.html.

Klages, Mary. *Woeful Afflictions: Disability and Sentimentality in Victorian America*. Philadelphia: University of Pennsylvania Press, 1999.

Knox, Richard A. "Gene May Help Explain the Origin of Homosexuality." *Boston Globe*, July 16, 1993, 1.

Kobler, J. "Sex Invades the Schoolhouse [with Editorial Comment]." *Saturday Evening Post*, June 29, 1968.

Kohlberg, Lawrence. "Stage and Sequence: The Cognitive Developmental Approach to Socialization." In *Handbook of Socialization Theory and Research*, edited by David Goslin. Chicago: Rand McNally, 1969.

Kong, Dolores. "Researcher Finds Clue in Brains of Gay Men; Reports Difference in Nucleus Linked to Sex." *Boston Globe*, August 30, 1991, 3.

Kramer, Peter D. *Listening to Prozac*. New York: Viking Penguin, 1993.

Krueger, Gretchen. "'For Jimmy, and the Boys and Girls of America': Publicizing Cancers in Twentieth-Century America." *Bulletin of the History of Medicine* 81.1 (2007): 70–93.

Kulynych, Jennifer. "Psychiatric Neuroimaging Evidence: A High-Tech Crystal Ball?" *Stanford Law Review* 49 (1997): 1249–70.

Kumbier, Alana. "The Chronic Popularity of Illness Lit." *Bitch*, Winter 2005, 72–77.

Lasch, Christopher. *The Culture of Narcissism: American Life in an Age of Diminishing Expectations*. New York: Norton, 1979.

LeBlanc, Lauraine. *Pretty in Punk: Girls' Gender Resistance in a Boys' Subculture*. New Brunswick: Rutgers University Press, 1999.

Lemanczyk, Sarah. "After School Specials." *On the Media*, NPR, January 14, 2005.

Lemann, Nicholas. "The Battle over Boys: Will Feminists or Their Foes Win the Teen-Age Soul?" *New Yorker*, July 10, 2000.

Leonard, Mary. "Are 90s Teens This Terrible: Parents Who Rocked 'n' Rolled through the '60s Are Endorsing Increasingly Harsher Measures to Keep Their Children in Line." *Boston Globe*, March 2, 1997, D2.

"Let's Learn to Make Love: Class Discussion Threatens National Teachers Strike." *Newsweek*, January 8, 1973.

Levant, Ronald F. "The Masculinity Crisis." *Journal of Men's Studies* 5.3 (February 28, 1997).

LeVay, Simon. "A Difference in Hypothalamic Structure between Heterosexual and Homosexual Men." *Science* 253 (1991): 1034–37.

Levine, Elana. *Wallowing in Sex: The New Sexual Culture of 1970s American Television*. Durham: Duke University Press, 2007.

Leykin, Yan, Ricardo F. *Muñoz, and Omar Contreras*. "Are Consumers of Health Information 'Cyberchondriacs'? Characteristics of 24,965 Users of a Depression Screening Site." *Depression and Anxiety* 29.1 (January 2012): 71–77.

Library of Congress. "Promoting Literacy, 1980–2002: News from the Center for the Book." http://www.loc.gov/loc/lcib/0209/cfb.html. Accessed September 28, 2007.

———. *Television, the Book, and the Classroom: A National Seminar, April 26, 1978*. Washington, DC: Library of Congress, 1978.

Linton, Simi. *Claiming Disability: Knowledge and Identity*. New York: New York University Press, 1998.

Lipsitz, George. *Possessive Investment in Whiteness: How White People Profit from Identity Politics*. Philadelphia: Temple University Press, 1998.

Lipsyte, Robert. "For Teen-Agers, Mediocrity?" *New York Times*, May 18, 1986, BR30.

List, S. S. "When Our Daughters Discover Love and Sex." *McCall's*, September 1973.

Longmore, Paul. "Conspicuous Contribution and American Cultural Dilemmas: Telethon Rituals of Cleansing and Renewal." In *The Body and Physical Difference: Discourses of Disability*, edited by David T. Mitchell and Sharon L. Snyder, 134–58. Ann Arbor: University of Michigan Press, 1997.

Lorde, Audre. *The Cancer Journals*. San Francisco: Aunt Lute Books, 1997.

———. *Sister Outsider: Essays and Speeches*. New York: Crossing, 2007.

Lore, Diane. "Teen Use of Drugs for Depression on the Rise." Cox News Service, May 14, 1999.

Love, Heather. *Feeling Backward: Loss and the Politics of Queer History*. Cambridge: Harvard University Press, 2007.

Lowry, Lois. *A Summer to Die*. New York: Houghton Mifflin, 1977.

Luker, Kristin. *When Sex Goes to School: Warring Views on Sex—and Sex Education—since the Sixties*. New York: Norton, 2006.

MacLeod, Anne Scott. *American Childhood: Essays on Children's Literature of the Nineteenth and Twentieth Centuries*. Atlanta: University of Georgia Press, 1995.

Maeoff, Gene I. "Dismay over Those Who Shun Reading." *New York Times*, September 28, 1982, C1.

Mahler, Margaret, Fred Pine, and Anni Bergman. *The Psychological Birth of the Human Infant: Symbiosis and Individuation*. New York: Basic Books, 1975.

Males, Mike. *Framing Youth: Ten Myths about the Next Generation*. Monroe: Common Courage Press, 1999.

Mansfield, Stephanie. "8 Years in Germ-Free Chamber: Youth in the Glass Cubicle Dies." *Washington Post*, May 29, 1980, A1.

Marill, Alvin H. *Movies Made for Television, 1964–2004*. Lanham: Scarecrow Press, 2005.

Martin, Emily. *Flexible Bodies: Tracking Immunity in American Culture from the Days of Polio to the Age of AIDS*. New York: Beacon, 1995.

———. *The Woman in the Body: A Cultural Analysis of Reproduction*. Boston: Beacon, 1987.

Mayberg, Helen S. "Functional Brain Scans as Evidence in Criminal Court: An Argument for Caution." *Journal of Nuclear Medicine* 33.6 (1992): 18.

McAlister, Melani. *Epic Encounters: Culture, Media, and U.S. Interests in the Middle East since 1945*. 2nd ed. Berkeley: University of California Press, 2001.

McCarthy, Anna. *The Citizen Machine: Governing by Television in the 1950s*. New York: New Press, 2010.

McColm, Euan. "All-American Monsters: Reared on a Diet of Violent Films, Sick Rock Music, and Neo-Nazi Fantasies in a Country Where Owning a Gun Is a God-Given Right." *Daily Record* (Glasgow, Scotland), April 22, 1999, 1–2.

McDaniel, Lurlene. *I Want to Live*. New York: Random House, 1995.

———. *No Time to Cry*. New York: Bantam, 1993.

———. Personal email with Julie Passanante Elman. February 22, 2008.

———. *Six Months to Live*. New York: Bantam, 1987.

———. *So Much to Live For*. New York: Bantam, 1991.

———. *Till Death Do Us Part*. New York: Bantam, 1997.

———. Webpage. http://www.randomhouse.com/features /lurlene/about_lurlene.html. Accessed December 14, 2007.

McDowell, Edwin. "New U.S. Law Is Intended to Promote the Love of Books." *New York Times*, December 29, 1986, C13.

McGee, Micki. *Self-Help Inc.: Makeover Culture in American Life*. New York: Oxford University Press, 2005.

McGowan, William. "A Sense of Belonging." *New York Times Magazine*, August 23, 1987.

McKenzie, John, and Antonio Mora. "Kids' Antidepressants." *Good Morning America*, ABC, April 30, 1999.

McKernan, Ruth. "A Global Map of the Mind." *Independent*, December 10, 1992, 14.

McPherson, William. "David's Choice." *Washington Post*, February 28, 1984, A17.

McRuer, Robert. "As Good as It Gets: Queer Theory and Critical Disability." *GLQ: A Journal of Lesbian and Gay Studies* 9.1–2 (2003): 79–105.

———. *Crip Theory: Cultural Signs of Queerness and Disability*. New York: New York University Press, 2006.

———. "Critical Investments: AIDS, Christopher Reeve, and Queer/Disability Studies." *Journal of Medical Humanities* 23.3–4 (2002): 221–37.

McRuer, Robert, and Abby L. Wilkerson, eds. Special issue, *GLQ: A Journal of Lesbian and Gay Studies* 9.1–2 (2003).

McVicker, Steve. "Bursting the Bubble." *Houston Press Online*, April 10, 1997. http://www.houston-press.com/1997-04-10/news/bursting-the-bubble/. Accessed June 17, 2008.

Medovoi, Leerom. *Rebels: Youth and the Cold War Origins of Identity*. Durham: Duke University Press, 2005.

Merriam, E. "We're Teaching Our Children That Violence Is Fun." *Ladies' Home Journal*, October 1964.

Meserve, Jeanne, and Eileen O'Connor. "Clintons Lead Discussion at White House Teenager Conference." CNN, May 20, 2000.

Metzl, Jonathan. *The Protest Psychosis: How Schizophrenia Became a Black Disease*. New York: Beacon, 2011.

Mickenberg, Julia L. *Learning from the Left: Children's Literature, the Cold War, and Radical Politics in the United States*. New York: Oxford University Press, 2005.

Miller, Toby. *Cultural Citizenship: Cosmopolitanism, Consumerism, and Television in a Neoliberal Age*. Philadelphia: Temple University Press, 2006.

———. *Makeover Nation: The United States of Reinvention*. Columbus: Ohio State University Press, 2008.

———. *The Well-Tempered Self: Citizenship, Culture, and the Postmodern Subject*. Baltimore: Johns Hopkins University Press, 1993.

Milner, Murray. *Freaks, Geeks, and Cool Kids: Teenagers, Schools, and the Culture of Consumption*. New York: Routledge, 2006.

MindFreedom International. Website. http://www.mindfreedom.org. Accessed July 19, 2008.

Mitchell, David T., and Sharon L. Snyder. *Narrative Prosthesis: Disability and the Dependencies of Discourse*. Ann Arbor: University of Michigan Press, 2000.

Monar, Hedi. "Wooing the Young Reader." *New York Times*, August 7, 1988, ED10.

Montgomery, Lori. "Young Lawbreakers Signal Their Certain Future as Felons." *Philadelphia Inquirer*, April 16, 1996, D01.

Moran, Jeffrey P. *Teaching Sex: The Shaping of Adolescence in the 20th Century*. Boston: Harvard University Press, 2002.

Moriearty, Perry L., and William Carson. "Cognitive Warfare and Young Black Males in America." *Journal of Gender, Race and Justice* 15 (2012): 281–314.

Moyer, Christine S. "Cyberchondria: The One Diagnosis Patients Miss." Amednews.com, January 30, 2012. http://www.amednews.com/article/20120130/health/301309952/1/.

Muñoz, José Esteban. *Cruising Utopia: The Then and There of Queer Futurity*. New York: New York University Press, 2009.

Murray, Gail Schmunk. *American Children's Literature and the Construction of Childhood*. Woodbridge: Twayne, 1998.

Nash, Ilana. *American Sweethearts: Teenage Girls in Twentieth-Century Popular Culture*. Bloomington: Indiana University Press, 2006.

———. "Hysterical Scream or Rebel Yell? The Politics of Teen-Idol Fandom." In *Disco Divas: Women and Popular Culture in the 1970s*, edited by Sherrie A. Inness. Philadelphia: University of Pennsylvania Press, 2003.

National Cancer Institute, U.S. National Institutes of Health. "Childhood Cancers: Questions and Answers." http://www.cancer.gov/cancertopics/factsheet /Sites-Types/childhood. Accessed January 15, 2008.

National Institute of Mental Health Child Psychiatry Branch. Website. http://intramural.nimh.nih.gov/chp/ brainimaging/index.html. Accessed May 29, 2008.

National Institutes of Health. "NIH Faculty Profile, Jay Giedd." http://gpp.nih.gov / Faculty/Mentors/ NIMH /JayGiedd.htm. Accessed May 29, 2008.

National Library of Medicine. "HTA 101: Introduction to Health Technology Assessment." www.nlm.nih.gov/nichsr/hta101/ta10103.htm. Accessed December 4, 2006.

"A Nation of Lookers-Into." *Economist*, September 27, 1986, 26.

Neal, Mark Anthony. *Soul Babies: Black Popular Culture and the Post-Soul Aesthetic*. New York: Routledge, 2002.

Nelson, Alondra. *Body and Soul: The Black Panther Party and the Fight against Medical Discrimination*. Minneapolis: University of Minnesota Press, 2011.

"New Age Killer Kids." *Advertiser*, January 18, 1996.

Nielsen, Kim E. *A Disability History of the United States*. New York: Beacon, 2012.

Norden, Martin F. *The Cinema of Isolation: A History of Physical Disability in the Movies*. New Brunswick: Rutgers University Press, 1994.

O'Connor, Eileen. "Medical Expert: Brain Damage Could Have Contributed to School Shooting Spree." CNN, November 10, 1999. http://www.cnn.com/HEALTH/9911/09/brain.holes/. Accessed June 5, 2008.

O'Connor, John J. "ABC's 'No Greater Gift' about Organ Donorship." *New York Times*, September 10, 1985, C22.

———. "Saturday Is No Picnic for the Kids." *New York Times*, September 30, 1973, 137.

———. "Those Adaptations—Faithful or Fudged?" *New York Times*, February 29, 1975, D29.

———. "TV: ABC Presents Its New Fare for Children." *New York Times*, October 13, 1972, 78.

———. "TV: 'Blind Sunday' Is a Fine Drama." *New York Times*, April 21, 1976, 48.

———. "TV Weekend." *New York Times*, November 12, 1976, 71.

Ordover, Nancy. *American Eugenics: Race, Queer Anatomy, and the Science of Nationalism*. Minneapolis: University of Minnesota Press, 2003.

Oshinsky, David. *Polio: An American Story*. Oxford: Oxford University Press, 2006.

Ouellette, Laurie. *Better Living through Reality TV: Television and Post-Welfare Citizenship*. London: Wiley-Blackwell, 2008.

Palladino, Grace. *Teenagers: An American History*. New York: Basic Books, 1996.

The Paperback Revolution. Website. http://www.crcstudio.org/paperbacks/. Accessed March 11, 2008.

Patton, Cindy. *Fatal Advice: How Safe-Sex Education Went Wrong*. Durham: Duke University Press, 1996.

PBS. "Profiling School Shooters." *PBS Frontline* website. http://www.pbs.org/wgbh/pages/ frontline/shows/kinkel/profile/. Accessed June 11, 2008.

Pearl Jam. *Jeremy*. Music video. Dir. Mark Pellington. 1992.

Penley, Constance. *NASA/Trek: Popular Science and Sex in America*. New York: Verso, 1997.

Perlman, Allison. "Reforming the Wasteland: Television, Reform, and Social Movements, 1950–2004." PhD diss., American Studies Department, University of Texas at Austin, 2007.

Peterson, Karen S. "Raising Sons in the Age of Columbine." *USA Today*, September 20, 1999, 8D.

Prescott, Heather Munro. *A Doctor of Their Own: The History of Adolescent Medicine*. Boston: Harvard University Press, 1998.

President's New Freedom Commission on Mental Health. Website. http://www.mental-healthcommission.gov/. Accessed June 11, 2008.

Price, Joyce Howard. "School Shooter Took Mood-Altering Drug." *Washington Times*, March 25, 2005, A03.

———. "Scientist Links Brain Anomaly, Homosexuality." *Washington Times*, August 30, 1991, A3.

Progressive Labor Party. "A Position Paper of the International Committee against Racism (InCAR) (1993)." http://www.plp.org/pamphlets/violinit.html. Accessed July 19, 2008.

Project on the Decade of the Brain. Website. http://www.loc.gov/loc/brain/. Accessed May 29, 2008.

Puar, Jasbir K. "The Cost of Getting Better: Suicide, Sensation, Switchpoints." *GLQ: A Journal of Lesbian and Gay Studies* 18.1 (2012): 149–58.

Purdum, Todd S. "What They're Really Fighting About." *New York Times*, August 24, 2004.

Quart, Alissa. *Branded: The Buying and Selling of Teenagers*. New York: Basic Books, 2004.

Rabinovitz, O. "How to Talk to Your Parents about Sex." [ed. by M. Brenton]. *Seventeen*, March 1971.

Radway, Janice. *Reading the Romance: Women, Patriarchy, and Popular Literature*. New York: Verso, 1987.

Rajan, Kaushik Sunder. *Biocapital: The Constitution of Postgenomic Life*. Durham: Duke University Press, 2006.

Ramlow, Todd. "Bad Boys: Abstractions of Difference and the Politics of Youth Deviance." *GLQ: A Journal of Lesbian and Gay Studies* 9.1–2 (2003): 107–32.

Rapp, Rayna. *Testing Women, Testing the Fetus: The Social Impact of Amniocentesis in America.* New York: Routledge, 2000.

Reagan, Leslie J., Nancy Tomes, and Paula A. Treichler, eds. *Medicine's Moving Pictures: Medicine, Health, and Bodies in American Film and Television.* Rochester: University of Rochester Press, 2007.

Reed, Fred. "Does a Drug Lead Boys to Kill? It's Time We Found Out." *Washington Times,* January 17, 2000, C2.

Reiff, Philip. *Triumph of the Therapeutic: Uses of Faith after Freud.* Chicago: University of Chicago Press, 1966.

Reilly, Michael. "A Wii Warm-Up Hones Surgical Skills." *New Scientist,* January 19, 2008. http://www.newscientist.com/article/mg19726396.100-a-wii-warmup-hones-surgical-skills.html. Accessed April 4, 2013.

Reissman, Catherine K. "Women and Medicalization: A New Perspective." In *The Politics of Women's Bodies: Sexuality, Appearance, and Behavior,* edited by R. Weitz. New York: Oxford University Press, 2003.

Rembis, Michael. *Defining Deviance: Sex, Science, and Delinquent Girls, 1890–1960.* Urbana: University of Illinois Press, 2011.

Restak, Richard. *The Naked Brain: How the Emerging Neurosociety Is Changing How We Live, Work, and Love.* New York: Harmony Books, 2006.

Reuben, D. R. "Everything You Always Wanted to Tell Your Teenager about Sex but Were Afraid to Bring Up." *Ladies' Home Journal,* November 1975.

Rich, Adrienne. "Compulsory Heterosexuality and Lesbian Existence." In *Blood, Bread, and Poetry.* New York: Norton, 1994.

Ringle, Ken. "Technology Isn't Enemy of Books, Report Says; Conquering Illiteracy Set as Nation's Aim." *Washington Post,* December 8, 1984, A12.

Roberts, Dorothy. *Killing the Black Body: Race, Reproduction, and the Meaning of Liberty.* New York: Vintage, 1998.

Rojas-Burke, J. "PET Scans Advance as Tool in Insanity Defense." *Journal of Nuclear Medicine* 34.1 (1993): N13.

Romero, Michele. "Music Review: Jeremy." *Entertainment Weekly,* September 25, 1992. http://www.ew.com/ew/article/0,,311872, 00.html.

Rose, Jacqueline. *The Case of Peter Pan, or The Impossibility of Children's Fiction.* Philadelphia: University of Pennsylvania Press, 1992.

Rose, Nikolas. *The Politics of Life Itself: Biomedicine, Power, and Subjectivity in the Twenty-First Century.* Princeton: Princeton University Press, 2006.

Rose, Tricia. *Black Noise: Rap Music and Black Culture in Contemporary America.* Middletown: Wesleyan University Press, 1994.

Ross, Andrew, and Tricia Rose. *Microphone Fiends: Youth Music and Culture.* New York: Routledge, 1994.

Rowan, C. T. et al. "Sex Education: Powder Keg in Our Schools." *Reader's Digest,* October 1969, 73–78.

Ryan, Joal. "Accused Teen Killer Deploys Pearl Jam Defense." *E! Online*, September 13, 1997. http://www.eonline. com/news/article/index.jsp?uuid=95258bfd-610a-49ce-b449-64a0962f3ab4. Accessed May 1, 2008.

Sandel, Michael J. *The Case against Perfection: Ethics in the Age of Genetic Engineering*. Cambridge: Belknap, 2009.

Savage, Jon. *Teenage: The Creation of Youth Culture*. New York: Viking Adult, 2007.

———. *Teenage: The Prehistory of Youth Culture, 1875–1945*. New York: Penguin, 2008.

Savran, David. *Taking It Like a Man: White Masculinity, Masochism, and Contemporary American Culture*. Princeton: Princeton University Press, 1998.

Saxton, Marsha. "Disability Rights and Selective Abortion." In *The Disability Studies Reader*, edited by Lennard J. Davis, 2nd ed., 105–16. New York: Routledge, 2006.

Scarry, Elaine. *The Body in Pain: The Making and Unmaking of the World*. Oxford: Oxford University Press, 1987.

Schaefer, Eric. *"Bold! Daring! Shocking! True!": A History of Exploitation Films, 1919–1959*. Durham: Duke University Press, 1999.

Schramm, Wilbur, ed. *The Impact of Educational Television*. Urbana: University of Illinois Press, 1960.

Schrum, Kelly. *Some Wore Bobby Sox: The Emergence of Teenage Girls' Culture, 1920–1945*. New York: Palgrave Macmillan, 2006.

Schulte, Stephanie Ricker. *Cached: Decoding the Internet in Global Popular Culture*. New York: New York University Press, 2013.

———. "Occupying a Node of Our Own: Protecting and Producing the Public through Personal Technology." Paper presented at the annual meeting of the Society for Cinema and Media Studies, Chicago, March 6–10, 2013.

Schwartz, Neena B. "Genes, Hormones, and Sexuality." *Gay and Lesbian Review Worldwide* 15.1 (January/February 2008).

"The Second Sexual Revolution." *Time*, January 24, 1964.

Sedgwick, Eve Kosofsky. *Touching Feeling: Affect, Pedagogy, Performativity*. Durham: Duke University Press, 2003.

Sender, Katherine. *Business, Not Politics: The Making of the Gay Market*. New York: Columbia University Press, 2005.

Serlin, David. *Replaceable You: Engineering the Body in Postwar America*. Chicago: University of Chicago Press, 2004.

"Sex-Education Controversy." *Christianity Today*, October 10, 1969, 34.

"Sex Education in School: Debate Splits Town in Wisconsin." *Life*, September 19, 1969.

"Sex in the Classroom." *Time*, July 25, 1969, 50.

"Sexual Preference Linked to Brain Region, Study Says." *Gazette* (Montreal), November 18, 1994, A12.

Shales, Tom. "Hewitt's Difference: Quality TV for Kids." *Washington Post*, October 12, 1977, B1.

———. "The Initiation of James." *Washington Post*, January 10, 1978, B1.

———. "Life and Love in a Bubble." *Washington Post*, November 12, 1976, B12.

Shapiro, Joseph P. *No Pity: People with Disabilities Forging a New Civil Rights Movement*. New York: Times Books, 1994.

"Should Sex Education Be Offered in Grade School? GH Poll." *Good Housekeeping*, July 1969, 12.

Showalter, Elaine. *The Female Malady: Women, Madness, and English Culture, 1830–1980*. New York: Pantheon, 1985.

Siebers, Tobin. *Disability Theory*. Ann Arbor: University of Michigan Press, 2008.

Siegfried, Tom. "Adolescents' Risky Rebellion Reflects Rewiring in the Brain." *Dallas Morning News*, August 22, 2000.

Simon, Paul. "The Boy in the Bubble." *Graceland*. 1986. Compact disc.

Smith, Ken. *Mental Hygiene: Better Living through Classroom Films, 1945–1970*. New York: Blast Books, 1999.

Smith-Rosenberg, Carroll. "The Female World of Love and Ritual: Relations between Women in Nineteenth-Century America." *Signs* 1.1 (1975): 1–30.

Snyder, Sharon L., and David T. Mitchell. *Cultural Locations of Disability*. Chicago: University of Chicago Press, 2006.

Somers, Margaret. *Genealogies of Citizenship: Markets, Statelessness, and the Right to Have Rights*. Cambridge: Cambridge University Press, 2008.

Somerville, Siobhan B. *Queering the Color Line: Race and the Invention of Homosexuality in American Culture*. Durham: Duke University Press, 2000.

Sontag, Susan. *Illness as Metaphor*. New York: Vintage Books, 1979.

Spelman, Elizabeth V. *Fruits of Sorrow: Framing Our Attention to Suffering*. New York: Beacon, 1997.

Spigel, Lynn. "From Domestic Space to Outer Space: The 1960s Fantastic Family Sit-Com." In *Close Encounter: Film, Feminism, and Science Fiction*, edited by Constance Penley, Elisabeth Lyon, Lynn Spigel, and Janet Bergstrom. Minneapolis: University of Minnesota Press, 1991.

———. *Make Room for TV: Television and the Family Ideal in Postwar America*. Chicago: University of Chicago Press, 1992.

Stanton, W. "Bring Back the Stork!" *Good Housekeeping*, August 1973.

Stephens, Tony. "Pen and Paper v. the Electronic Society; Literacy: Are Standards Falling?" *Sydney Morning Herald*, March 2, 1987, 6.

Stern, Alexandra Minna. *Eugenic Nation: Faults and Frontiers of Better Breeding in Modern America*. Berkeley: University of California Press, 2005.

Stewart, Kathleen. *Ordinary Affects*. Durham: Duke University Press, 2007.

Stiker, Henri Jacques. *A History of Disability*. Ann Arbor: University of Michigan Press, 1999.

Stockton, Kathryn Bond. *The Queer Child, or Growing Sideways in the Twentieth Century*. Durham: Duke University Press, 2009.

Strangers with Candy. Comedy Central. April 7, 1999–October 2, 2000.

Strauch, Barbara. *The Primal Teen: What the New Discoveries about the Teenage Brain Tell Us about Our Kids*. New York: Doubleday, 2003.

"Study Links Genetics, Male Homosexuality Research: Canadian Scientists Say Gay Men Have More Ridges in Fingerprints." *Los Angeles Times*, December 26, 1994.

Suplee, Curt. "Brain May Determine Sexuality: Node Seen as Key to Gay Orientation." *Washington Post*, August 30, 1991, A1.

———. "Neurobiology: Seasonal Advantage on the SAT?" *Washington Post*, November 18, 1991, A2.

Szasz, Thomas. "Anatomy of a Teenaged Shooting." Letter to the Editor. *New York Times*, March 10, 2001. http://query.nytimes.com/gst/fullpage.html?res=9501E5DC113AF930A25750C0A9679C8B63. Accessed June 6, 2008.

Tahse, Martin. Interview. *Talk of the City*. KPCC Radio. DVD Special Feature. ABC's *After School Specials*. DVD.

———. Telephone interview with the author. Washington, DC. February 22, 2007.

Tanner, Lindsey. "Break a Leg? Try 'Wiihabilitation.'" NBC News, February 2, 2008. http://www.nbcnews.com/id/ 23070190/#.UV3pmluc7AU.

Taylor, Paul. "Emergence: Signs of Immune System Are Found in Boy Who Lived in Plastic Bubble." *Washington Post*, February 11, 1984, A1.

TeenScreenTruth. Website. http://www.teenscreentruth.com.

Tenver, E. "Talk to Your Teen-Agers about Sex." *Reader's Digest*, December 1979, 128–31.

Thomas, Virginia. "Mosaic 2000: An Educational Dragnet." Heritage Foundation, November 10, 1999. http://www.heritage.org/research/commentary/1999/11/mosaic-2000-an-educational-dragnet. Accessed June 11, 2008.

Thornton, Davi Johnson. *Brain Culture: Neuroscience and Popular Media*. New Brunswick: Rutgers University Press, 2011.

Tongson, Karen. *Relocations: Queer Suburban Imaginaries*. New York: New York University Press, 2011.

Treichler, Paula A. *How to Have Theory in an Epidemic: Cultural Chronicles of AIDS*. Durham: Duke University Press, 1999.

Treichler, Paula, Lisa Cartwright, and Constance Penley, eds. *The Visible Woman: Imaging Technologies, Gender, and Science*. New York: New York University Press, 1998.

Trites, Roberta Seelinger. *Disturbing the Universe: Power and Repression in Adolescent Literature*. Iowa City: University of Iowa Press, 2000.

Turkel, Simon. "Anatomy of a Teenaged Shooting." Letter to the Editor. *New York Times*, March 11, 2001. http://query.nytimes.com/gst/fullpage.html?res =9B00E5D-C113AF930A25750C0A9679C8B63. Accessed June 6, 2008.

"TV Highlights." *Washington Post*, February 5, 1975, B11.

U.S. Congress. Senate Committee on the Judiciary. Subcommittee to Investigate Juvenile Delinquency. *Juvenile Delinquency (Motion Pictures)*, *Juvenile Delinquency (Comic Books)*, and *Juvenile Delinquency (Television Programs)*. (Three separate volumes.) 83rd Cong., 2d sess., 1954.

———. *Juvenile Delinquency (Television Programs)*. 84th Cong., 1st sess., 1955.

U.S. Equal Employment Opportunity Commission. "Remarks of President Bush at the Signing of the Americans with Disabilities Act." http://www.eeoc.gov/eeoc/history/35th/videos/ada_signing_text.html. Accessed March 19, 2012.

U.S. Public Health Service. "The Surgeon General's Call to Action to Prevent Suicide." 1999. http://www.surgeongeneral.gov/library/calltoaction/ calltoaction.htm. Accessed May 9, 2008.

U.S. Senate. Hearings Before the Committee on Interstate and Foreign Commerce. 86th Congress, January 27–28, 1959, 69.

U.S. Surgeon General. *Television and Growing Up: The Impact of Televised Violence; Report to the Surgeon General, United States Public Health Service*. Washington, DC: National Institute of Mental Health, 1972.

United Press International. "Quest for Normal Life." Photograph. *New York Times*, March 31, 1978, A14.

Voight, Cynthia. *Izzy Willy Nilly*. New York: Atheneum, 1986.

Wacquant, Loïc. *Punishing the Poor: The Neoliberal Government of Insecurity*. Durham: Duke University Press, 2009.

Wailoo, Keith, Alondra Nelson, and Catherine Lee, eds. *Genetics and the Unsettled Past: The Collision of DNA, Race, and History*. New Brunswick: Rutgers University Press, 2012.

Walsh, David. *Why Do They Act That Way? A Survival Guide to the Adolescent Brain for You and Your Teen*. New York: Free Press, 2004.

Walsh, Shushannah. "DNA of Newtown Shooter Adam Lanza to Be Studied by Geneticists." *ABC World News*, December 27, 2012. http://abcnews.go.com/US/dna-newtown-shooter-adam-lanza-studied-geneticists/story?id=18069343.

Warhol, Robyn R. *Having a Good Cry: Effeminate Feelings and Pop-Culture Forms*. Columbus: Ohio State University Press, 2003.

Warner, Michael. *The Trouble with Normal: Sex, Politics, and the Ethics of Queer Life*. New York: Free Press, 1999.

Washington, Harriet A. *Medical Apartheid: The Dark History of Medical Experimentation on Black Americans from Colonial Times to the Present*. New York: Doubleday, 2007.

Weber, Brenda. *Makeover TV: Selfhood, Citizenship, and Celebrity*. Durham: Duke University Press, 2009.

Weinberger, Daniel R. "A Brain Too Young for Good Judgment." *New York Times*, March 10, 2001.

Weisbard, Eric, with Jessica Letkemann, Ann Powers, Chris Norris, William Van Meter, and Will Hermes. "Ten Past Ten." *Spin*, August 2001. http://www. fivehorizons.com/archive/articles/spin801.shtml. Accessed May 7, 2008.

Wertham, Frederic. "How Movie and TV Violence Affects Children." *Ladies Home Journal*, February 1960.

Wexler, Bruce. *Brain and Culture: Neurobiology, Ideology, and Social Change*. Boston: MIT Press, 2006.

White House, Office of the Press Secretary. Press release, April 20, 2000. http://clinton4.nara.gov/WH/ New/html/20000420.html. Accessed June 6, 2008.

White, Patrick. "Sex Education; or How the Blind Became Heterosexual." Special issue of *GLQ: A Journal of Lesbian and Gay Studies*, edited by Robert McRuer and Abby Wilkerson, 9.1–2 (2003): 133–47.

White, Ryen W., and Eric Horvitz. "Cyberchondria: Studies of the Escalation of Medical Concerns in Web Search." November 2009. http://research.microsoft.com/apps /pubs/default.aspx?id=76529.

Whitfield, Jamie. "Missions of Mercy Inspire Lurlene McDaniel's Angelic Series." First Person Bookpage. http://www.bookpage.com/0007bp/lurlene_mcdaniel. html. Accessed October 10, 2007.

Wilkerson, Abby L. *Diagnosis: Difference: The Moral Authority of Medicine*. Ithaca: Cornell University Press, 1998.

Will, George F. "Tempting Readers." *Washington Post*, June 6, 1991, A21.

Williams, Raymond. *Marxism and Literature*. New York: Oxford University Press, 1977.

Wright, Bradford. *Comic Book Nation: The Transformation of Youth Culture in America*. Baltimore: Johns Hopkins University Press, 2001.

Yemma, John. "Imaging Moves Scientists Closer to 'Brain Atlas.'" *Boston Globe*, June 22, 1996.

Young, Laurens D. "Anatomy of a Teenaged Shooting." *New York Times*. Letter to the Editor. March 10, 2001. http://query.nytimes.com/gst/fullpage.html?res= 9C06E5D-C113AF930A25750C0A9679C8B63. Accessed June 6, 2008.

Zoglin, Richard. "Now for the Bad News: A Teenage Timebomb." *Time*, January 15, 1996.

Stutter, 79–83, 85
Subculture, youth, 3, 24, 26
Suffering, 122, 125; nobility of, 110–11
Suicide, 63, 137, 142
Superpredators, 8, 25, 135, 150, 157–58, 163
Surveillance, 9, 11, 25, 30, 162, 163, 164
Sycamore Year (1974), 78
Szalavits, Maia, 160

TA. *See* Technological assessment
Tahse, Martin, 64, 66–67, 69, 77–78, 79, 80,
  186n14, 186n17
"The Take-Over Generation," 38
Teasdale, Nancy, 144–45
Technological assessment (TA), 41–42, 44, 56
Technological progress, 29, 31, 32, 34–37,
  42–43, 133, 138; celebratory discourse of,
  30, 33, 38, 39, 40, 41, 44, 46, 56, 59, 60,
  134; citizenship and, 60; rehabilitative
  edutainment and, 60
Technology, 22, 23, 25, 30, 59, 134, 168; aliteracy and, 119; neuroimaging, 139–40,
  143, 153, 199n96
Teen-Age Crime Wave (1955), 11
Teenager: consumers, 4, 26, 160, 177n5; craziness and pathology, 131, 132, 133, 140, 144,
  145, 147, 148, 159–60; educational books,
  144–45; emotional habitus, 97, 129, 132;
  excessive emotionality, 25, 96, 97, 121, 129,
  131; Gen-X, 119; identity crisis, 2, 13, 15–16,
  68, 99, 170, 171; impulsive behavior, 142,
  144, 146, 147, 149; inner-city, 152; magazines, 76; male white, 150, 152–56, 158, 159;
  masculinity crisis, 154–55; mental illness
  and, 148, 159, 160, 161, 162; nonwhite, 6, 8,
  11, 19, 25, 26, 27, 104, 163, 178n21; pharmaceutical industry and, 3, 9, 25, 132, 150, 159,
  160, 161, 163; school shootings by white,
  25, 153, 156, 158; sexuality and, 3, 6, 66, 75,
  169–70; tried in adult courts, 163; violence, 73, 150, 165; white, middle-class, 4,
  8, 9, 10, 11, 20, 24, 25, 26, 70, 82, 91, 105–6,
  122, 126, 152. *See also* Boyhood; Girls;
  Rebel; Youth activism; Youth reading
Teenagers: An American History (Palladino),
  177n5

Teen angst, 12, 13, 27, 48, 64, 96, 123–24,
  125–26
Teen Brain Book: Who and What Are you
  (Carlson, Teasdale), 144–45
TeenScreen Program, 162–63
Teen sick-lit, 24–25, 93, 96–97, 169, 190n3;
  AIDS in, 190n4; cultural stereotypes in,
  99–100; emotional management and,
  121–24, 128, 129; endorsement of, 122–23,
  125; heteronormativity in, 95, 106, 110,
  116, 126–27; plotlines, 100; realism, 101–4,
  121; rehabilitation strategies in, 112, 121;
  romance in, 111–16; social issues and, 104,
  130; white female protagonists in, 94, 105,
  106–8, 170. *See also* McDaniel, Lurene;
  specific authors
Television (TV): adult oriented, 72; children's, programming, 65, 66, 68, 71, 72,
  73, 74; commercial, programming, 73,
  77, 177n7, 188n26; damaging effect of,
  programs, 65, 66, 90; disability and,
  programming, 60, 66–71; "disease-of-
  the week," programming, 23, 24, 32, 44,
  47–48, 59, 63, 70, 169; educational, 72,
  73, 78, 90; educational value of, 63, 64,
  65, 66; fantastic family sitcoms, 40; movies, 22, 23–24, 26, 32; movies and social
  critique, 48; overcoming narratives in,
  programming, 60, 80–83, 88; partnership between books and, 118; realism, 4,
  13, 24, 32, 48; regulation, 23, 59–60, 65,
  71–72, 75, 77, 78; sex-themed, programming, 47–48, 59, 60, 64, 65, 72, 74, 77, 78;
  socially responsible, 23, 60, 64, 65, 66, 76,
  77; titillation and sexuality in, programming, 77, 78; violence, 73, 74
*Television and Growing Up: The Impact of
  Televised Violence* (Surgeon General,
  1972), 73
Testing the Current (McPherson), 49
3-2-1 Contact (1980), 73
Tiger Beat, 76, 79
Time, 76, 97, 140, 144, 157
Time capsule, Library of Congress, 93, 125
Tolerance, 67, 79, 91, 92, 165
Trauma, 101, 104, 105

Travolta, John, 1, 32, 46
Treichler, Paula, 48
TV. *See* Television
Tween, 178n14

U.S. News & World Report, 144
USA Today, 135

Veterans, 15–16, 31, 38, 51, 71
Vetter, Carol Ann, 33
Vetter, David, III, 1, 23, 29, 32, 41, 182n3;
    depression of, 43; isolation of, 42, 48,
    49, 50; life of, 33–34, 36–37, 49–50; news
    coverage, 30, 31, 36–37, 42, 46. *See also*
    Bubble boys
Vetter, David Joseph, 33
Videogames, 119, 172
Vietnam War, 4, 13, 22, 31, 47, 170; veterans,
    31, 38, 51, 71
Violence, 25, 31, 59, 72, 135; African
    Americans and, 156, 157–58; brain
    physiology and, 152–53, 156; domestic,
    63; Latinos and, 156; masculinity and,
    200n104, 202n134; media, 13, 73, 74, 75,
    151; race and, 152, 156, 157–58; school,
    warning guides, 161–62, 202n134; teen,
    73, 150, 165; TV, 73, 74. *See also* School
    shooting
Violence Initiative, 156–57, 158
Vogue, 140
Voigt, Cynthia, 94

Wacquant, Loïc, 164
Wakefield, Dan, 77
Walsh, David, 145–46
*The War against Boys: How Misguided
    Feminism Is Harming Our Young Men*
    (Sommers), 155
Ward, Ingeborg L., 141
Washington Post, 1, 46, 49, 73, 77, 83, 146;
    cartoon, 74
Washington Times, 159
Watergate, 4, 47, 170
Wealth, 29, 179n43

WebMD, 127, 172–73, 174
Weekly Standard, 157
Weinberger, Daniel R., 152
Welcome Back, Kotter (1975-1979), 46
Wertham, Frederic, 12
White, Patrick, 57
White, Ryen W., 168
White House Conference on Mental Health,
    160
White House Conference on Teenagers:
    Raising Responsible and Resourceful
    Youth, 160
White Man's Burden (1995), 153
Whiteness, 105–6, 122, 155, 164; aliteracy and,
    121; heteronormative masculine, 153. *See
    also* Angry white male; Teenager; Teen
    sick-lit
Wholeness, 14
Why Do They Act That Way? (Walsh),
    145–46
Wii, 172, 203n9
The Wild One (1953), 11
Williams, Paul, 56
Willpower, 88, 89, 91, 101, 135, 171
World War II, 4, 11, 14, 35; post, 8, 11, 12, 21,
    27, 31, 38, 171, 177n7; veterans, 15–16

YA. *See* Young adult literature
*Yes, Your Teen Is Crazy! Loving Your Kid
    without Losing Your Mind* (Bradley), 131,
    144
Young adult literature (YA), 4, 22, 24, 26;
    economy of, problem novel, 129; emo-
    tional instruction through, 121–22, 123;
    Harlequin paperback, 100; multicultural
    protagonists in, 104; national health
    and, 95–96, 97; partnership with TV, 118;
    problem novel, 63, 67, 94, 97–99, 98, 120,
    121–24, 129; proliferation of, 98; series
    fiction, 193n41. *See also* Realism; Teen
    sick-lit; *specific authors*
Youth activism, 26, 71, 160, 161
Youth reading, 118; national health and, 95–
    96, 97; programs, 93, 99, 117–19, 190n7

ABOUT THE AUTHOR

Julie Passanante Elman is Assistant Professor of Women's and Gender Studies at the University of Missouri.